THINKING
ABOUT
TERRORISM

To my family

THINKING
ABOUT
TERRORISM

The Threat to Civil Liberties
in Times of
National Emergency

MICHAEL E. TIGAR

Defending Liberty
Pursuing Justice

Cover design by ABA Publishing.

Printed in the United States of America.

11 10 09 08 07   5 4 3 2 1

Library of Congress Cataloging-in-Publication Data

Tigar, Michael E., 1941-
    Thinking about terrorism / Michael E. Tigar.
      p.   cm.
    Includes bibliographical references and index.
    ISBN 978-1-59031-842-3 (alk. paper)
    1. Terrorism. 2. State-sponsored terrorism. 3. International Criminal Court.
    I. Title.

  K5256.T54 2007
  345'.02—dc22   2007019852

Discounts are available for book ordered in bulk. Special consideration is given to state bars, CLE programs, and other bar-related organizations. Inquire at Book Publishing, ABA Publishing, American Bar Association, 321 North Clark Street, Chicago, IL 60610-4714.

www.ababooks.org

CONTENTS

PREFACE

Two Kinds of Terrorism

This is a book about terror and terrorism. I am a lawyer and law teacher, but I wrote this book for everyone concerned with the issues that these terms raise. What are terror and terrorism? How have we faced them, and how might we face them more effectively and more in harmony with constitutional history and tradition? How can we learn from the rest of the world's reaction to terror and terrorism? I have titled the book *Thinking about Terrorism* because that is what we need to do. Of course, we should face the threat of terrorism and take constructive action, but action without thought can only make the problem worse.

Since September 11, 2001, political leaders, the media, and public figures have brought the words terror and terrorism into daily discourse. We live under warnings of different colors based on federal declarations of alleged degrees of danger of terrorist attack. There is debate whether laws, and the Constitution itself, must yield to new interpretations based on the threat or existence of terrorism. We are told there is a "war on terror." This war has no well-defined enemy. The assertion that this war exists is not accompanied by a statement of what will constitute victory, or when that might occur. Because, as we shall see, terror and terrorism have existed in all periods of United States history, the war is by its own rather circular definition indefinite.

In the name of combating terror and terrorists, the President authorizes searches and seizures without a judicial warrant. When a newspaper reveals these warrantless searches, the executive branch threatens the editors with prosecution. Some detention centers are so secret that even the Red Cross cannot perform its historic international duty of visiting captives to ensure they are being treated humanely. In these centers, captives are tortured. The level of violence in countries with large Muslim populations increases. Here in the United States, attitudes towards Muslims—and Middle Eastern and South Asian people generally—have hardened. Ethnic and religious slurs are commonplace in the media and in public discourse.

Hardly anybody feels safe in the midst of this turmoil. The situation has become intolerable. Yet, the dangers we face—of all kinds—will not go away. In a series of essays in this book, I will analyze recent events, and place them in a historical context. The problems we face and the fears that bedevil us are not new. They are old in several important ways.

The international problems we face are the same as those faced by every Western nation that has tried to impose its will on the Middle East. The politics of petroleum have dominated that process since World War I. The problems of presidential invasion of personal liberty, justified by claims that only in this way can some danger be averted or overcome, have been part of American legal and constitutional history at least since the early 1800s. The September 11, 2001, attack was a predictable result of past events that must be studied to be understood.

On the international front, wars in Iraq and Afghanistan—and armed conflict elsewhere in the Muslim world—have provoked increased violence. Michael Scheuer, a former CIA official, has chronicled some results of these conflicts. The perceived injustice of American occupation has fueled recruiting for Muslim extremist groups. Committed young people welcome the opportunity to learn the fighting trade in combat against the most sophisticated army in the world.[1] We must remember that the United States was arming and training Islamist fighters to resist the USSR in Afghanistan twenty years ago. Among those fighters were the people who now work closely with Osama bin Laden. In his 1982 State of the Union address, President Reagan proclaimed, "We support the mujahadeen."

I have worked in the fields of domestic and international human rights, and on the legal limits of executive and congressional power, for forty years. Lawyers, by virtue of their training and socially determined position, are in charge of remembering. Some lawyers remember past events in order that they can be repeated. This is sometimes called precedent, which Jonathan Swift said, "is a maxim among . . . lawyers, that whatever hath been done before, may legally be done again: and therefore they take special care to record all the decisions formerly made against common justice and the general reason of mankind."

There is another and better way of remembering. Lawyers in this century have remembered the horrors of aggressive war, war crimes, crimes against humanity, genocide, and torture in order to express and apply norms that punish those who commit such acts and, one may hope, restrain those who would commit them. When lawyers remember in this way, they are listening to the voices and stories of people who have been oppressed, and using their learning and skill to fashion, apply, and support remedies and preventive measures. There are many examples of courageous lawyer conduct, but among the most evocative as I write these words in 2006 is the conduct of military lawyers faced with the reality of unlawful detention and torture at United States military facilities in the period beginning with the conflict in Afghanistan and continuing during the Iraq conflict. Military lawyers are commissioned officers. They wear a uniform. They have taken an oath to support and defend the Constitution. They know as well as anybody what warfare means. Yet, a number of them spoke out, first against the Department of Defense proposals to violate or circumvent provisions of the Geneva Conventions and customary international law, and then against proposals to deny detainees any semblance of a fair trial.

In this book, I draw on historical parallels to the present time. If we can see how problems like the one we face today were addressed, well or not so well, perhaps we will better understand what to do now. In analyzing past events, there is nothing that can harm us in the present moment. Liberated from our fears, we can better see how to address issues.

I do insist on certain themes. First, executive power must never be unchecked. The power to order military action or to infringe on personal rights to privacy, liberty, and security is not confided to one branch of government. This is a fundamental understanding of the American constitutional system. It is a lesson about governance that has been painfully learned the world over.

Second, the United States is part of the international community. In that community, there are rules of conduct. A decision to go it alone in violation of basic international standards brings bad consequences sooner or later. The United States cannot continue policies that the rest of the international community opposes. However, that is simply a selfish reason for acting or not acting. The rules of conduct developed in the past six or seven decades deal fundamentally with the desire, shared by almost all the world's people, for human rights and economic and social justice. Torture, killing of civilians in aggressive war, support for state-sponsored terrorism, arbitrary detention, and denial of fair procedures bring the state that practices them into disrepute. These practices fuel anger and bring supporters to the banners of those engaged in terrorist acts. They invite others to commit similar acts. When Israel launched full-scale attacks on Lebanon as a consequence of the acts of the Islamist group Hezbollah, hundreds of civilians were killed. The killings were the product of air raids, accompanied by the use of deadly cluster bombs. Israeli Prime Minister Ehud Olmert rebuked European leaders who criticized Israel, saying that NATO bombings in Bosnia had killed 10,000 civilians, and therefore, "Don't preach to us about the deaths of civilians." Prime Minister Olmert's response was in one sense beside the point. Many trenchant critics of killing civilians do so with clean hands, but his aim at European political leaders was apt.

As I was writing this book, and casually talking to friends about it, someone said, "Are you one of those people who thinks terrorists are simply misunderstood, or do you think they should be held accountable?" "Both," I replied. How, then, are we to understand, and how are we to make terrorists accountable? I answer the question more fully in the closing paragraphs of this book. The journey from here to there runs through a series of essays on aspects of this issue.

My experience as an advocate tells me that I will not convince you of anything by presenting unvarnished arguments. The entire history of persuasive discourse reinforces this view. In our rhetorical tradition, recitation precedes revelation. Evidence comes before conclusions. This order of things leads to fairer, more rational decisions. In Biblical history, there are parables that illustrate rules of conduct. On a grander scale, the Old Testament—which is significant in the Christian, Jewish, and Muslim communities—sets the stage by telling the early history of the people Israel. It is not until about the second chapter of Exodus that the voice attributed to God starts laying down detailed rules of conduct. In the Buddhist tradition, young Prince Siddhartha witnesses poverty, sickness, old age, and death and then undergoes significant experiences before reaching enlightenment and beginning to teach.

So this book tells stories, some based on my own experience and some from other sources. From these stories, I hope to draw out definitions of terrorism that make sense and to describe ways of dealing with terrorism that are likely to succeed and that are unlikely to provoke results worse than the evil they confront.

The book deals with two distinct types of terrorism: state-sponsored and group or individual. The distinction is important for historical and practical reasons. Conduct by states is subject to special rules of international law that are designed to respect the territorial integrity of states and discountenance undue interference in their internal affairs, while recognizing and enforcing norms that all states must observe even in dealing with so-called internal problems. Conduct by states and state actors—public officials—is the subject of special consideration in treaties and by transnational institutions.

Individual or group terrorism must be distinguished from civil war and from criminal conduct that does not deserve to be so characterized. The significant dangers to personal liberty that are committed in the name of a war or campaign against terrorism serve as a warning. Careful classification is an important initial step in combating terrorism. Classifications that are overinclusive may be used to justify use of state power against innocent or even constitutionally protected activity.

I hope that the stories in this book, and the conclusions I draw from them, help to fuel a constructive debate. I understand that there is danger. I also understand that executive action is being taken against a great many people and institutions that do not pose significant danger. One needs to count the costs. A couple of decades ago, the Texas folklore philosopher John Henry Faulk was asked to speak at a gathering in Austin, Texas. Just before his talk, the audience heard a presentation by the then-director of the FBI who painted a picture of various threats facing the country and called for law enforcement action that included surveillance, infiltration, and all manner of related activity.

When it was his turn, John Henry rose and said something like this:

You know, not many people know this, but I was in law enforcement. I was United States Marshal. I was nine years old. My territory stretched along the banks of what is now Lake Austin, from the Faulk homestead and inland for a mile or more. So it was that Billy Johnson and I were patrolling one day, and we decided to check out the chicken house. We opened the door and went in, and the door slammed behind us. We did not notice that the latch slipped into place as the door shut.

Billy felt around up in the nesting boxes above the height of his head, and all of a sudden he screamed, "Chicken snake!" He had put his hand up there and touched a snake. We ran for the door and, the door being shut, we crashed right through it. We were hollering "Chicken snake! Chicken snake!"

You may well ask, me being marshal and all, where was my courage. It was running down my leg into my tennis shoe. Billy and I were scratched and bruised from our encounter with the door and the ground.

Our hollering excited the attention of my grandmother, who came running out the back door. "John Henry, what on earth is going on?" she asked.

"Grandma," I said, "Billy found a chicken snake in the henhouse."

"John Henry Faulk," grandma said, "don't you know a chicken snake can't hurt you."

"Yes, ma'am," I said, "but it can scare you so bad you could hurt yourself."

Given the ways in which the terms terror and terrorism can be and have been manipulated for political advantage, there is a great danger of harming the very ideas of constitutional liberty, separation of powers, and principles of international order.

Note

1. MICHAEL SCHEUER, IMPERIAL HUBRIS: WHY THE WEST IS LOSING THE WAR ON TERROR (2004). Scheuer is a CIA veteran.

ACKNOWLEDGMENTS

Material in this book has previously appeared, although with major changes, in *Law & the Rise of Capitalism* (2d ed. 2000), *Fighting Injustice* (2002), and in lectures and speeches I have delivered to academic and bar audiences. I have been greatly assisted by Natalie Hirt, a law student at Duke, and by Jennifer Dodenhoff and Maria del Cerro, law students at Washington College of Law. Jane Tigar contributed ideas and sources on issues of executive power. The law libraries at Duke and Washington College of Law provided valuable assistance. In footnotes, I have tried to direct the reader to source materials on which I relied. In more than fifty years of writing and speaking on these topics, I cannot represent with confidence that I have acknowledged all the people and works that have influenced me. Many of the ideas here are based on being privileged to represent clients engaged in seeking social change; to them, a special thank you.

PART ONE

State-Sponsored
Terrorism and Its
Perpetrators

A. Defining Terrorism—History, Logic, France, and Mark Twain

If we are to condemn terrorism, and punish its practitioners, we must have a working definition. Terror and terrorism are evocative words. It is easy to use such words figuratively and therefore, imprecisely: He was dressed "fit to kill"; "You are torturing me with your lack of concern"; and so on. In the 1950s, it was fashionable to use terms like communist, communist sympathizer, and fellow traveler to castigate people with liberal or left-wing political views. Americans feared the political and military power of the Soviet-Chinese bloc. Therefore, hanging the communist label on a political opponent was a useful political ploy. The label was used against civil rights leaders, labor organizers, student protesters, and college teachers concerned with global issues of peace and disarmament, just to name a few.

Today, terrorist and terror have become epithets or insults and are used often with no sense of a specific meaning. We accept this sort of imprecision in daily speech, because we understand what we are doing. We might call somebody a bastard or a son of a bitch and everybody understands we do not mean the terms literally. However, the terms terror and terrorism are being used in a dual and, therefore, dangerous way. They are epithets, but they are also words used increasingly in laws and judicial decisions as the predicate for governmental conduct directed against individuals and groups.

An epithet's force derives from what it evokes beyond or in addition to what it means. Therefore, an epithet is inherently vague as a description of something. When an epithet becomes a popular way to insult certain kinds of people—as happened with the anticommunist epithets of the 1950s—it is also inherently overbroad. Vagueness and overbreadth are undesirable qualities in laws that are directed at political activity. Indeed, they are the hallmarks of unconstitutionality.

In order to put these thoughts in perspective, let us survey the use of terror and terrorism as evocative ideas in historical and social contexts. The very idea of terror comes to our tradition in images of fear. To give you an idea of the myriad ways in which the term *terror* can be and is used, we can take a brief historical tour. From England, we inherited a crime called "affray," which still exists under that name in some American states. The word *affray* is derived from the French word *effrayer*, which means to make somebody frightened. According to Sir William Blackstone, the English legal scholar who had such a great influence on American lawyers in the late 1700s, affray is committed by "the fighting of two or more persons in some public place, to the terror of His Majesty's subjects." Affray was also defined around that time as "a public offense to the terror of the people, and is an English word, and so called, because it affrighteth and maketh men affraid." The states that maintain the crime of affray require that prosecutors prove somebody was actually frightened. However, the offense potentially reaches so broadly as to label almost anyone who brawls in public a terrorist.

Some American states drew on the old definition of affray to make it unlawful for people to display weapons in ways that alarm people. Turning again to Blackstone, it seems that since the 1400s the English monarchs had prohibited people from that sort of conduct, on pain of having their weapons confiscated or even of being jailed. The obvious purpose of such laws is to enforce the state's monopoly on the legitimate use of violence and, in so doing, to discourage vigilantism and even organizing for a potential violent uprising. The historic prohibition on displaying arms has sometimes been argued as a history-based limit on the constitutional right to bear arms.

Throughout American history, terror and terrorist have been chameleon words. From the earliest days of the American labor movement, they were epithets hurled at labor organizers and strikers. Doubtless, some labor leaders were involved in violent acts against property and people, but judges, prosecutors, and employers used the terrorism epithet to brand all organized workers. In the late nineteenth and early twentieth centuries, judicial opinions were rife with this sort of rhetoric. Judges doubted that unions should even exist, and described entire unions as terrorist. Charismatic and effective labor leaders, such as Harry Bridges of California, were the targets of prosecutorial speeches that sounded the union terrorism theme. The various criminal syndicalism laws under which labor organizers and radical spokespersons were prosecuted contained references to terrorism.

Of course, the rhetoric calmed down once Congress had passed the Norris-LaGuardia Act in 1932, which guaranteed the right to strike, and then the Wagner Act in 1935, which provided a legal basis for union organization. The Supreme Court finally focused on the vagueness and overbreadth of criminal syndicalism laws in 1969. Its opinion invalidating Ohio's law against "advocating . . . violence, or unlawful methods of terrorism" put an end to what had become only a small trickle of prosecutions.

However, labor leaders and radicals were not the only recipients of the terrorist sobriquet. Among other perpetrators of terror recognized in Supreme Court opinions were: monopolies and trusts, the Ku Klux Klan, federal tax collectors, police who conduct unlawful searches, mobsters who influence a jury, courts of justice who should be a "terror to evil doers," patent holders, and Native American attackers.[1]

The observant reader will note that this recital itself contains a significant ambiguity. The word terror has been with us a long time. Terrorism might be something different. An *ism* is a set of ideas—a suffix that one adds to somebody's name, to a word, or concept, such as Marxism, Arianism, Jansenism, Protestantism, Catholicism, and so on.

Terror became terrorism in European usage, during the French Revolution.[2] The victorious revolutionaries sought to impose their views on those who resisted them. By 1798, the Académie Française had officially accepted that terrorism meant the system or rule of terror. Novelists and essayists in England penned denunciations of the French political trials. These trials began predominantly against aristocrats. Then as the factions within the Revolution split apart, former allies tried and executed their enemies. These events and the debate that surrounded them helped to define the term terrorism in a certain context. However, some critics noted that those who used the term as an epithet against the revolutionaries in France did not come to their task with clean hands.

The English conservatives of the time, who were among the most vocal critics and sedulous invokers of the term terrorism, presided over a political system that defined more than one hundred crimes as capital offenses, and had during the preceding one hundred years been engaged in violent governmental actions to drive peasants from their lands. In a celebrated passage from *A Connecticut Yankee in King Arthur's Court*, Mark Twain's protagonist finds himself in a country where peasants were oppressed and bound to the land. He summoned up an image of the French Revolution:

> Why, it was like reading about France and the French, before the ever-memorable and blessed Revolution, which swept a thousand years of such villainy away in one swift tidal wave of blood—one: a settlement of that hoary debt in the proportion of half a drop of blood for each hogshead of it that had been pressed by slow tortures out of that people in the weary stretch of ten centuries of wrong and shame and misery the like of which was not to be mated but in hell. There were two "Reigns of Terror," if we would but remember it and consider it; the one wrought murder in hot passion, the other in heartless cold blood; the one lasted mere months, the other had lasted a thousand years; the one inflicted death upon ten thousand persons, the other upon a hundred millions; but our shudders are all for the "horrors" of the minor Terror, the momentary Terror, so to speak; whereas, what is the horror of swift death by the ax, compared with lifelong death from hunger, cold, insult, cruelty, and heartbreak? What is swift death by lightning compared with death by slow fire at the stake? A city cemetery could contain the coffins filled by that brief Terror which we have all been so diligently taught to shiver at and mourn over; but all France could hardly contain the coffins filled by that older and real Terror—that unspeakably bitter and awful Terror which none of us has been taught to see in its vastness or pity as it deserves.[3]

This passage tells us, I think, many things about terror and terrorism. The lessons we can find in it are easier to see and accept because Twain wrote about events so long ago that they cannot make us frightened or angry today, at least unless we are French, or perhaps English. Yes, it is true. When a spate of killings and hatred has pitted class against class, religion against religion, race against race, the scars seem to remain for a long time. Today, in the West of Ireland, in Bosnia, or in countless other places in the world, someone will point to a certain place and tell you that on that very spot someone else's great-great grandfather was killed for a very bad reason, and the crime has not been expiated or expunged to this day. However, for readers of this book, who are mostly in the United States, the French Revolution remains an object of study and not an event that excites or revives a sense that there is vengeance yet to be taken.

Twain's most significant target is moral relativism. He does not give us a definition of terrorism, but perhaps would begin with the one in a legal dictionary: "The use or threat of violence to intimidate or cause panic, esp[ecially] as a means of affecting political conduct."[4] We shall see this definition is not quite right but it will do to start. Twain argues, the excesses of the French Revolution were the product of the terror that the French ruling class visited for centuries on the French peasantry. The Revolution's violence was briefer and less terrible than what it responded to and avenged. In this passage and the discussion that precedes it, Twain does not so much justify the French terror as tell us that it was the understandable product of what had gone before. If we are to condemn the revolutionaries, he tells us that we must also condemn the conduct to which they reacted.

Americans can look back at their own history for a selective memory about violence. History books are full of stories about settler bravery. Yet, they tell us relatively little about the terror practiced against Native American populations who sought to assert their rights through peaceful means and were told the courts were not open to them.

Beyond moral relativism is the second and distinct question of inevitability. This is the issue of causation. One may condemn the revolutionaries' terror, but in order to learn from those events, one should first understand from whence it came. Twain says it was a predictable response. This is a variation on Santayana's dictum that those who do not remember the past are condemned to repeat it. Decrying terrorism and punishing terrorists may be and often is a worthy endeavor, but to forestall, discredit, and prevent terrorism in any given social and historical contexts, we must understand its root causes. Twain's novel, *A Connecticut Yankee in King Arthur's Court*, is a product of Twain's most productive years. Most people remember the book for its humor, but its political commentary is sharp and insightful. Twain warned that revolutionary violence is the inevitable consequence of subjugating human beings.

Twain's discussion of the French Revolution is simply one passage in his book. If we look at those events more closely, we can refine our definitions of terror and terrorism, and take a more critical stance towards them. The violence that attended and followed overthrow of the French monarchy was inevitable, as Twain rightly says. It is hard to imagine a great social change that is not preceded, accompanied, and followed by violent clashes between supporters of the old regime and partisans of change. There have been exceptions. For example, the end of apartheid in South Africa was accompanied by appointment of a Truth and Reconciliation Commission, which heard the confessions of past violent acts by all parties and issued amnesty in exchange. Even there, waves of violence swept the country for several years.

Such upwellings of violence may or may not fit the definition of terrorism. Let us revisit the definition quoted above. The first part of the definition, "the use of violence to intimidate or cause panic," sweeps broadly. It would include ordinary criminal offenses of extortion and robbery, both of which may involve putting somebody in fear. Much criminal conduct involves scaring people, but it is unhelpful to define all such activity as terrorism. The second part of the definition, "especially as a means of affecting political conduct," is more helpful. In historical contexts, terrorism describes a certain way of making people bow to the political will of the perpetrator. We can and will refine the definition, but the limitation to a political context is both useful and historically sound. If we accept the limitation, then we can make important distinctions. When the French monarchy fell, French workers and peasants rioted in many parts of the country. They invaded the chateaux of royalty and aristocrats, and seized the land they had tilled as tenants. Although the human targets of this violence were no doubt frightened, it would be unhelpful to characterize all this conduct as terrorist. If one accepts that France was in the throes of a genuine civil war, violence on both sides is to be expected. We are, or should be, searching for definitions of terror and terrorism that single out, for particular condemnation, violence that lays no claim to legitimacy. Later, we return to this theme in the context of conflict over state power.

The reign of terror to which the revolution's critics referred was the organized use of public show trials and public executions by the new holders of state power. Twain's discussion conflates this state-sponsored violence with the more spontaneous outbreaks of peasant worker violence and in doing so obscures, rather than illuminates, a workable definition of terrorism. I think it is important to have a definition that meets certain criteria, so that we can legitimately condemn all terrorism, properly so called, and at the same time point out how some political leaders selectively brand conduct as terrorist in order to serve their own ends.

To see Twain's discussion in context, let us examine the upwellings of violence during the French Revolution. We need to examine who practiced what may properly be called terrorism and for what purpose. Those who have watched the movie or read Dickens's *Tale of Two Cities*, or read or seen *The Scarlet Pimpernel*, may have an image of a revolution fomented by poor peasants who worked the land, and directed at topping the aristocracy and ending its privileges. Indeed, the shock troops of the revolution were drawn from the poorest class, and it was in part to placate that class and manipulate political opinion that the revolutionary government resorted to show trials and the spectacle of public executions.

In 1789, facing bankruptcy after years of bad harvests and agricultural crises, Louis XVI summoned the Estates-General for the purpose of raising new taxes. There is every indication that the bourgeois deputies elected in the countryside—where 89 percent of the population lived—were prepared, based on the sentiment in their districts, to use this opportunity to curtail noble prerogatives, particularly those relating to taxation and manorial rights. On July 12, 1789, a poor woman encountered by a British traveler told him, "Something was to be done by the great folk for such poor ones, though I know not who or how, but God send us better, for taxes and feudal services are crushing us."

What was done is familiar history. Within the context of the Estates-General, the Third Estate and elements of the nobility transformed themselves into a National Assembly with the declared task of formulating a constitution. On the night of August 4, 1789, in a decree finally promulgated—after extensive debate and the addition of clarifying amendments and commentary—the following November 3, the Assembly expressed itself on the issue of property law:

> The National Assembly destroys entirely the feudal regime, and decrees that all rights and liabilities, feudal and personal, tending . . . to servitude . . . are abolished without indemnity, and all others are declared repurchasable, and that the price and means of repurchase will be fixed by the National Assembly. The rights not abrogated by this decree will continue nonetheless to be enforceable until they are compensated for.

Succeeding articles abolished the noble right to fish and hunt in streams and woods and the right to hold court.

The opening sentence of the decree assured the peasantry that the feudal system was abolished. The very word feudal was apparently coined by the revolutionaries. What was this feudal system, and for whose benefit was it to be dismantled? Personal servitude hardly existed in 1789; here, the decree only confirmed a state of fact. The lords' rights of fishing, hunting, and justice were an anachronistic nuisance; their final abolition simply made it easier to reorganize the theory of land law. The feudal dues that weighed so heavily on the peasants—their rent, the portion of the harvest due the seigneur, the money payments due on sale of the land—were declared purchasable, not abolished. The National Assembly promised to set fair prices at some future time so that, with a single payment, a peasant might become a proprietor of the land he and his family had farmed for generations. When the committee on feudal rights finally reported on September 4, the intent of the decree became clearer. The Assembly, the committee recommended, ought to make clear that it was abolishing the illegitimate prerogatives of the nobility and creating a uniform, indivisible "right of property"—the right to use and abuse what one owned. The right of property was to be a relation between a person and a thing: *persona* and *res*. All personal obligations associated with ownership or with an estate in land were but deformations of this legal idea.

If this view, which animated the subsequent legislation of the Assembly, had been preceded or followed by a distribution of land to the peasantry in full ownership—as was demanded at various times in the streets and in the Assembly itself—the impact would have been profound. However, this was never the intention of a majority of the Assembly. Two years after the decree, a village in the south complained that there had been no change in actual conditions. The villagers expressed their fear that there would be no liberation from the "odious regime" [of feudal rights] for a thousand years."

Those nobles who held parcels of land and exercised feudal rights over them were ruinously and inescapably in debt to the financiers of the rising bourgeoisie. These financiers were clients both of the lawyers in the National Assembly and of the nobility who were "of the robe" and allied with the Third Estate. They cared little for the right to hunt, fish, and dispense justice, but they insisted that the dues that were exacted from the tillers of the land and secured the debts owed them be redeemable in cash. Who had that cash? The merchants and bankers held the cash.

In sum, the workers and peasants who were the Revolution's shock troops would find that the result of all this change was not any great leveling of social differences, but rather the substitution of one set of owners for another. The new owners would be the merchants and bankers who, in fact, had carried the inefficient and corrupt nobility on their backs, by paying taxes and with loans to support the nobles' style of life. In July 1789, thinking that the power had already passed as far toward the people as the merchant class and their allies could stand, Abbé Sieyes wrote: "All can enjoy the advantages of society, but only those who contribute to the public establishment are the important shareholders of the great social enterprise. They only are the active citizens, the true members of the Association."

Sieyes was an important publicist for the Revolution. He candidly admitted that the leaders of the National Assembly would use the term Third Estate in two quite different senses. One was the inclusive sense of all who were not allied with the king and nobles. This was a useful rhetorical device for investing the populace with a sense of participation in the new order. The other use of the term was limited to those in leadership positions or, as one legislator put it, "There are no true citizens except owners." Other voices, like that of Jean Marat, were only heard briefly: "What will we have gained, to have destroyed the aristocracy of the nobles to replace it with that of the rich?"

The historians who have chronicled the Revolution trace the details of the National Assembly's retreat from initial statements of high principle. The slave trade was declared abolished, only to be re-recognized in deference to the interests of French entrepreneurs with sugar holdings in the Caribbean. The National Assembly sharply limited the right of laborers to organize. When women organized to claim equal rights in private and public life, the National Assembly responded by outlawing their organization with the following justification:

> Since when has it been permissible for women to abandon their sex, and to make themselves into men? Since when is it seemly to see women abandon the pious cares of housekeeping, the cradle of their children, to come into the public square, to ascend the platform and harangue passersby, to take up the duties which nature has confided to men only?

Despite the decidedly conservative tilt that the National Assembly was taking, the Revolution had powerful foreign and domestic enemies. Leaders of other European countries feared the spread of republican ideas as inimical to royal and noble prerogative. They could see disturbing parallels between their own situations and those of the French aristocracy in 1789. Significantly, the so-called reign of terror did not begin until June of 1793. That summer saw an interesting alignment of political forces.

On the right, the remnants of the old nobility had the support of foreign powers to conduct military action against the revolutionary government. On the left, the Jacobin party sought to solidify its power by supporting populist measures that would gain—regain—the political support of the French masses.

In the middle were French business interests, termed the Girondins because their historic and financial base was in the Gironde—the area around Bordeaux that was a commercial and seafaring center. The

Girondins had assiduously sought to preserve and extend a system of rules that favored the merchant class.

By the end of June, an avowedly dictatorial government, dominated by the Jacobins, was in place. Girondin leaders had been arrested. The government instituted conscription to raise an army to deal with military challenges.

Then, on August 5, 1793, the government formally adopted "the terror" as an instrument of policy, suspending legal guarantees. Offenses against the state were vaguely defined, and tried before a "revolutionary tribunal." The targets of this terror were the former royalty, former nobility, Girondin leaders, and other people deemed disloyal. Death sentences were carried out by the guillotine. Dickens's graphic portrayal of prisoners going to their death in wooden carts—tumbrels—past crowds of jeering spectators is accurate.

Maximilien Robespierre became the most influential member of the revolutionary government. He said, "Terror is nothing other than prompt, severe, inflexible justice."

The reign of terror went on in full force until the summer of 1794 when the Girondin faction toppled the Jacobin leadership and, in a counterterror, executed the Jacobin leaders, including Robespierre. On a somewhat smaller scale, the counter-terror continued with the use of political trials and executions for several years.

The conservative trend continued. In 1804, the French Council of State issued the Napoleonic Code, putting into statutory law the rules about free contract and property that essentially reflected the Girondin agenda. When presenting the Code's final draft, one of its architects, Jean Portalis, traced the history of the French Revolution in decidedly revisionist terms:

> It was our discoveries in the arts, our first success in navigation, and the ferment happily born of our successes and discoveries of every sort that produced, under Louis XIV, Colbert's rules on manufactures, the law of waterways and forests, the regulation of commerce, and that of the maritime trade.
>
> Good was born of good. When the legislator has focused his concern and attention on a few important matters, he feels the necessity and has the desire to encompass all. There were judicial reforms, civil procedure was corrected, a new order was established in criminal justice, and the vast project of giving a uniform code to France was conceived. . . .
>
> Thus was the spirit that moved among us, thus our knowledge and resources, when suddenly a great revolution erupted. All

10

abuses were attacked at once, all institutions questioned. At the voice of the orator, institutions seemingly unshakeable crumbled; they were without roots in the sentiments of the people. Power found itself quickly conquered by opinion.

It was, one must admit, one of those decisive times which occur sometimes in the history of nations, and which alter the position and the fortune of a people. . . . Among all the reforms proposed, the idea of uniform legislation particularly occupied the attention of our deliberative assemblies.

But how to prepare a code of civil laws in the midst of the political troubles agitating our country? The hatred of the past, the impatient desire to live for the present, the fear of the future led to the adoption of the most exaggerated and violent measures. Caution and prudence, the attitudes of conservatism, were replaced by the desire to destroy everything.

Certain unjust and oppressive privileges, which were but the property of a few men, had weighed on the heads of all. To recover the advantages of liberty, the country fell for a brief moment into license. To suppress the odious system of privilege and preference and to prevent its rebirth, some sought to level all fortunes after having leveled all social ranks. . . .

But more moderate ideas came back to the fore; the first laws were corrected, new plans demanded: it was understood that a civil code must be prepared with wisdom, and not imposed with furor and haste.

This remarkable recasting of history makes the Revolution a bump in a road that was already headed for significant social change, portrays aristocratic privilege as a relatively minor annoyance, and relegates the social upheavals of 1789 through 1794 to the status of a rather unfortunate interruption of things as they must be.

From this sketch, we can evaluate Twain's discussion, and perhaps further the search for a meaningful definition of terrorism. The violence that attended the Revolution's early years was indeed the release of the pent-up anger Twain spoke of, but it cannot usefully be called terrorist in every aspect. It was part of a civil war directed at seizure of state power. It is true, and I will discuss it in later chapters, that some activity directed at the state apparatus by revolutionary groups can legitimately be called terrorist. However, it is not useful to call all such activity by that name, and doing so runs up against some principles of international law that I will deal with later.

The Terror, named as such by its practitioners—Robespierre and others, was the systematic use of state power. The judicial, legislative, and police organs of the State were aimed at a loosely defined group of enemies. To some extent, the Jacobins had understandable reason for taking repressive measures. Their government faced foreign and domestic enemies intent on overthrowing the new government. However, their terror had wider and somewhat more sinister goals. The laws on which it was based cast the net wider than reason could justify. The trials of those caught in the net were a farce. The public executions were a show. All of this was designed to terrorize even those who broadly shared the Revolution's goals but might want to advocate some modest change. More significantly, it seems to me, the Terror was a way of lying to the great mass of people who had supported the idea of fundamental social change and who hoped their lives would become better as a result of it.

I say "lying" advisedly. Even the Jacobins, the most radical wing of Revolutionary thought, had no intention of satisfying the leveling, egalitarian demands of the French workers and peasants. The Jacobin leadership believed the rising discontent of this constituency could be appeased by the visible spectacle of rounding up, trying, and executing those branded as partisans of the old order and sworn enemies of the new one.

The Terror was state-sponsored violence conducted against political enemies in disregard of fair substantive and procedural standards and used as a means of spreading fear among the regime's opponents. It had the additional goals, no doubt intended, of solidifying support for the regime by appealing to the prejudices held by the mass of people, and deflecting attention from the regime's failure to address fundamental social problems. The French Terror shared this quality with that practiced by many holders of state power, of scapegoating its victims. Twain's discussion focuses too much on the widespread popular antagonism to the former regime, and too little on the excesses perpetrated by the new one.

What of Twain's critique of the old regime? He surely captures in words its history of tyrannical oppression. Should we not utterly condemn the French royalty and aristocracy for their state-sponsored terrorism? Is it historical or moral relativism not to include those events in our definition? I answer no, though hesitantly. The religious and political persecutions that characterized French history in the three centuries that led to 1789 have been documented. Understanding them is essential to analyzing the roots of late eighteenth-century violence in France.

In defining state-sponsored terrorism in a way that is useful to us today, I would add something to the words above. I suggest: systematic state-sponsored violence, conducted against political enemies, and in disregard of historically determined fair substantive and procedural standards. I have added "historically determined."

Most people believe, and I agree with their judgment, that the French Terror was wrong in fundamental ways. One legitimate basis of condemnation is that its practitioners knew better, in light of the historically determined standards of their own time. One premise of this book is that we must find a consistent and understandable way to identify and condemn terrorism, and to devise ways of combating it that do not sacrifice fundamental values in the process. Any such discussion must begin by finding a place to stand, and thinking about what to do. Where to stand asks the obvious question about different personal and historical perspectives.

What to do is a harder question, and I will explore different answers in the remainder of this book. I will describe the kinds of tribunals that have been invoked and created to address issues of terrorism, and the origin and application of legal principles proposed and used. It is relatively easy to express fear, indignation, concern, anger, and other emotions called out by instances of state-sponsored and individual terrorism. It is equally easy to speak in platitudes and generalities on this subject. Professor Caleb Foote once reminded us, "The great stoic philosopher Epictetus in one of his writings imagined himself facing a wrestler. The strong man boasted to him 'See my dumbbells,' to which the philosopher impatiently retorted, 'Your dumbbells are your own affair. I desire to see their effect.' "[5] In the terrorism debates, we have seen plenty of dumbbells. We need to consider thoughtful, practical solutions and approaches.

B. How to Judge State-Sponsored Terror—Where to Stand and What to Do

"A place to stand" is another name for point of view. When jurors are making a life-death decision, we ask them to think about where they will stand. I said to the jurors in the Terry Nichols trial penalty phase:

> I feel now when I think about that evidence as though I'm standing before you and trying to sweep back a tide of anger and grief and vengeance. And I'm given pause by the fact that I feel that way, and I wonder if sometimes you might feel that way. But when I think that, then I think also of the instructions that the Judge is going to give you, because those instructions, as we contemplate this tide

of anger and grief and vengeance, can get us all to higher ground, because the instructions will tell you that neither anger nor grief nor vengeance can ever be a part of a decision reached in a case of this kind.[6]

I was asking them to stand in a place from which they might see the human connection between themselves and Terry Nichols. However, viewing and judging is two-sided. Those who judge must have a certain perspective, and they must also try to see where the person being judged in the perspective of that person's historical circumstance and life history. Suppose a jury is summoned in a case where a wife subjected to years of humiliation and brutal treatment from her husband finally took his life. There is a famous story by Susan Glaspell of such a case that arose about 1900. She mockingly titled her story *A Jury of Her Peers*, considering that the jury in the case consisted of twelve white men of property. Glaspell later wrote a play, *Trifles*, which captures this idea of empathy and a place to stand.

This concept also applies when we apply our definition: systematic state-sponsored violence, conducted against political enemies, and in disregard of historically determined fair substantive and procedural standards. To have answers that are persuasive and that point us towards solutions for today's problems, we must understand the pleas of victims and the justifications interposed by alleged perpetrators. In the end, we may be impatient with the latter. The norms against torture, genocide, and crimes against humanity are by now held nonderogable. Pleas of necessity or superior orders are held relevant to punishment and not guilt. However, that principle itself is a product of historical development.

When we look at the conduct of a government in ancient Greece or Rome, we would not think it right to judge that government by today's standards. Supreme Court Justice Robert Jackson discussed this idea in a celebrated case. He spoke of the requirements of "a relation between some mental element and punishment for a harmful act," and of a "concurrence of an evil-meaning mind with an evil-doing hand." It is meaningless to condemn someone for conduct that they did not know was wrong, and unfair to punish them for it.[7]

We can see the same idea at work in one of the most famous series of dramas in Greek literature, the Oedipus cycle of Sophocles. The Oedipus cycle consists of three plays, written at different parts of the poet's life. He probably wrote *Antigone* first, *King Oedipus* more than a decade later, and *Oedipus at Colonus* toward the end of his life. In *King Oedipus*,

Sophocles shows us Oedipus's relationship with his mother, the killing of his father, and his being cast out of civilized society. It is quite clear that Oedipus did not know any of the facts that would have made his conduct a violation of secular or god-made law. Yet, he is punished.

In *Oedipus at Colonus*, we see the old king near the end of his life. He meets Theseus, King of Athens, and rages about the injustice of punishing people who do not know or appreciate the wrongfulness of their conduct:

Was I the sinner?
Repaying wrong for wrong—that was no sin,
Even were it wittingly done, as it was not.
I did not know the way I went. They knew;
They, who devised this trap for me, they knew!

Why did Sophocles change focus from conduct as the basis of punishment to intention as the basis of culpability? George Thomson, the eminent classical scholar, suggests an answer in his book, *Aeschylus and Athens*, that I find persuasive: Greek philosophy, at the point somewhere between the authorship of these two plays, began to explore the difference between nature and norm, *physis* and *nomos*. Thomson ties the introduction of this distinction between norms we make up and the reality of the world around us to the introduction of money as the abstraction of commodities in the Greek economy, the social basis for abstracting moral rules from human experience.

Whether or not one agrees with Thomson, the shift in emphasis between the plays is striking. Oedipus arraigns the system of punishment based on whether it takes account of the supposed ability to choose between right and wrong courses of conduct. While there may be debate over the ability of people to choose the right, Oedipus's argument is that the system of justice must treat actors as if they could choose. A system that punishes without providing such an opportunity simply gives the function of identifying targets of punishment to blind forces of fate or chance, or worse yet, to malign vengeance-seekers.

I carry these insights into our discussion by introducing the phrase "historically determined" to mean that in order to brand state repression as terrorist, the state actors must act wrongfully in accordance with the standards of their own time. We must be able to say that they knew or should have known that their conduct was wrongful. This is a familiar standard in judging official conduct.

In the discussion that follows, I want to underline the essential contradiction between the two sets of fundamental ideas that underlay the French Revolution and all the other movements to create so-called democratic nation-states in Western Europe. That contradiction runs through the justifications and criticisms of state terror in the ensuing two centuries.

By now, we are familiar with international tribunals that have tried government officials for crimes against humanity, war crimes, and crimes against the peace, torture, genocide, and related offenses. Usually, the crimes charged are not written down in any penal code. The tribunal relies on universally accepted standards of conduct that were developed and known before the conduct the defendant is alleged to have committed. In order to guard against a charge that the tribunals are unfair, the prosecution must prove either that the defendant knew the conduct was wrong or that the standard was so clear that he or she must have known.

We can test this definition—systematic state-sponsored violence, conducted against political enemies, and in disregard of historically determined fair substantive and procedural standards—against the French Terror. Did the Jacobin leaders understand that their conduct was wrongful? The answer must be yes, judged by the standards of that historical time.

As of 1790, ideals of liberty and procedural fairness were well-established in France, England, and the United States. Fairness in trial procedures, limits on the exercise of police power, and substantive protections of dissent were common themes of the political struggles in those countries. As one of its first actions, the French National Assembly issued the "Declaration of the Rights of Man and of the Citizen" on August 26, 1789. The declaration became a beacon light in the definition of human rights and remains part of French fundamental law to this day.

The Declaration's introduction declared:

The representatives of the French people, constituted in the National Assembly, considering that ignorance, forgetting or disregard of the rights of man are the sole causes of the public misfortunes and of the corruption of governments, have resolved to set out, in a solemn declaration, the natural, inalienable and sacred rights of Man, in order that this Declaration, continuously presented to all Members of the social body, will ceaselessly recall to them their rights and duties; in order that the acts of legislative and executive power, may be at all times compared with the goal of every political institution, and be respected; in order that the demands of citizens, founded henceforth on simple and incontestable principles, will be directed always at the maintenance of the Constitution and the happiness of all. Therefore, the National Assembly recognizes and declares, in the presence and under the auspices of the Supreme Being, the following rights of Man and of the Citizen. . . .[8]

Seventeen articles followed guaranteeing social equality, the right to fair treatment before the law, separation of powers, free speech and press, and proclaiming that governmental abuse of power was not only prohibited but would be punished.

We have already seen that the declaration's noble words were more or less quickly gainsaid by the legislative and executive action of the National Assembly's ruling party. However, they had equally obviously endorsed the declaration's words and understood their meaning.

Therefore, it would be easy, even with imperfect historical hindsight, to say that those who engineered and directed the Terror acted with knowledge that their conduct was wrongful and indeed contrary to the most basic principles of social justice.

To say this, however, is only to say that French authorities disregarded their own basic principles and their own express understanding. However, suppose that we are confronted with a government that commits terrorism—as we have defined the term—and has a legal structure that does not guarantee fundamental rights. Can the leading figures in such a government plausibly say that their conduct should not be judged by any standards other than their own internal law? The answer is no, certainly not in this century.

To explain this answer, we must survey the development of transnational legal norms. The French revolutionaries did not invent the idea of universal rights. They simply gave voice—a somewhat hypocritical voice, as matters turned out—to ideas that had been brewing for at least two centuries. During the 1600s, a number of legal writers had constructed theories of natural right, which they variously termed "the rights of man," "the law of nations," or "jus gentium"—the law of all people.[9] The English Revolution and its aftermath had severely limited royal power and recognized—if not always fully—rights to free expression, religious tolerance, and procedural fairness. The voices of French legal philosophers had been a part of this chorus.

Sir William Blackstone, the most influential eighteenth-century legal scholar, wrote of the law of nations as:

[A] system of rules, deducible by natural reason, and established by universal consent among the civilized inhabitants of the world; in order to decide all disputes, to regulate all ceremonies and civilities, and to insure the observance of justice and good faith, in that intercourse which must frequently occur between two or more independent states, and the individuals belonging to each.[10]

The writers on universal rights gave different justifications for the theory. All of them, including Hugo Grotius, included a heavy dose of religion-based natural law ideas. While rejecting constrained religious ideologies identified with particular sects and creeds, these writers called out the image of "Nature and Nature's God,"[11] to use a phrase that found its way into the American Declaration of Independence. In order to invest their analysis with legitimacy, most seventeenth- and eighteenth-century universal rights theorists also rooted their analysis in a discussion of how human history showed that recognition of these rights was consistent with historically determined norms of human conduct and concepts of human needs. Some of this discussion was also rhetorical, in the sense of giving progressive ideas the stamp of inevitability and signaling that the social changes to come were irresistible.

The universal, or at least transnational, nature of the new norms was the product of a long historical process. One defining characteristic of the feudal and royal societies of Europe during the medieval period was their particularism. Despite royal efforts to extend control over all parts of the royal domain, local control over markets and modes of production remained dominant. The merchant class that was to lead the charge for a new social organization was transnational. It sought and obtained concessions for its trade based on a consistent set of ideas about free commerce, much of which went by the name law merchant. So, the rhetoric about fundamental ideas of liberation went with the practical notion of liberating commerce and manufacture from feudal and royal constraints.

The ideology of universal rights clashed sharply with the politics of nationhood. "Vive la France" was the rallying cry, and not "Vive l'humanité." So much has been written about the drive towards nationhood and national identity that we do not need to trace that history here. The nation-state is the preferred and dominant form of bourgeois democratic governance. The leaders of revolutionary change recognized that the desire to see allegedly universal principles put into practical application depended on the existence of a state apparatus that would enforce them. In that time and place, legitimating these claims in this way meant securing their adoption as the legal ideology of a nation-state in which the bourgeoisie controlled state power. To be sure, all the European powers pursued or continued their colonial adventures. Napoleon had imperial ambitions that went beyond the borders of France. However, the fundamental premise remains true.

One can see the contradiction. Once codified, so-called universal principles were no longer universal, they were simply the law of a particular place. They were not principles of a transnational class, but rules established to protect a particular group. That group needed protection against its erstwhile feudal opponents and against those within the nation-state whose interests were in opposition to the newly victorious government. As we have seen in the brief sketch of French revolutionary legislation, among those whom the government sought protection against were the very peasants and workers who had helped bring it to power. The powerful leaders of every nation-state looked to the state for protection against the leaders of other states—to protect commerce, colonies, and territory. The contradictions between different national groupings triumphed over their common interest in establishing and defending transnational principles favorable to commerce.

We can now begin to see how the division into nation-states helped to submerge the idea of human rights, that is, of claims for justice based on "dialectical arguments that have their roots in experience, to a definite view of human flourishing and good human functioning," that is, upon the view that humans have needs for such things as "political rights, money, shelter, and respect."[12] The nation-state, by claiming the right to a monopoly of force within its borders—as extended by its colonial claims—asserted that the only valid claims for such things were those that it recognized as such.

This departure from the theory of universal and natural right was not completely surprising. Although Grotius traced the details, Jean Bodin had foretold it in his 1576 treatise on sovereignty:

> All men are linked to one another and participate marvelously in the universal Republic. All the kingdoms, empires, tyrannies, or republics of the world are united by none other than the authority of reason and the rights of all people. And thus, the world is like a great city and all men together speak with one voice, so that they know they are of the same blood, and under the protection of the same reason. But because this empire of reason has been weakened and constrained, one cannot know how to bring together all nations in one single republic. For that reason, princes have recourse to arms and treaties.[13]

Then, let us trace the ways in which the themes of universal norms were traduced. This discussion is essential for seeing the struggle to

19

adopt a consistent, defensible, and uniform set of principles to identify and condemn state-sponsored terror. For Blackstone, the law of nations included provisions relating to individual rights, at least with respect to mercantile transactions and the rights of hostages. Moreover, Blackstone wrote that the law of nations had been incorporated into the law of England, and was therefore part of the law of the land to be applied by English courts in deciding cases between individuals. That is, there were certain transcendent norms that a legitimate sovereign was bound to respect.

In a sense, Blackstone's definition quoted above was true when he wrote it, and continued to be true. British courts did apply general principles of transnational law in deciding certain private law questions, and in admiralty cases, as did courts of most other countries. In the nineteenth century, judges and legal scholars continued to think of mercantile law principles as transnational in character, and to look to the old merchant law sources.

But the dominant themes of nineteenth century legal writing were that the nation-state was the exclusive source of rights, and any transnational or supranational rules were the product of consent given by treaty or custom. The English legal philosopher Jeremy Bentham penned an influential statement of this view in 1776. Indeed, Bentham is credited with having coined the word *international*, discussing the law of nations in his book, *Principles of Morals and Legislation*. Two brief passages from that book summarize Bentham's view, which was also the dominant theme of international law for more than a century. Bentham wrote:

> The word international, it must be acknowledged, is a new one; though, it is hoped, sufficiently analogous and intelligible. It is calculated to express, in a more significant way, the branch of the law which goes commonly under the name of the law of nations: an appellation so uncharacteristic that, were it not for the force of custom, it would seem rather to refer to internal jurisprudence. The chancellor D'Aguesseau has already made, I find, a similar remark: he says, that what is commonly called droit des gens, ought rather to be termed droit entre les gens.[14]

Bentham makes his point again by saying that dealings between individuals from different states are a matter of the internal law of one or the other of those states, as indeed are dealings between sovereigns in their private capacity. Then, he says, "There remain then the mutual transactions between sovereigns as such, for the subject of that branch of jurisprudence which may be properly and exclusively termed international."

Lest one mistake Bentham's intention, one can look at the writings of d'Aguesseau on which he relies. D'Aguesseau wrote that the terms "law of nations," "law of all peoples," and "jus gentium" were misleading, because they did not describe the legal relationships involved. One should rather speak of law among peoples, because the legal relationships were between nation and nation, rather than involving the rights of individuals as such.

Bentham had prefigured his views in an essay he wrote between 1774 and 1776, criticizing lectures that Blackstone gave at Oxford. The young Bentham concluded that in great measure, the law of nations "isn't law at all." John Lind was young Bentham's collaborator, in a systematic critique of Blackstone that was never completed. In a further discussion of Blackstone's views, Lind wrote (in a passage reviewed and probably approved by Bentham):

> The fact is, the term, law of nations, however allowable in common conversation, should never find a place in a philosophical discussion of law: and that for this plain reason, that nations have no common superior upon earth, from whom they can receive a law.
>
> 'Tis strange how this confusion of terms disfigures even arguments which would otherwise have merit. Even Montesquieu falls into the same error as our Author [Blackstone] in confounding compacts and principles with Laws. There is a difference, however: the mistakes of Montesquieu are the mistakes of a man of genius: whilst those of our Author speak only the servile copyist.[15]

The theory of international law made clear that sovereigns were arbiters of their own conduct within their borders, and that no individual had rights against any sovereign except as the sovereign should decide to accord. Relations among sovereigns were to be regulated by treaties and other instruments, by observance of customary law norms based on tacit consent of states as shown by their consistent practice and warfare as a sanction or as an instrument of policy.

In such a system, there was no basis for speaking of international human rights, except as any particular sovereign chose to interpret and apply them. This method of analysis effectively neutralized any claim that one could judge the misconduct of a nation-state based on standards external to that nation-state's own laws and institutions. In the United States, supporters of slavery, displacement of Native Americans, and anti-alien measures directed primarily at Asians embraced this theory that there were no external standards by which to judge such conduct. The judges who confronted these issues often acknowledged, more or less vaguely, that conduct such as slavery raised serious moral issues but they professed to find no binding transnational rule forbidding it.[16]

A second aspect of the Bentham theory deserves our notice. Under that view of international law, only nation-states are bearers of rights. The idea of individual human rights has no place, unless a nation-state takes up the individual's cause. This concept still exists today, although no longer as the exclusive means by which individual rights may be asserted. In the International Court of Justice, for example, only states can be parties. The rights of individuals are adjudged when a state takes up the cause. Thus, a French seaman, a Congolese politician, and Spanish shareholders[17] come before the court only indirectly because France, the Republic of Congo, and Spain, respectively, assert their interests. Without such a champion, the right-bearer has no remedy in that tribunal. Today, of course, such transnational tribunals as the European Court of Human Rights and the Inter-American Court of Human Rights do accept petitions from individuals, as I discuss below.

Even in the nineteenth century, the Benthamite idea was never fully realized. The Supreme Court held in 1886 that a British subject could assert rights in U.S. courts under a treaty between the United States and Britain, rejecting the claim that only Britain could enforce those rights.[18]

The campaign to abolish the slave trade was transnational. Many people remember a ship called *Amistad*. There was a movie of that name based on the story of this vessel that carried a cargo of African slaves. The ship set sail from Havana in June 1839. The slaves on board rose up and killed the captain and one crew member and took charge of the ship. Two months later, *Amistad* fetched up at Montauk, on Long Island, New York. Complex litigation followed, as Spanish and Portuguese merchants sought to claim the Africans as their property, and others claimed parts of the ship and her cargo. The Supreme Court eventually heard the case. A key part of the Court's decision recognized that the Africans' status depended on "invariable principles of justice and international law."[19]

In 1900, the Supreme Court decided another case that put the matter more clearly. During the Spanish-American War in 1898, U.S. naval forces had seized Cuban fishing vessels as prizes of war. The vessel owners sued to get their boats back; they won in the Supreme Court. The case means far more than that two small boats were returned to their owners. The Court held that principles of customary international law, that is law not embodied in treaties, must be found and applied when governmental conduct is challenged. Moreover, individuals, such as these boat owners, could invoke the protection of international law even during a time of armed conflict such as the Spanish-American War.[20]

In the twentieth century, we have seen a revival and expansion of the older idea of a law of all peoples that defines and protects fundamental human rights, and that can be used as a means of judging the conduct even of sovereign states and their leaders. This movement gained impetus from the Nuremburg Trials of the Nazi leaders in the wake of World War II. As that war drew to a close, and Allied victory seemed certain, British Prime Minister Winston Churchill, American President Harry Truman, and Soviet leader Joseph Stalin considered what should be done to the leaders of Nazi Germany. Those civilian and military leaders had been responsible for the concentration camps in which six million leftists, gypsies, Jews, and others labeled as social outcasts had perished. They had committed war crimes, crimes against humanity, and genocide, or so it seemed.

All three Allied leaders wanted to take decisive action to rebuke and repudiate such conduct, and to make clear that no person, no matter how exalted a position he or she held, and no nation could permissibly engage in it. For a time, the idea seemed to be that the Allied military authorities should round up those considered culpable and execute or imprison them. However, under American prodding, the Allies instead devised a court to try the alleged wrongdoers according to prevailing standards of procedural fairness. Thus, the Treaty of London that established a judicial procedure was born first, and then the actual trials, which took place in Nuremburg, Germany.

The trials, and the treaty that authorized them, accomplished several important things. First, presentation of solid evidence of the Nazi crimes placed beyond all but the most captious criticism any claim that the Nazi holocaust did not occur. Most, if not all, publicized trials teach lessons. Sometimes, those lessons say negative things about the process. However, fair trials, fairly conducted, can teach important lessons about historical events and the benefits of rational analysis of complex events. A trial in the adversary system hears only evidence that is relevant and that meets some minimum standard of reliability. Adversaries challenge one another's proof. Facts and law are decided by people who are, so far as a fallible and imperfect system can guarantee it, relatively unbiased. In the old English phrase, the jurors must be "indifferent as they stand unsworn."

Second, the treaty and the trials enunciated and applied precise rules forbidding state conduct that would merit the name state-sponsored terror.

Third, the treaty and trials made clear that conduct approved and conducted by the leaders of one sovereign state—in this case Nazi Germany—could and would be condemned according to a set of transnational rules external to that state's own legal system. In short, there was a place to stand to condemn the Nazi leaders' conduct.

Fourth, and closely related, the treaty and tribunals rejected the idea that high-ranking officials were immune from prosecution and punishment. Even a head of state cannot commit or authorize acts of state terror with impunity.

The London Treaty and Nuremburg gave us, to use the phrase with which this chapter begins, a "place to stand." Having such a place in 1946—when the London Treaty was signed—does not end our inquiry. I have insisted on using the phrase "historically determined" in defining terror. Let us see what that means in this context. In the first Judiciary Act of 1789, the U.S. Congress included a law that has become known as the Alien Tort Claims Act (ATCA). It says that federal courts can hear a lawsuit by an alien for a wrongful act that is done in violation of the law of nations or treaty of the United States.

The Supreme Court examined the ATCA in *Sosa v. Alvarez-Machain*.[21] The Drug Enforcement Administration recruited Mexican nationals to kidnap Alvarez and forcibly bring him to the United States to be tried for the torture and murder of a DEA agent. He was acquitted, and sued the people who had kidnapped him and their American handlers. The Supreme Court held that the kidnapping did not rise to the level of a fundamental violation of the law of nations and that Alvarez, therefore, had no claim under the ATCA. However, the Supreme Court majority went on to analyze the ATCA in a way that gives vital support to future claims based on more fundamental rights.

The Court noted that in 1789 the law of nations recognized only a relatively few private rights. However, the Court held that the historical and legal developments sketched above had expanded the list and that further expansion could be expected. Thus, although Alvarez did not win his lawsuit, his case provides the basis for lawsuits about such basic claims as torture and genocide. The norm that forbids torture began to take shape in the nineteenth century. By now, the norm is well-established in customary law to the extent that it is termed fundamental. Transnational jurists term it a *jus cogens* norm, which simply means that it is binding on all states and cannot be ignored based on claims of necessity or convenience. Several international treaties further define and prohibit torture and provide remedies for victims.

Just as slavery was an accepted practice at one time, and then progressively limited until its abolition, torture is today universally condemned. This is not to deny that both slavery and torture are practiced in many parts of the world, and even justified by practitioners and apologists. Of course, criminal homicide also occurs, and is sometimes excused or justified on various grounds, but nobody claims that the norm against murder does not exist or should not exist.

So, I suggest, we have found a place to stand when we wish to evaluate state conduct and characterize it as impermissible state-sponsored terror. We can look back at the French reign of terror and say that it certainly violated the French Republic's own declared norms of state conduct. Maximilian Robespierre could not claim that he did not understand the assertedly universal norms he had helped to proclaim, nor plausibly deny that he had transgressed them.

It would be more difficult to say that the French state violated norms of state conduct that were generally accepted and were therefore part of the customary law of nations. Certainly the English, among whom one found France's most vocal critics, did not have a judicial system that guaranteed basic rights. Felony defendants in England did not have a right to defense counsel until 1802. As noted above, more than one hundred crimes were punished by the death penalty. Many of these capital offenses had been created in the early 1700s as part of a campaign to put down peasant revolts by criminalizing traditional means of rural livelihood, such as hunting and gathering, on lands owned by wealthy people. Political persecution of dissenters was still going on, though not to the degree that it was practiced in France and not with such dire consequences as the guillotine. In short, there is room for disagreement about the French reign of terror and, therefore, Mark Twain's view that it was, if not justified, certainly understandable.

Let us return for a moment to the proposed definition: systematic state-sponsored violence, conducted against political enemies, and in disregard of historically determined fair substantive and procedural standards. The term systematic denotes a deliberate use of unlawful violence as a means of social control. Therefore, such violence would be the conscious instrument of governance. All holders and users of state power may, from time to time, depart from accepted standards in their use of violence against people and property. If such deviations are recognized as wrongful, and subject to meaningful review and correction, one would not characterize them as instances of state terror. Legitimate holders of state power have a near-monopoly on the legitimate use of violence. I say "near-monopoly" because all legal systems recognize that private persons can engage in justified use of force, for example in self-defense. As we have seen, in today's world, historically determined standards would include the prohibitions against torture, disappearances, extrajudicial killing, ethnic cleansing, genocide, and crimes against humanity, among other serious violations of established norms.

Seen in this way, terrorism is not a specific criminal act. Rather, it is a term applied to systematic behavior that may include a number of specific offenses that are recognized by almost all legal systems. As we shall see, terrorism might also encompass other ordinary crimes, such as rape and even theft. When we can legitimately say that a series of acts deserve the name terrorism, then there is added reason to pursue and punish the perpetrators, and if they are tried, to add to their punishment on account of the nature and motivation of their conduct.

As we think about responses to terrorism and accountability of perpetrators, we can review some different approaches taken by and on behalf of victims, and make a preliminary evaluation of their value. I begin with a list as a prelude to evaluating the legitimacy and effectiveness of different approaches:

- Judicial proceedings against state actors and even against states themselves have been instituted in domestic courts of the country concerned and other countries, and before international tribunals. Tribunals have been created by treaty and by United Nations General Assembly resolution. These proceedings may be civil or criminal. In the rest of this book, I discuss many of these tribunals and cases.
- Economic and political sanctions may be used against states that practice terrorism, either unilaterally or under the collective security umbrella of the United Nations. Unilateral sanctions raise serious questions under international law.
- Civil conflicts, civil wars, or uprisings—the terms are somewhat interchangeable—challenge the exercise of lawless state power. These are instances where people suffering from oppression exercise their historic right of self-defense. However, in such

conflicts, both sides may commit acts legitimately classified as terrorist.

- Military intervention either as a matter of collective security or unilaterally. Examples include Somalia, the former Yugoslavia, Afghanistan, and Iraq. When an intervention takes place under the collective security apparatus of the United Nations, there is a stronger argument to justify it than when one or more nation-states take action without UN authorization. In this book, I discuss military intervention only briefly. The reader can well judge the propriety and effectiveness of recent interventions without resorting to modes of analysis that transnational law may provide.

C. Judicial Proceedings—*Letelier-Moffitt*

On September 21, 1976, Orlando Letelier and Ronni Karpen Moffitt were killed when a bomb exploded in their car as they drove down Massachusetts Avenue in the District of Columbia. Letelier left a wife and four sons. Ronni's husband, Michael, was in the car and seriously injured in the blast.

In litigation about the death, the court found:

Following the election of Salvador Allende as president of Chile in 1970, Orlando Letelier served variously as Ambassador of the Republic of Chile in the United States, Minister of Foreign Relations, Minister of Interior, and finally Minister of Defense. When the military junta headed by General Augusto Pinochet came to power in September 1973, Letelier was imprisoned until approximately February of 1974. At that time, he was expelled from Chile and after a stay in Venezuela made his way to the United States in January 1975. While in the United States, he served as Director of the Transnational Program at the Institute for Policy Studies in Washington, D.C. During 1975 and 1976 up until the time of his death, he not only worked at the Institute, but also taught at a local university and engaged in various political activities, which included speaking and writing in opposition to the Pinochet government.[22]

Ronni and Michael Moffitt worked with Letelier at the Institute for Policy Studies.

The military coup in Chile overthrew Salvador Allende, a democratically elected President who was a member of Chile's Socialist Party. The coup plotters had the support of the United States, which had provided and continued to provide assistance that helped bring about the coup and then assisted in the brutal tortures, disappearances, and extrajudicial killings that followed and were a means of enforcing social control. Orlando Letelier had been so effective at mobilizing support for a return to democratic rule in Chile that President Pinochet issued a decree on September 10, 1976, assertedly revoking Letelier's Chilean nationality. Under the definition developed in this book, Chile's military government practiced state-sponsored terrorism. This conclusion has been amply reinforced by evidence in many forums.

The car bombing was done on orders of the Chilean secret police and with the approval of President Pinochet. A Chilean secret agent, Michael Vernon Townley, recruited three Cuban émigrés living in the United States and rigged a radio-controlled bomb under Letelier's car.

In August 1978, my law partner, Sam Buffone, and I sued the Republic of Chile and the individual perpetrators of the bombing, on behalf of Orlando's widow Isabel, their four sons, and Michael Moffitt's and Ronni's parents. We brought the lawsuit in federal district court under the Foreign Sovereign Immunities Act of 1976 (FSIA). This law had been passed by Congress to regulate lawsuits against foreign states in U.S. courts. In 1978, few people thought it provided a means to redress state-sponsored terrorism that took the form of assassination.

The military government of Chile did not answer the lawsuit. Instead, it filed a diplomatic note, drafted by a Washington, D.C., law firm, claiming that the federal court did not have the power—subject matter jurisdiction—to hear the case. The junta did not file its note with the court, in order to maintain its claim that it did not recognize the court's power. Rather, it sent the note to the State Department, which forwarded it to Judge Joyce Hens Green. The junta's primary claim was that a sovereign state is immune from suit for the acts alleged against it. When a litigant makes such a claim, the court assumes that all the allegations in the complaint are true and then asks, "If so, does this court have the power to give relief?"

Judge Joyce Hens Green began her analysis of the immunity question by citing Chief Justice John Marshall's opinion for the Supreme Court in *The Schooner Exchange v. McFaddon*, a case decided in 1812.[23] She then described how the law had changed in the intervening century and one-half.

The Schooner Exchange teaches interesting lessons about the forces in play in a case like *Letelier-Moffitt*. It began when two Maryland residents, John McFaddon and William Greetham, somehow found out that a French military ship had docked in the port of Philadelphia on July 22,

1811. The ship bore the name *Balaou,* and was commanded by an officer of the Emperor Napoleon's navy. *Balaou* had been on a voyage to the Caribbean from Europe, and came into Philadelphia after encountering difficult weather and in need of repair and provisions. It must have been quite a voyage. Then, as now, the port of Philadelphia is at least eighty miles up Delaware Bay and the Delaware River from Cape May, New Jersey. The bay and river waters present quite a challenge to sailors.

McFaddon and Greetham told a compelling story. The *Balaou,* they said in their federal lawsuit, was really their ship, the *Schooner Exchange.* Their ship had been on a peaceful trading voyage to Spain when on October 27, 1809, she was overhauled and seized by agents of Emperor Napoleon. Given that the United States and France were at peace in 1809 as in 1811, the seizure looked very much like piracy. Therefore, it would have been in violation of the law of nations, and the pirates, if ever they were found, would have been punishable in whatever court first acquired custody of them.

Neither the French government nor the vessel's captain responded to the lawsuit. However, the French government made a protest to the American State Department, like the procedure the Chilean junta later followed. In the *Exchange* case, however, the celebrated Attorney for the United States for Pennsylvania, Alexander J. Dallas, appeared in federal court and requested that McFaddon and Greetham's claim be dismissed. Dallas prevailed in the trial court, but the circuit court reversed, and the case came to the Supreme Court with Mr. Dallas's request for an expedited hearing.

One of McFaddon and Greetham's complaints was that it did not appear that Mr. Dallas represented anybody with a claim on the vessel. However, all the courts overlooked this fact, and the practice of the United States appearing to assert the interests of a friendly foreign sovereign had been established.

Chief Justice Marshall, for all the Justices, wrote that foreign flag ships on peaceful journeys, who take refuge in American ports and while there do not commit any wrongs, are immune from seizure. In sum, Emperor Napoleon's France had sovereign immunity from McFaddon and Greetham's claims. This immunity derives from general principles of international law and is for the federal courts to decide as a matter of federal law.

For 150 years, the federal courts struggled with the concept of immunity. By the mid-twentieth century, it was a general rule that foreign states were immune from acts done as an expression of their sovereignty, which was sometimes rendered in Latin as *iure imperii,* but not for acts of a commercial, nonsovereign nature, *iure commercii.* This supposed distinction was complicated by the increasing involvement of modern states in ventures such as aviation, shipping, banking, and public utilities, and by the post World War II recognition that sovereigns were not free under any conditions to commit certain acts such as genocide, war crimes, and crimes against the peace.

The U.S. State Department, in the tradition of Alexander J. Dallas, regularly evaluated claims of sovereign immunity asserted by nation-states who were sued, and would file letters agreeing with or dissenting from the nation-states' claim. The courts gave these letters great deference. Although the United States was not in a state of war with any sovereign during this period, the State Department was somewhat more friendly to some governments than to others.

The Foreign Sovereign Immunities Act of 1976 came from concern about the politicization of immunity law. Under the FSIA, a sovereign state is not immune from suit for personal injury, death, or property damage, except when the claim arises from "malicious prosecution, abuse of process, libel, slander, misrepresentation, deceit, or interference with contract rights," or the product of a "discretionary function." These exceptions mirror those in the Federal Tort Claims Act, which authorizes suits against the United States. That is, Congress wanted to treat foreign sovereigns the same as the United States in federal courts. Judge Green found that Chile did not have immunity as to the *Letelier-Moffitt* claim. She rejected the claim that the killings might be a discretionary act, noting that there is no discretion to commit an illegal act, much less blowing up people on the streets of Washington, D.C.

So, the case went forward. Chile declined to appear further. However, its default did not translate into automatic victory. Under the FSIA, you cannot get a default judgment against a foreign state unless you prove your case to the judge. This provision helps to ensure that if a foreign government does not choose to appear for whatever reason, it will not suffer a financial loss without a federal judge having reviewed the law and the facts.

At the hearing, we presented proof of the assassination and of the Chilean government's complicity in it, as well as of the financial damages the Letelier and Moffitt families suffered. Judge Green awarded compensatory damages totaling $2,953,475 to the Letelier and Moffitt families, and attorney fees to our law firm. That judgment was entered November 5, 1980. We then turned to other provisions of the FSIA to see how we might collect this judgment. We found that all of Chile's assets in the United States were immune from seizure under the law. We enlisted the help of lawyers in France and the Netherlands to see about seizing

Chilean copper cargoes or taking other steps to collect. The government of France's socialist president, François Mitterand, graciously received us at the Elysée Palace—France's White House—but would not assist. We tried to collect by seizing a LAN-Chile airplane, but the court held that LAN-Chile was not sufficiently culpably involved to make its assets available to satisfy the judgment.

Then, on December 14, 1989, Patricio Aylwin was elected President of Chile, as the military junta began to loosen its grip of Chilean society. The long period of repression meant that leftist organizations could not realistically compete for the presidency. The junta left in place legal provisions that continued military control of many civilian institutions. However, Aylwin's election was a step forward. President Aylwin expressed the hope that Chile's relations with the United States could be improved. One major obstacle was that Congress had passed legislation forbidding military aid to Chile until there was progress towards justice in the *Letelier-Moffitt* case. Senator Kennedy was even ready to propose an amendment to the FSIA that would have helped the Letelier and Moffitt families seize Chilean assets in the United States to satisfy the judgment.

Finally, the American and Chilean governments agreed to create a bilateral international tribunal that would examine the evidence and determine what payment Chile should make to the families. The commission studied the court records and awarded an amount that approximated the judgment plus some additional funds because of the delay in payment. Thus, the *Letelier-Moffitt* case became an example of accountability for state-sponsored terrorism.

D. Judicial Proceedings—Pinochet, not Kissinger

The *Letelier-Moffitt* case was neither the beginning nor the end of the story of impunity and accountability for Chilean state-sponsored terrorism. For many years, historians and journalists documented U.S. official involvement in the Chilean military coup and cooperation with the junta. Then, on September 18, 2000, in response to a bill sponsored by Congressman Hinchey, the executive branch issued a detailed report on these issues. Along with and following the report, the Clinton administration declassified thousands of relevant documents. From these documents, it is possible to tell the story that follows:

Chile had a long tradition of democratic governance. By the late 1960s, it was apparent that a leftist political alliance dominated by the Chilean Socialist Party might well come to power.[24]

On September 4, 1970, Dr. Allende, the leader of the leftist coalition party, won a slight plurality of the votes (36.3 percent) in Chile's presidential election. In accordance with the Chilean Constitution, the Chilean Congress in joint session, would determine the next president among the first and second contenders in the absence of a clear victor. Traditionally, the Congress had confirmed the candidate with the highest popular vote after the requisite thirty-six day period. Accordingly, on October 24, 1970, the Chilean Congress was expected to ratify Dr. Allende as Chile's first Socialist president.

On September 8, 1970, Henry Kissinger, who was then serving as Assistant for National Security Affairs to President Richard Nixon, requested that the U.S. Embassy in Chile submit "a cold blooded assessment of the pros and cons and problems and prospects involved should a Chilean military coup be organized now with the U.S. assistance."

On September 12, 1970, assessing the situation for Chile, U.S. Ambassador to Chile Edward Korry stated, "[The] Chilean military will not move to prevent Dr. Allende's accession, barring [the] unlikely situation of natural chaos and widespread violence." The Central Intelligence Agency in Santiago was convinced that the military in Chile in its present state was unwilling to seize power. Edward Korry is an interesting figure in the ensuing drama. He had been a journalist covering mainly European issues before entering diplomatic service. He thought an Allende government was dangerous: "Castroism without Castro" was the phrase he used.

Dr. Kissinger, assisted by CIA director Richard Helms, proceeded on two tracks in an effort to prevent Dr. Allende from assuming office. Track I comprised covert political, economical, and propaganda activities approved by the 40 Committee, a subcabinet level body of the executive branch chaired by Dr. Kissinger whose overriding purpose was to exercise control over covert operations abroad. These activities were designed to induce Dr. Allende's opponents in Chile to prevent his assumption of power, either through political or military means. Track II activities were directed "towards actively promoting and encouraging the Chilean military to move against Allende."

Track II was organized, coordinated, and operated by Kissinger and others outside the normal channels for covert operations. With the exception of Kissinger himself, who was chairman of the 40 Committee, and top CIA officials, the 40 Committee was entirely excluded and kept uninformed of Track II. Moreover, the State Department was not informed of Track II. Defendant Kissinger issued orders directly to the CIA, which were carried out by the CIA's station in Santiago and its collaborators.

In the month after September 12, Tracks I and II moved together. Ambassador Korry was authorized to encourage a military coup and intensify contacts with the Chilean military officers to assess their willingness and support of a coup. Ambassador Korry also was authorized to make his contacts in the Chilean military aware that if Dr. Allende were seated, the military could expect no further military assistance from the United States.

On September 21, 1970, Ambassador Korry reported to Kissinger that "General Schneider would have to be neutralized, by displacement if necessary" in order to effect a coup and prevent Dr. Allende from assuming office.

On September 23, 1970, the CIA Santiago office reported to the CIA in Washington, D.C., that General Rene Schneider, commander-in-chief of the Chilean military, would be a stumbling block achieving the goal of promoting a coup in Chile. Between October 4 and October 20, 1970, the CIA made about twenty-one contacts with key military and *carabinero* (police) officials in Chile. Certain Chileans who were inclined to stage a coup were given assurances of a strong support by the United States both before and after a coup.

Under the orders and supervision of Kissinger and Helms, the CIA established, maintained contacts with, and worked with three different groups of coup plotters. Key individuals included retired General Roberto Viaux and General Camilo Valenzuela, Commander of the Santiago Garrison. All groups made it clear, and Kissinger was aware, that any coup would require the elimination of General Schneider, who felt deeply that the Chilean constitution required that the Army not intervene in the constitutional process.

Kissinger and Helms obtained information about the extremist right-wing officer, General Viaux, who had ties to *Patria y Libertad* (Fatherland and Freedom), the most prominent right-wing paramilitary group in Chile, and was willing to accept a secret U.S. commission to remove General Schneider. Kissinger knew of General Viaux's intent, military training, and of the human rights abuses he had committed and was likely to commit.

The CIA provided *Patria y Libertad* with $38,000 between September 4 and October 24, 1970, "in an effort to create tension and a possible pretext intervention by the Chilean military."

Within the first weeks of October 1970, Kissinger and Helms came to regard General Viaux as "the best hope for carrying out the CIA's Track II mandate." As late as October 13, 1970, the CIA gave General Viaux $20,000 in cash and promised him a life insurance policy of $250,000.

On October 14, 1970, the CIA Santiago office reported to the CIA Washington, D.C., office that General Viaux planned "to kidnap . . . General Schneider 'within 48 hours' as part of a coup plan which counts with the cooperation of Valenzuela."

Although the term kidnap was initially employed, Kissinger, Helms, or anyone acting under their direction never gave any instruction to leave General Schneider unharmed, which would have both been reasonable and necessary if they truly wished to prevent such harm, especially given the CIA's delivery of deadly weapons to the coup plotters. In the language of the law, it was foreseeable to Kissinger and his associates that there was a substantial risk to human lives—General Schneider's among them.

On October 15, 1970, Kissinger gave specific instructions to the CIA to "continue keeping the pressure on every Allende weak spot—now, after the 24th of October, after 5 November, and into the future until such time as new marching orders are given." Kissinger knew that the CIA was in contact with the other groups of plotters who had demonstrated their continued commitment to leading a coup against Dr. Allende.

On October 16, 1970, CIA officials cabled the CIA Santiago station based on their conversation with Kissinger. The cable, which was conveyed verbatim to General Viaux, reiterated the "firm and continuing policy [of the United States] that Allende be overthrown by a coup." It stated that Washington's objectives were to send a message to General Viaux to "discourage him from acting alone," to "continue to encourage him to amplify his planning," and to "encourage him to join forces with other coup planners so that they may act in concert either before or after October 24" (the day that the Chilean Congress was to meet to confirm Dr. Allende as president). The cable reassured General Viaux, "you will continue to have our support."

The October 16, 1970, Washington, D.C., CIA cable to its officers in Santiago stressed that the CIA's "operating guidance" was to continue their work of promoting a successful coup in spite of "other policy guidance" that they may receive from other branches of the U.S. government. Reflecting his concern for secrecy, Kissinger expressed in an October 15, 1970, cable that: "It is imperative that these actions [the plan to kidnap General Schneider and assist in promoting a coup in Chile] be implemented clandestinely and securely so that the USG [United States Government] and American hand will be well hidden."

On October 16, 1970, a cable also informed the CIA Santiago station that it should expect delivery of six gas masks and six tear gas canisters that had been requested by one of the groups of coup plotters to carry out General Schneider's kidnapping. The gas masks and the tear gas had been dispatched from Washington, D.C., through special courier.

Kissinger and Helms maintained contact with all groups of plotters. On October 17, 1970, members of the Valenzuela group expressed their willingness to sponsor a coup and informed the CIA through U.S. Army Attaché Paul Wimert of their plan to kidnap General Schneider. They also requested eight to ten tear gas grenades, three 45-caliber machine guns, and 500 rounds of ammunition to accomplish the task. On October 18, 1970, four days before General Schneider was murdered, Wimert met with a Viaux associate and delivered a supply of six tear gas grenades to members of the Valenzuela group, as previously requested.

On October 19, 1970, submachine guns and ammunition were sent by "sterile" diplomatic pouch to members of the Valenzuela faction. That same day, the CIA Santiago office created an "emergency channel" of communication with General Viaux. "Sterile" is a term of art indicating that the guns and ammunition had no identifying markings and that their method of transport was secure from inspection.

On the evening of October 19, 1970, the Valenzuela group, aided by some in the Viaux group, and equipped with the tear gas grenades delivered by the CIA, attempted to kidnap General Schneider as he left an official dinner. The attempt failed because General Schneider left in a private car rather than his official vehicle. A member of the group assured U.S. Army Attaché Wimert that another attempt would be made on October 20, 1970.

On October 20, 1970, another attempt to kidnap General Schneider was made, following payments by the CIA of $50,000 each to General Valenzuela and his chief associates. These payments were authorized on the condition that the Venezuela group would make another kidnapping attempt, but they again failed to kidnap General Schneider during their October 20, 1970, attempt. The CIA Santiago office reported the failed attempt to kidnap General Schneider to the CIA in Washington, D.C.

At 2 a.m. on October 22, 1970, U.S. Army Attaché Wimert delivered three "sterile" submachine guns with ammunition to a member of the Valenzuela group for yet another kidnapping attempt. At or about 8 a.m. that same day, a Viaux-led kidnapping group finally succeeded in removing General Schneider by fatally wounding him as his automobile was intercepted on his way to work. He died two days later. An unloaded machine gun was found at the scene of the killing. That same day, the CIA Santiago office reported to the CIA in Washington, D.C., that the assailants who shot General Schneider used the same kind of weapon delivered several hours earlier by U.S. Army Attaché Wimert to a member of the Valenzuela group. Furthermore, the report stated that the CIA Santiago office "know[s] that General Valenzuela was involved," and is "certain" that numerous other associates were involved.

On October 23, 1970, the CIA commented on the attack on General Schneider, saying, "It was agreed . . . that a maximum effort has been achieved, and that now only the Chileans themselves can manage a successful coup. The Chileans have been guided to the point where a military solution is at least open to them."

Bruce MacMaster, a CIA employee, made efforts on behalf of the CIA to obtain hush money for jailed members of the Viaux group after the assassination and before the coup plotters could implicate the CIA. According to a memorandum at the time, "In an effort to keep prior contact secret, maintain good will of the group, and for humanitarian reasons, $35,000 was passed."

After the Schneider killing, U.S. Army Attaché Wimert and CIA Santiago Chief Henry Hecksher retrieved the payments of $50,000 that had been paid to General Valenzuela and his associates. U.S. Army Attaché Wimert also retrieved the guns with the serial numbers filed off, the ammunition, the tear gas, and the gas masks, and went to the port town of Valparaiso and dumped them all in the ocean.

At some point as the plot to kidnap General Schneider was unfolding, Ambassador Korry became aware of it and went to Washington, D.C. He reported meeting with Kissinger and President Nixon. After the death of General Schneider, Korry asked Wimert whether the United States had been involved and was told that it had not.

Salvador Allende became President after all. The socialist reforms of his administration were controversial, and U.S. officials continued their efforts to destabilize and ultimately overthrow his government. The record of U.S. officials' involvement in the events that led to the coup that took place on September 11, 1973, and those that the coup predictably engendered, is well-documented by materials that were declassified and released in 2000. Those with questions should read the CIA's report of September 23, 1970, issued because of legislation sponsored by Rep. Hinchey and available on the CIA Web site.

The coup was led by military officers—General Augusto Pinochet foremost among them. The military seized the presidential palace, took Allende into custody, and killed him. The Costa-Gavras motion picture *Missing*, starring Jack Lemmon and Sissy Spacek, recounts post-coup events in dramatic fashion.[25]

Henry Kissinger and the CIA provided at least $6.5 million between 1970 and 1973 to destabilize the Allende government. They developed a plan to penetrate and bribe all the major Chilean political parties, support antiregime demonstrations, finance the opposition press and other groups, implement a false propaganda campaign, and maintain a close relationship with possible coup plotters within the military. The CIA also encouraged several coup plotters by telling them that "if [a] military junta took over [Chile], [the] U.S. could help in many ways: Financially, with food, agricultural loans, etc." Government officials knew that a coup would result in massive repression against civilians. On October 1, 1973, the U.S. Navy Section in Valparaiso, Chile, characterized the coup d'etat in a very positive light and claimed ownership for the coup, referring to the event as "our D-Day" and as being "close to perfect."

Following the coup, the Chilean secret police, the Directorate of National Intelligence (DINA), punished the new regime's opponents and sought to deter further opposition through indiscriminate arrests, torture, execution, and disappearances. These events are documented in reports later issued by the new government installed after Pinochet's departure from the Presidency of Chile. At the time these repressive measures were being used, the U.S. Defense Department reported to senior American officials that the DINA's methods were "so notorious as the [government of Chile's] chief instrument of repression, and so tied by its operations and training to abusive activities, that elimination, or a complete overhaul, seems the only remedy." Other officials reported that DINA interrogation and torture "techniques are straight out of the Spanish Inquisition and often leave the person interrogated with visible bodily damage."

American officials, including Henry Kissinger, knew of the DINA abuses. On September 20, 1973, the Assistant Secretary of State for Inter-American Affairs informed Kissinger that the Chilean government was holding 5,000 political prisoners in the National Stadium. CIA officials reported that General Pinochet was conducting a severe campaign against leftists and perceived political enemies in the early months after the coup, as evidenced by the CIA's report of the location of twenty-seven bodies that showed signs of torture and mutilation, and had been dumped into a river. Two months after the coup, Kissinger received notice that 13,500 individuals had been arrested, 7,000 to 8,000 had been held in the National Stadium, 2,000 individuals had left Chile in search of asylum, between 100 and 320 executions had occurred, and as many as 3,000 individuals had died. These numbers were much higher than the "official" numbers being released at the time by the dictatorship, yet

U.S. authorities did not release this information to the public. As late as 1975, the CIA was still reporting that serious abuses were common, evidenced by its finding that 3,811 political prisoners had been or were being held.

The Hinchey report contains many details of the way that American officials cooperated with the DINA during the rest of the 1970s by providing money, encouragement, and receiving intelligence product in exchange. On the political front, Kissinger was a leader in seeking to help the junta and played a role in authorizing the CIA to "assist the junta in gaining a more positive image, both at home and abroad." The CIA paid for Chilean military spokesmen to travel to other countries, promote the junta's propaganda, and spread projunta material in U.S. media outlets. In turn, the CIA supplied its own promilitary dictatorship propaganda by using U.S. media assets. The United States also provided assistance to a multicountry project called Operation Condor, which helped intelligence chiefs from several South American countries carry out programs of state-sponsored terrorism. Until the Congress, reacting to the *Letelier-Moffitt* case, barred such sales, the United States also stepped up sales of military equipment to the junta.

Dr. Kissinger showed the world two faces about reports of the junta's human rights record. In a 1976 speech to the General Assembly of the Organization of American States, he publicly advised Pinochet to achieve some progress on human rights to improve Chile's image with the U.S. Congress. In a private meeting with Pinochet, Kissinger spoke differently. He said, "[t]he speech is not aimed at Chile. I wanted to tell you about this. My evaluation is that you are a victim of all left-wing groups around the world, and that your greatest sin was that you overthrew a government which was going Communist. . . . We welcomed the overthrow of the Communist-inclined government here. We are not out to weaken your position."

The catalog of arrest, tortures, disappearances, and killings is not yet complete, but the victims numbered in the thousands, with the greatest number occurring during the first few years of the junta's rule. A 2004 report listed some 28,000 victims.

In 1988, the junta allowed a plebiscite on October 5, 1988, in which voters could vote yes or no on whether Pinochet should serve another eight-year term as President—55 percent voted no. A national election was held and Patricio Aylwin was elected president. Aylwin was sworn in, and Pinochet left office on March 11, 1990. However, Pinochet had seen to it that he would be a senator for life with immunity from prosecution, and that he would remain as commander-in-chief of the Army until 1998. Other transitional measures helped to ensure that the Chilean Senate would be dominated by the right wing for some years.

Because of fears that the Chilean military would again seize power and its continuing grip on important elements of state power, for some time there was no real accountability for the state-sponsored terrorism of the Pinochet years. A 1991 report on abuses was incomplete and unaccompanied by measures to bring responsible parties to justice. Rather, it required transnational action to open up the possibility of finding the facts and assessing responsibility. In Spain, human rights lawyer Juan Garcés became counsel for more than 4,000 victims of the Pinochet era. His clients fell into three categories: survivors of torture and unlawful imprisonment, relatives of those who were known to have been killed, and relatives of those who disappeared and were not accounted for. Under generally accepted principles of human rights law, relatives of the disappeared have standing to sue for their own anguish caused by not knowing what happened to their loved ones.

Under Spanish law, a private person can initiate a criminal prosecution, subject to the decision of an examining magistrate to accept the case and pursue it. The state prosecutor can support the case, stay neutral, or try to derail it, but the magistrate has substantial independence. Garcés was fortunate in that Judge Baltasar Garzón decided that the case must be pursued. Garcés used the court procedures to assemble an impressive dossier of Pinochet's involvement in the crimes of his regime.

Garcés's case came before investigating magistrate Baltasar Garzón. Garzón has been the investigating magistrate, with power to direct criminal prosecutions, in a number of cases involving terrorism. He has pursued Argentine participants in Operation Condor, Basque separatists, and al Qaeda supporters. His rulings provided crucial support to Garcés's efforts.

Of course, Pinochet's crimes—like those of other Garzón targets—were directly carried out by thousands of armed operatives, secret police, uniformed police, and members of the military. However, when we think about the didactic and deterrent effect of criminal prosecutions, selecting high-profile—indeed iconic—defendants is a wise use of prosecutorial resources. Such prosecutions provably help to influence the conduct of other highly placed perpetrators.

By 1998, Garcés and Garzón had assembled a substantial criminal case against Pinochet for violation of Spanish laws against torture that are based on international norms. Why is it that a Spanish court could proceed against crimes committed in Chile? To begin with, all states have the jurisdiction to prescribe norms against torture and crimes against humanity, wherever and by whomever those offenses are committed, just as they have the power to legislate against the earlier-defined offenses of slavery and piracy. One can argue that all states are obliged to take these norms into their own legal systems. As to jurisdiction to punish, most states recognize their own power to prosecute crimes against their citizens, and crimes that take place outside their territory but with a predictable and intended effect in the territory. Many victims of the Pinochet era in Chile were Spanish nationals.

However, there is a broader principle—that of universal jurisdiction. In the eighteenth century, it was accepted that piracy was a crime against all of humanity, and that a pirate when caught could be brought into any forum and tried there. In later years, other offenses have joined the list, and today it is understood that the power and duty to punish international criminals is not limited by the boundaries of nation-states. The law's maxim is *aut daedaere, aut judicare*—send the alleged criminal to another state for prosecution or try him. I discuss this topic in more detail later in this book.

When Garcés learned that Pinochet had gone to London for medical treatment in the fall of 1998, he obtained from Garzón an Interpol warrant to arrest Pinochet to be held for extradition to Spain. The Spanish government was a somewhat reluctant player in this situation, but Judge Garzón was fully behind it. Pinochet called on the American lawyers who had represented him and the junta, as well as British counsel. He invoked his alleged immunity from prosecution.

As is usual in extradition cases, the demanding state (in this case, the Kingdom of Spain) was represented in the British courts (the rendering state) by the British crown. Jane Tigar and I were asked to help the British lawyers in resisting Pinochet's immunity claim. The case went twice to Britain's highest court, the House of Lords, and resulted in a judgment that Pinochet was not immune for any acts that occurred after 1988, when Britain signed the torture treaty. Under an ongoing conspiracy theory, and given that most of the disappeared had never been accounted for, this decision allowed the case to go forward.

The next stage was a hearing before the Bow Street magistrate. There has been a magistrate sitting in Bow Street, London, for more than 200 years. Sir John Fielding, the brother of writer Henry Fielding, served as magistrate in the eighteenth century. For Pinochet's hearing, the magistrate was Roland Bartle, a conservative jurist. Dame Margaret Thatcher, Britain's former prime minister, spoke out in support of Pinochet and some feared that her comments would influence the magistrate.

The comments did have an effect, but not the one that Dame Thatcher wanted. Bartle resented the efforts to sway his consideration of the law. In this extradition proceeding between two states who were both members of the European Community, he was obliged to accept the allegations of fact in the Spanish documents and to apply settled legal principles. However, because of the publicity surrounding the case, and the importance that Pinochet's immunity claim had achieved, he dealt with the issues at some length. Speaking of the treaties that established new procedures for extradition, he wrote in his October 8, 1999, judgment:

> These Conventions represent the growing trend of the international community to combine together to outlaw crimes which are abhorrent to civilised society whether they be offences of the kind to which I have referred or crimes of cruelty and violence which may be committed by individuals, by terrorist groups seeking to influence or overthrow democratic governments or by undemocratic governments against their own citizens. This development may be said to presage the day when, for the purposes of extradition, there will be one law for one world.

Point by point, Magistrate Bartle rejected the defense contentions and held that Pinochet could stand trial in Spain for torture and for conspiracy to commit torture, and that the families of disappeared persons could be considered as torture victims. Pinochet's factual arguments were matters for defense in the trial court in Spain. However, Britain's Home Secretary had the last word and decided that Pinochet was in too frail a physical condition be extradited to Spain to stand trial. Pinochet returned to Chile.

The British proceedings had, however, done their work. The House of Lords decision denying Pinochet immunity was followed up in Chile by judicial decisions attacking his claims of immunity in the courts of that country. Hundreds, perhaps thousands, of cases were filed by victims and their families against Pinochet and other junta leaders and agents. The tide had turned, and it appeared possible that there could be accountability in Chile's own courts.

The political impact in Chile of the Pinochet proceedings had been of great concern to those of us who, from 1973 onwards, had opposed the junta and welcomed Pinochet's departure from the presidency. In 1998, when the extradition proceedings began in London, I spoke to many people involved in the Chilean democratic movement. Some were concerned that the public attacks on Pinochet would provoke the Chilean military to take action. However, Chilean human rights leaders supported what Garcés and the British courts were doing.

When I returned home from the London magistrate hearing in 1999, I pondered this question of accountability. When the Hinchey report came out, on September 18, 2000, with the executive branch conceding that U.S. conduct towards Chile had been wrong, I felt encouraged. With some overstatement, I said this in a talk at Washington College of Law:

> I want to talk about bringing it home. When you attack a human rights abuser who is in a position of power, you may recall what the Duke of Norfolk said to Sir Thomas More: "By the Mass, Master Moore, it is perilous, this striving with kings." It is perilous to contest the power of those who are wielding power right now, as distinct from those who have been left, or been removed from, office. More prosaically, during the years when Harold Macmillan was British Prime Minister, Deputy Prime Minister Richard A. Butler did most of the defending of the Tory Party in the House of Commons. Macmillan would wander into the chamber from time to time, usually in a fuzzy sweater. One morning, as Butler was holding forth, Macmillan entered the House. Harold Wilson, who was the shadow Prime Minister jumped up and said, "Stop ragging the monkey, here comes the organ grinder now!" It is time to engage the responsibility of the organ grinder. That is to say, we have had the years of the Cold War. We live in the middle of the metropolitan country, whose policies have permitted, encouraged, financed, and derived the benefit of tortures, disappearances, forcible relocations, murders, and displacements of whole populations. And so the question is, whether under American law, it is possible to engage the responsibility of the individuals and entities who have done these things.

Based on these ideas, and after thorough factual and legal research, students at Washington College of Law, in a clinical program on human rights impact litigation, began lawsuits against Henry Kissinger and other U.S. officials for complicity in the 1970 assassination of General René Schneider, and in the tortures and disappearances under the Pinochet regime. There was at least one irony in suing Henry Kissinger in the courts of his own country. He had resisted efforts of French judicial authorities to question him about his involvement in human rights abuses in Chile. He had written an article in *Foreign Affairs*[26] attacking the very idea of universal jurisdiction and supporting the contentions made in that context by Augusto Pinochet. Indeed, Kissinger's article contained a flattering photo of Pinochet and criticized the British proceedings. Kissinger said:

> The appropriate solution was arrived at in August 2000 when the Chilean Supreme Court withdrew Pinochet's senatorial immunity, making it possible to deal with the charges against him in the courts of the country most competent to judge this history and to relate its decisions to the stability and vitality of its democratic institutions.

The evidence of Kissinger's culpable involvement in the Schneider assassination and the postcoup crimes of the junta was powerful. George W. Bush had become President while the case was being prepared. The Bush administration's Justice Department took over Kissinger's legal defense. After several years of litigation, the U.S. Court of Appeals for the District of Columbia Circuit held that Kissinger's complicity could not be litigated in U.S. courts. That court invoked the political question doctrine, holding that the matters were not suitable for judicial action but rather belonged to the executive's unreviewable discretion.[27]

These holdings were questionable invocations of a vague and often-criticized doctrine. The Supreme Court has often held that senior executive officers, including the President, are accountable for actions taken in violation of the constitution, laws and treaties of the United States. Such executives may have a qualified immunity from suit, based on showing that they could not have known their conduct was unlawful. Uncritical invocation of the political question doctrine converts that qualified protection into an absolute wall against relief for victims. In the famous *Steel Seizure* case, the Supreme Court rebuked President Truman and his agents for venturing beyond their lawful powers, even during a time of military conflict.

As for the contention that cases touching on foreign relations are beyond the power of courts to decide, the Supreme Court has firmly held that "it is error to suppose that every case or controversy which touches foreign relations lies beyond judicial cognizance."[28] As Justice O'Connor said in one of the cases rebuking the Bush administration for claiming an unreviewable power to detain suspected terrorists:

> [W]e necessarily reject the Government's assertion that separation of powers principles mandate a heavily circumscribed role for the courts in such circumstances. Indeed, the position that the courts must forgo any examination of the individual case and focus exclusively on the legality of the broader detention scheme cannot be mandated by any reasonable view of separation of powers, as this

approach serves only to condense power into a single branch of government. We have long since made clear that a state of war is not a blank check for the President. . . . Whatever power the United States Constitution envisions for the Executive in its exchanges with other nations or with enemy organizations in times of conflict, it most assuredly envisions a role for all three branches when individual liberties are at stake.[29]

The Supreme Court's assertion of power to find and apply transnational law in the service of human rights traces all the way to the earliest years of our national existence.[30] All three branches of government share responsibility for foreign affairs. With specific reference to torture and to covert action—the very issues in the Kissinger litigation—Congress has repeatedly condemned the former and ordered limits on the latter.

In the end, the Kissinger litigation demonstrates a significant problem with invoking the power of national courts for redress against the wrongs committed by that nation's leaders, at least until the generation of wrongdoers has left power and their place taken by those anxious to learn the past's lessons in the service of a more just future. The Kissinger litigation should cause us to consider that national judicial power, so important in the civil rights struggles, has limits.

It is ironic that the Bush administration and conservative federal judges would hold that U.S. complicity in torture, disappearances, assassination, and other emblems of state-sponsored terrorism are beyond the reach of judicial power at the same historical moment that the administration was planning military action with the avowed intention of displacing a tyrannical regime and supporting accountable and democratic institutions. Courts of a given nation-state are assigned a place to stand, within the governmental structure of that nation-state. From that place, they are adjured to look outside their own system to transnational principles. We have examined historical examples of national courts struggling with this obligation to look outside.

When a national court system refuses to apply the legal ideology of human rights in an even-handed manner, its actions inevitably degrade the idea of transnational norms and contribute to an argument that such norms are always cynical instruments of major powers' ambition. I do not hold such a pessimistic view, and believe that struggle within national tribunals is an important part of the campaign to achieve respect for these historically and socially determined norms. However, I also argue in later essays for establishment of truly transnational forums where responsibility can be assessed.

E. Judicial Proceedings—the French Cases[31]

No intelligent person denies that the Nazi Holocaust represented state-sponsored terrorism against leftists, gays, gypsies, Jews, and others. The treatment of Holocaust victims meets our definition: systematic state-sponsored violence, conducted against political enemies, and in disregard of historically determined fair substantive and procedural standards.

Few question that collaboration with the Nazi regime was more wide-spread than most people are now willing to admit. In the early 1990s, I became interested in criminal prosecutions in France of wartime Nazi collaborators, for studies on how a prosecutorial and judicial system can address perpetrators of state-sponsored terrorism when the accused are citizens of the country in which the trials are taking place. The broader question is whether national judicial systems can ever adequately address such activities near the time it occurs or even years later.

Three criminal cases in France are useful examples for study. To see these cases in perspective, one must examine how the legal rules under which they were conducted came into being. As World War II ended, the victorious Allies faced the question of what to do about Nazi leaders. There was some sentiment for summarily executing them. In the end, they were tried at Nuremberg. Japanese leaders were tried at Tokyo. It cannot be said that the trials were uniformly fair: for example, particularly in the Tokyo cases, the right to counsel was not meaningfully afforded the defendants. In addition, some of the war crimes charged against the defendants represented conduct, such as failure to limit civilian casualties from bombing, that the Allies had committed.

However, the trials were an opportunity to spell out state and individual responsibility for acts that merit the name terrorism. They were didactic, in the sense that laying out the evidence of the Nazi Holocaust could place beyond the pale of all but the most captious criticism any claim that the holocaust and the death camps did not happen.

Of course, the Nuremberg and Tokyo trials were examples of victors judging the vanquished. If the idea of accountability was to gain wider acceptance, and the claims of immunity or impunity to be rejected, it would be important for other trials in other forums to follow. The United States did not set a good example. It welcomed Nazis who could provide scientific and technical information, and ignored or concealed their involvement in persecution. The laws that permitted revocation of citizenship of those who entered the United States, based on proof of their involvement in Nazi persecution, were selectively and at times capriciously enforced. Other countries as well provided refuge for persecutors.

The story of France's pursuit of Holocaust perpetrators shows the interplay of political forces, accountability, and judicial review. There were three iconic war crimes trials in France: Klaus Barbie, Paul Touvier, and Maurice Papon. Barbie, known as the "butcher of Lyon" was a Gestapo agent, and his trial could be regarded as an episode, long after Nuremberg, in the ongoing hunt for Nazi criminals. However, Touvier was thoroughly French, and Papon was not only French but had served in important governmental posts after World War II. Therefore, the Touvier and Papon trials were occasions for serious inquiry and debate in France about collaboration with Nazi terror. The evidence in these trials teach us how easily state actors can become complicit in terrorist acts against a perceived enemy. They remind us how fragile the institutions designed to protect and promote human rights are, and how accountability can be hard to find.

The prosecution of Paul Touvier for crimes against humanity consumed the attention of lawyers, scholars, and journalists. Many French people—judges among them—had and continue to have difficulty facing the truth of Vichy France collaboration with Hitler's atrocities during the World War II. The Touvier case tells us a compelling story of the ways in which French political figures have struggled with the legacy of the German occupation and resistance to it. The opinions of jurists give some hint of the stark power of crime against humanity as a revolutionary concept in international penal law, and in the movement to vindicate and extend international human rights.

For the trial lawyer, the Touvier case illustrates once again that the story of a criminal case lies in the details of proof. Touvier's claims—to have not been involved, to have acted from good motives, to have been an honorable soldier—were stripped from him one by one. This was done by the quiet force of facts, and not by rhetoric, prosecutorial excess, or judicial overreaching.

1. Vichy France—The Background[32]

On May 10, 1940, Germany invaded France. On June 14, 1940, German troops entered Paris by the Porte de la Villette. That night, SS Standartenführer Helmut Knochen installed himself and his command at the Hotel du Louvre.

The French National Assembly met in disorder at Vichy. Under the influence of Vice-Premier Pierre Laval, the Assembly voted full emergency and constitution-making power to Premier Henri Phillipe Petain, a war hero with the rank of Marshal. Petain formed a government on

July 12, 1940, which quickly made peace with the Germans in exchange for nominal sovereignty and independence in a part of France.

On June 17, the Vichy government passed its first law regulating the freedom of foreigners, with major emphasis on Jews who were not French citizens. On July 22, a new law provided for revoking the naturalization of Jews who had obtained French citizenship after August 1927. Certainly, the Vichy government did not automatically and completely heed the German will in formulating and executing genocidal policies. Some Vichy ministers were more compliant than others. Petain's feeble efforts to control some of his ministers resulted in German counterpressure, to which Petain usually yielded.

Members of the Vichy government attempted at times to resist German importuning concerning the persecution, roundups, detention, execution, and deportation of Jews and other targets of Aryan dominance. These efforts became feebler and less availing after German troops entered Vichy territory in November 1942. Laval, whom Petain had removed from the government in 1940, rejoined it under German pressure.

In January 1943, a new military police detachment, the Milice, was established in the Vichy zone. It was under the command of the most virulently pro-Nazi members of the Petain cabinet, and reported directly to Darnand, Secretary of State for the Maintenance of Order. The Milice was the direct outgrowth of the Service of the Legionnaire Order (SOL). The SOL celebrated its goals and functions in a theme song—a sort of homage to Petain. The last stanza went:

SOL, make pure France's lot:
Bolsheviks, freemasons, enemies
Israel, ignoble rot
Nauseated France vomits you out

The Milice occupied an increasingly important role in the Vichy government during 1943 and 1944, right up to the liberation of Paris in August 1944. Its actions included the assassination of Georges Mandel on July 6, 1944. Mandel had been a cabinet officer under the Third Republic, and an opponent of the Vichy France reorganization. His assassination was, according to the Milice official version, in retaliation for the Resistance having killed Philippe Henriot on June 28, 1944. Henriot was Vichy France secretary of state for information and a virulent pro-Nazi. Henriot's important position within the Vichy establishment, as the war ended, evidenced that government's alliance with the Reich and its avowed dedication to anti-Jewish and antileftist pogroms. There was evidence that Mandel was also singled out for assassination because he was a Jew. At Touvier's trial, the defense attempted to show that Mandel was killed on Hitler's orders to bolster the theory that the crimes charged against Touvier had been ordered by the Gestapo.

The assassination of Mandel, an eloquent and visible symbol of anti-Vichy and anti-German sentiment, symbolizes essential truths about the Milice and Vichy government. The Milice's response to Henriot's death was evidence that it had become the state, and that it felt free to apprehend and punish people without the formality of a trial or even formal charges. Mandel was perhaps its most prominent target, but not its first. The Milice's dominant position was one of many items of evidence that the Vichy government was a pawn of Nazi Germany.

Among the first were seven Jews rounded up and shot in the early hours of June 29, 1944, at a cemetery near the town of Rillieux-la-Pape. This reprisal was conducted under the personal direction of Paul Touvier, and his role became the sole basis on which he was tried and convicted in Versailles in the spring of 1994.

Touvier's crime, if one credits the evidence against him, was a homicide aggravated by theft of the victims' goods. Touvier came to insist, when his fugitive days were ended and he finally faced his accusers, that the Germans had been so exercised over Henriot's death that they had commanded the assassination of dozens of Jews. Touvier claimed that he had managed to get the number down to just seven.

This claim led to a minute examination not only of Touvier's actions but of the Vichy–Third Reich relations during this critical period, and of the Milice's role in the closing days of the war. All of this factual examination was overshadowed by the Charter of the International Military Tribunal that defined the crime against humanity, the French Penal Code provisions that codified the offense, and the earlier case of Klaus Barbie.

2. The Crime Against Humanity

The 1945 London Treaty[33] that established the Nuremburg Tribunal also defined the crime against humanity in an annexed Charter. The Charter empowered the tribunal to "try and punish persons who, acting in the interests of the European Axis countries, whether as individuals or members of organizations, committed any" of a number of crimes, including "crimes against humanity." The crime against humanity was defined as "murder, extermination, enslavement, deportation, and other inhumane acts committed against any civilian population, before or during the war, or persecutions on political, racial or religious grounds in execution of or in connection with any crime within the jurisdiction of the Tribunal, whether or not in violation of the domestic law of the country where perpetrated."[34]

The quoted portions of the Charter actually deal with four distinct concepts, which sometimes have been confused in later discussions. The first idea is the competence or jurisdiction of the tribunal in relation to persons: the tribunal has power only over those persons who acted in the interest of the Axis powers during a certain time period. This is termed competence *ratione personae*.[35] One sees the same sort of definitional exercise in the United Nations Security Council resolution establishing the international criminal court for trial of human rights violations in the former Yugoslavia.[36]

Second, the Charter defines the tribunal's subject matter jurisdiction or competence *ratione materiae*. This competence extends to crimes against humanity, crimes against the peace, and war crimes.[37]

Third, the Charter provides a definition of specific offenses. This task is obviously essential given that no international legislative body had passed statutes criminalizing the potential defendants' conduct. That is, there was no written norm in existence when the Nazis took power in Germany that defined a crime against humanity. There were treaty provisions to which one might refer, although those dealt primarily with war crimes and to a lesser extent with crimes against the peace. However, the norms described in the Charter were not drawn from thin air. They could be justified by international consensus as norms of customary international law, and perhaps as peremptory norms.[38] The drafters of the United Nations resolution on the former Yugoslavia faced a similar task of defining terms. That resolution speaks expressly of the principle *nullum crimen sine lege*: no crime without a law, and the consequent need to "apply principles of international humanitarian law which are beyond any doubt part of customary law."

Fourth, in defining the crime against humanity, the Charter authorizes prosecution regardless of any provisions in the domestic law of the place where it was done. This principle has since been expanded. For example, the Yugoslavia resolution rejects the defense of superior orders for subordinates, except in mitigation of punishment, and rejects any defense of official position or compliance with local law on the part of an official.

When one parses the London Charter text by subject matter, it seems clear that the crime against humanity does not require that the actor have been an agent of state power. He or she need only have intentionally[39] done the forbidden conduct with the forbidden motivation or effect.

Most of the prohibited acts can most readily be done by those possessing state power. Such inhumanities have been committed and are being committed by members of nominally private groups as well. Examples would include Afrikaner groups in South Africa seeking to destabilize the existing government, KKK and Nazi groups in the United States, death squads in El Salvador and Guatemala, and other organizations devoted to committing terrorist acts as defined elsewhere in this book.

The Soviet scholar G. I. Tunkin has spoken of "responsibility of individuals for crimes against humanity."[40] Piracy has long been known as an individual crime against the law of nations.[41] Engaging in the slave trade might also fall into that category. The Genocide Convention expressly mandates punishment of "private individuals" who violate its terms.[42] Thus, while the prosecution of crimes against humanity has historically focused on state actors, there is no reason that they should be the only ones susceptible of being charged with such offenses. Americans may be accustomed to thinking of crimes against humanity as a broader version of criminal violation of civil rights, under the federal criminal laws.[43] These offenses require that the accused be, or be in concert with, a state actor. That requirement springs from the notion that constitutional rights are valid against "state" and not "private" action.[44]

Limiting criminal responsibility to state actors can also cause difficulty in a time of fragmented public authority and real dispute over who is exercising state power, in fact and in law. The Touvier case illustrates the problem: the Milice, of which he was a member, was surely an agent of the Vichy government. Yet, Milice members had loyalties to the Nazis that surpassed those of many Vichy officials, and aspirations for their own future role in a reconstituted Europe. The same sort of ideology dominates a number of the most dangerous violent groups whose actions implicate the interests protected by the prohibition on crimes against humanity.[45]

The debate about whether non-state actors can commit crimes against humanity has, I think, been eclipsed by events. As the transnational community seeks to devise fair and just means to punish terrorist acts fairly and equitably, most people recognize that very destructive conduct that merits the label terrorist is being committed by groups that are informal in the sense that they do not proclaim allegiance to any particular state. Indeed, non-state actors may wield power to commit many kinds of crime that surpass the power of any particular nation to police and punish; examples include environmental degradation, financial fraud, oppression of workers, and even slavery. As I discuss later, rules that protect against unfairness must be enforced regardless of who is going to be prosecuted. However, the power and duty to prescribe and punish seems indisputable.

3. French Penal Code

In 1964, as the result of agitation led by Holocaust survivors and Resistance groups, the crime against humanity was added to the French Penal Code, and made imprescriptible; that is, not subject to the statute of limitations. The 1964 statute did not create the crime as a matter of French law. The 1964 law recognized that crimes against humanity had been defined in a United Nations resolution of February 13, 1946, and in the Charter of the Nuremburg tribunal.[46] Moreover, French law since 1810 had provided that torture and barbarity were aggravating circumstances in the commission of any offense.

The crime against humanity definition was clarified in 1992. Here are the most pertinent provisions:

Article 211-1. Genocide is an action, according to a concerted plan, directed at the total or partial destruction of a national, ethnic, racial or religious group, or of any particular group defined according to any other arbitrary criteria, through commission or causing others to commit, towards the members of such group, any of the following acts:

- a voluntary attempt against human life;
- grave assault against physical or psychic integrity;
- submission to conditions of existence of such a nature as to cause the total or partial destruction of the group;
- measures designed to prevent births;
- forced transportation of children.

Genocide is punishable by life imprisonment. . . .

Article 212-1. Deportation, enslavement, or massive and systematic summary executions, kidnapping of persons followed by their disappearance, torture or inhuman acts, inspired by political, philosophical, racial or religious reasons, and organized according to a concerted plan against a group within the civilian population, are punishable by life imprisonment. . . .

Article 212-2. When committed in time of war, according to a concerted plan, against those who fight the ideological system in the name of which crimes against humanity are perpetrated, acts included within Article 212-1 are punishable by life imprisonment . . .

Article 212-3. Participation in a group formed or in an association established in order to prepare for commission of the crimes defined by Articles 211-1, 212-1 and 212-2, when such participation is manifested by commission of one or more material facts, is punishable by life imprisonment. . . .

Article 213-5. Public action relative to the crimes defined in the present article, as well as any penalties duly imposed, are not subject to any statute of limitation.

Both natural and juridical persons—that is to say, incorporated and incorporated organizations—may be prosecuted for these offenses. The imprescriptibility provision means not only that prosecution is not barred by a statute of limitations, but that a judgment of conviction will not lapse if the defendant is a fugitive. Under French law, most judgments for serious crimes lapse if not carried out within twenty years.[47] When the crime against humanity was first included in the Penal Code in 1964, it included a provision that crimes against humanity are "imprescriptible by their nature." This formulation captures a basic idea about prosecuting state-sponsored terrorism that takes the specific form of crimes against humanity.

Again, nothing in the text of these statutes requires proof that the defendant acted on behalf of the state, much less that he or she was in the service of an Axis power. As noted above, French courts are free to apply the statutes in accordance with their text, rather than as limited by previous judicial decisions.

4. The Barbie Case—Too Clever by Half

To see the Touvier prosecution in perspective, we must take a brief detour into the case of Klaus Barbie. Barbie was an SS officer. In 1942, he became head of the Gestapo in Lyon, responsible for repression and reprisals against the Resistance, Communists, and Jews. He earned his title "butcher of Lyon." After the war, Barbie was briefly a fugitive. The American Counter Intelligence Corps employed him as an anticommunist expert. Later, he took refuge in Bolivia, where his skills proved useful to a series of rightist governments.[48]

Two historic forces came together to bring him to trial in France for crimes against humanity. In France, François Mitterand's government became willing to seek Barbie's return to France for investigation and trial. It did so under intense pressure from the Association of Sons and Daughters of Jewish Deportees in France headed by Serge and Beate Klarsfeld. Second, a new Bolivian government was willing to give him up.

Barbie was charged with crimes against humanity based on having presided over the murder and deportation of Jews and members of the Resistance. The litigation over these charges provides an essential backdrop to the Touvier case.

The examining magistrate rejected charges that Barbie had killed members of the Resistance, because these victims were in military opposition to the Nazis. They were not noncombatant victims. This decision was reviewed and corrected by the court of appeals, and then by the Cour de Cassation, which set the standards under which Barbie was to be judged. The Cour de Cassation decided that the crime against humanity should be defined in terms of victims and actors: victims might include the direct objects of systematic racial or religious persecution, but also those who opposed such persecution by any means. Thus, Resistance members, as soldiers fighting Nazism, could be victims of crimes against humanity.

However, not every persecutor would be guilty. The Cour de Cassation said that "the perpetrator of the crime against humanity should have acted within the framework of his affiliation with a policy of ideological hegemony such as the Third Reich's National Socialist ideology."[49] Under this definition, Barbie could be prosecuted because he was a Nazi officer and his victims were opponents of Nazism. Barbie's defense counsel, the leftist lawyer Jacques Vergès, had sought a broader definition of the crime against humanity: one that would have theoretically encompassed French colonial atrocities. Thus, he hoped to turn the trial into a demonstration that France's vaunted adherence to the rights of man and humanitarian principle was a charade.

The Cour de Cassation well understood this goal, and its decision was generally interpreted as foreclosing prosecutorial attacks on French colonial misconduct in Algeria, Tunisia, and Indochina, for example. While the language of the Cour de Cassation does not in terms preclude prosecution of French officials for their conduct in colonial areas, the major focus is clearly on Barbie as an adherent of Nazi Germany. In harmony with this reading, the prosecutor's theme at Barbie's trial was that Barbie's crimes stemmed from Nazi ideology. Vergès's efforts to expand the law's ostensible reach continued to produce controversy, however. Many people recoiled at the idea that French courts might ever be called upon to judge the conduct of true Frenchmen as state-sponsored terror. These fears came again to the surface in the later prosecution of Maurice Papon, which I discuss below.

Under the Cour de Cassation's interpretation of the law, Barbie was tried in 1987, convicted, and sentenced to life imprisonment. He died in prison in 1991. With the precise contours of the crime against humanity still unsettled by the Cour de Cassation's Barbie judgment, the proceedings against Touvier, which had been pending in a desultory way for years, began in earnest in 1989.

5. Touvier's Capture

The same political forces that had demanded the trial of Barbie agitated for official action against Touvier. A formal accusation for the crime against humanity had been issued against Touvier in 1973, but a team of officers to execute the warrant was not formed until 1988. Touvier had been a fugitive most of the years since 1944. He was finally arrested by French police on May 24, 1989, in the monastery of a breakaway Catholic sect.

Among the most telling documents at Touvier's trial were his diaries and scrapbooks, annotated with his thoughts during his long years in hiding. Arno Klarsfeld,[50] one of the civil advocates at the trial, noted that:

While, on July 3rd, Klaus Barbie was listening to the presiding judge Cerdini pronouncing, in the name of the French nation, the penalty of perpetual imprisonment, Paul Touvier, cloistered in an underground life he had deliberately chosen, was commenting in a green schoolboy's notebook on the torments and misfortunes of his alter ego of former days.

Only a short time before that verdict, having a premonition, Paul Touvier wrote in his notebook this phrase of Ernest Hemingway: "Never send to know for whom the death knell tolls, it sounds always for you."[51]

Yes, this phrase of Hemingway was surely a premonition, because two years later, adjutant Mathy and commandant Recordon sounded, by ringing the bell of the priory of Saint-François at Nice, the death knell of Paul Touvier's long escapade, calling him to account for the past that the holy waters of all the monasteries where he had taken refuge were not able—and would not know how—to purify.

6. Touvier's Flight, the Charges Against Him, and the Judicial Decisions

In September 1945, as the Allied forces entered Lyon, Touvier became a fugitive, knowing that he was sought for his role in the Milice. He was sheltered by Milice friends and sympathetic churchmen. He remained a fugitive until 1989, and even arranged for publication of a fake report of his death. In 1946 and again in 1947, he was declared a fugitive and sentenced to death by French tribunals for treason and assisting the

54

enemy. Under French law, as noted above, Touvier's sentences lost their effect in 1966 and 1967.

However, the judgments of conviction continued to carry collateral consequences, such as inability to own property. Therefore, Touvier could not take title to his dead father's house. After an intensive lobbying campaign by Touvier's friends in the Church, President Pompidou's staff came to believe Touvier's version of events and advised Pompidou to accord a pardon. Pompidou did so on November 23, 1971. To put matters in perspective, the granting of pardons and amnesties in France is much more usual than in the United States. On the other hand, Pompidou's mentor Charles DeGaulle's only recorded comment on Touvier was "Touvier? 12 bullets in his hide."

However, the pardon became so controversial that it probably contributed not only to new charges against Touvier, but to strengthening the movement to define and punish crimes against humanity under French law. In June 1972, a leading French newspaper found out about the pardon and published an article. More publicity followed. In 1973, Touvier was charged with crimes against humanity, as defined in the Charter of London and recognized under French penal law since it was added to the Code in 1964.

Appellate procedures in the case dragged on while Touvier remained a fugitive. A Paris Chambre d'Accusation found the charges against Touvier legally insufficient, because they were based on collaboration with the Vichy regime. That tribunal refused to hold that Vichy was a regime dedicated to racial or religious hegemony. That is, the court required that the accused be proven to have acted on behalf of a regime with such a purpose. It seemed judges were unwilling to issue a forthright denunciation of the Vichy regime, even as it operated when the Milice achieved its power and the Germans abandoned the pretense that Vichy was independent. No, as one party argued, the Vichy government was a "constellation of good intentions," in which there were those who were fanatical anti-Semites and Nazi supporters, but that essentially reflected a pragmatic response to a difficult situation.

On November 27, 1992, the Cour de Cassation quashed that decision. However, it also took a narrow view of crimes against humanity. Its opinion indulged in a cramped reading of history to avoid outright condemnation of the Vichy government as a pawn of Germany. The judges reasoned as follows:

> Whereas [the judges] observe that besides the criminal intent that must exist to form a common law crime, crimes against humanity must form part of the execution of a concerted plan, and be

accomplished in the name of a State systematically practicing a policy of ideological hegemony; the crime must also be committed against people because they belong to a peculiar racial or religious group or because they belong to a group that opposes this policy of ideological hegemony.

Considering that, to determine whether the actions charged against Touvier formed part of such a concerted plan, the judges, by means of the facts reported above, analyze the ideology of both the established government of the French State and that of the Milice, an organization set up by the so-called law of January 30, 1943; basing themselves on a "significant amount of bibliography," they are drawn to the conclusion that the Vichy State did not practice a policy of ideological hegemony, considering that its policy of collaboration with the National Socialist State of Germany was essentially pragmatic; that despite the anti-Semitic measures taken, it never proclaimed, as did Germany, that the Jew was the enemy of the State; that finally, the Milice, which was one of the organs of the "French State," and did have hegemonic ambitions and had among its aims the fight "against the Jewish leper for French purity" did not succeed in transforming the authoritarian State into a totalitarian State;

Whereas, the decision [under review] reports the statements made by Touvier, who, without denying his participation in the decision to execute the hostages, has always stated that this decision had been taken jointly with de Bourmont, then regional chief of the Milice of Lyon, after meeting with Knab, chief of the local Gestapo, who wanted to organize massive reprisals against the Jewish population after the assassination of Philippe Henriot; and that de Bourmont together with Touvier has succeeded to reduce the number of victims that the accused would have had been required to execute;...

Considering however in conclusion that while Article 6 of the Statutes of the Military Tribunal of Nuremberg says that the authors or accomplices of crimes against humanity are punished only if they have acted for a State belonging to the European Axis, the Chambre d'Accusation could not, without contradicting itself, declare at the same time that (i) the assassinations in this case were not a crime against humanity, and that (ii) the crimes have been committed at the instigation of a leader of the Gestapo, which is an organization declared criminal because it acted for a State that practiced a policy of hegemonic ideology.

In short, the charges against Touvier could proceed on the assumption that he was knowingly and intentionally carrying out the will of the Gestapo, which was indisputably an arm of the Nazi German state. Why did the judges think it necessary to avoid wholesale condemnation of the Vichy government, even as it operated in its latter days? Here, one confronts the same question that arises every time a nation-state makes a transition away from practicing state-sponsored terror, or looks back at its troublesome past. Under such circumstances, there will always be a large number of people—perhaps a majority—who were actively complicit in the old regime's crimes, benefited from the illegality, voiced support for the old ways, or whose silence abetted the regime. Some of these people may hold positions of power in the present day. The difficulty of asking a national tribunal to address such past issues is evident in the Touvier litigation as it was in the U.S. litigation over American complicity in Chilean state-sponsored terror. As I discuss below, this difficulty may be one justification for creating and empowering transnational tribunals to try terrorism cases and other violations of human rights.

In Touvier's case, the Cour de Cassation remanded the parties to the Chambre d'Accusation of the Cour d'Appel of Versailles, which formulated the charges Touvier faced at the Cour d'Assises in Versailles. The Cour de Cassation opinion caused a certain amount of shuffling among those who were seeking Touvier's trial. In France, private parties who are victims of the alleged crime have standing to participate in the judicial proceedings, including the trial. Most prominent among the lawyers for private parties in Touvier's case—and later in the case of Papon—was young Arno Klarsfeld. He is the son of Serge and Beate Klarseld who were among the most vocal and effective advocates for the 1964 penal code amendments and the prosecutions of collaborators. Arno Klarsfeld had initially seen the Touvier case as a chance to show that the Vichy regime was collaborationist from the outset, but he fell back—as did the other parties on the prosecution side—into claiming that the evidence also supported Touvier's personal collaboration with Nazi desires.

7. The Executions at Rillieux-la-Pape

Touvier's trial was an extraordinary spectacle. Touvier was confronted not only by the public prosecutor, but also by thirty-four civil lawyers, representing victims and victim groups.[52]

In June 1944, Touvier was twenty-nine years old and in charge of intelligence for the Milice over an area in which four million people lived. Touvier's dignified, almost regal, mien[53] at trial made one forget how he achieved his position of power within the Milice. During the early Vichy years, he held a clerical job with the railroad and lived with a prostitute whose husband was in jail. He joined the Milice in October 1943 and quickly achieved a leadership position. He wore fine clothes, drove a car requisitioned from a Milice target, and collected money and belongings from Jews and other targets of Milice hostility.

On the morning of June 28, he had been in Vichy, some 150 kilometers from Lyon. He returned to Lyon that afternoon, and set in motion the assassination of seven Jews. Touvier concedes this much. However, in his version, he returned to Lyon and was told by the Milice chief for Lyon, Victor de Bourmont, that the German Gestapo chief for Lyon, Werner Knab, had demanded that one hundred Jews be assassinated in reprisal for Henriot's death. Touvier said de Bourmont had bargained Knab down to thirty. According to his version, Touvier told de Bourmont that they should start with just seven, and see whether that would be enough. As Touvier told it, once the seven were killed, there were no more requests. The seven were Glaeser, Schusselman, Zeizig, Ben Zimra, Prock, Kryzkowski, and one man whose name has never been established. At his trial, Touvier could not recall the names of any of the seven. All seven were merchants.

The difficulty with Touvier's version is that there is almost nothing to corroborate it, even inferentially. Seven were killed, but one prisoner was spared. He was Edouard Goulard, a Resistance member but not a Jew. Although he was in custody, he was left behind when the group of seven Jews was taken out of the Lyon Milice headquarters in the Impasse Cathelin. He testified at Touvier's trial that Touvier had selected the seven to be killed, and made the decision to leave Goulard behind. The reprisals, then, were to be taken against Jews rather than against a known Resistance member, despite the Resistance having performed the assassination of Henriot. Indeed, five of the seven were rounded up based apparently on a list of names that Touvier supplied to the arresting Milice officers.

Here are some other witness statements to similar effect, all from members of the Milice who served with Touvier:

> I did not hear anything concerning this affair . . . I have only had echoes from which I remember this: contrary to the orders from Vichy that prohibited all reprisals for the death of P. Henriot, the

regional chief had on his own authority ordered the execution of ten Israelites at Lyon.

* * *

Touvier gave the orders concerning seizures [of the victims' property] and arrests. The fruits of these seizures (money, jewels, pieces of furniture, etc.) were brought back to the Milice headquarters where they were seized by Touvier and sold or exchanged by him. He also ordered many murders, among which were the execution of seven Jews at Rillieux towards the end of the month of June 1944. Touvier was an authoritarian man without scruples and a true bandit.

* * *

As from the time that Touvier became a member of the Service, arrests became more numerous, the chief he, himself, took the decisions . . . The emptying of Ziezig's store was governed and ordered by Touvier.

* * *

I think this execution was the work of the Milice. On the 28th of June 1944, I heard while I was on duty, information concerning a punitive operation undertaken as a result of the assassination of P. Henriot . . . I asked Touvier if I should stay at the headquarters of the Milice. On his affirmative response, I stayed at Impasse Cathelin, waiting for further orders. The sun had not risen yet, it was about three o'clock in the morning, and I was walking on the sidewalk of Impasse Cathelin with Reynaud, when I saw the soldiers of the Franc-Garde[54] coming down the street with the prisoners. I had seen some of them the night before in the prisons of the Milice and I recognized among them the Jews that the Service had arrested several days before. I recognize on the pictures you are showing me the same faces that I saw then. Under the orders of these soldiers whose names I do not know, the prisoners were loaded into a closed van that was parked in front of the Milice garage . . . I saw and heard the chief, Touvier giving orders. I heard him distinctly ask if the "boxes" were ready . . . Touvier left in a private car . . . I suppose that Touvier participated in the execution, having as I saw him, ordered the preparations. . . .

If there had been a German order, from Knab to de Bourmont to Touvier, someone at the time would have heard of it. Yet, as trial counsel argued, there was no trace of any such order. However, there was evidence that the killings and their aftermath matched Touvier's own method of operation. Here is a further excerpt from trial counsel's summation:

But let us say that [Touvier] had chosen to omit deliberately to tell others of his "tragic combat" (these are his words) directed at diminishing the number of victims: do you sincerely believe, members of the jury, that it could be possible that the agitation, the confusion, the number of comings and goings between his office and that of de Bourmont, that all of this stirring that he described in his answers to questions, could have passed unseen by the Milice members of the Impasse Cathelin? Do you believe that if there had been an order from the Germans these Milice members would have known absolutely nothing about it?

That passes the limits of understanding. How in the world can one believe in such blindness among the Milice members of the Second Service: the Service of information of the Milice! Of information!!

These Milice members were supposed to be the source of information of the Vichy regime. These Milice members were stationed as lookouts on the lookout for the least bit of information. Would they have let go such an important item of information?

But perhaps Touvier tried to keep this information secret, not from modesty, but for another reason? His defense counsel will certainly not fail to make such a claim. But when he will say so, you will ask yourself why? Why would Touvier want to keep such information secret? You will ask yourselves: does that sound true?

Close your eyes, ladies and gentlemen of the jury. You are during summer of 1944, not far from the place where the Saône and the Rhône come together. You are at Impasse Cathelin, at the corner of St. Hélène street, quite near to the Perrache train station [Lyon's main train terminal]. Touvier goes to see his second in command Reynaud and says: "We need seven Jews."

You heard him, as he repeated this phrase fifty years later, here, in this proceeding, in front of you.

What would be, under these conditions, the normal answer of Reynaud?

"Seven Jews, but for what, Paul?"

And this is the question that Reynaud or the other Milice members, facing the request of Paul Touvier, would have asked.

60

But now, supposing that there really had been a German demand, ask yourself whether Touvier could have answered: "Bestir yourself, Reynaud, I need seven Jews to execute. Go, run, hurry and bring back seven Jews!"

How is it that Paul Touvier could possibly have responded in such terms, he, so attentive to his image, he, who changed his clothes several times a day, not being able to change his consciousness. (And you recall what a suit cost at that time, ladies and gentlemen of the jury. You recall the testimony of M. Jeanblanc who told you the shock he felt when he saw his own suit on a Milice member who had stolen it from him, during what Touvier called, according to the hearings, a "loan" or a "search." At that time, M. Jeanblanc told you that it was necessary to save for more than a year, in order to afford a suit.)

And so, why would someone like Paul Touvier, so concerned about his image, have degraded this image by failing to make to Reynaud, in case there had really been a German demand, the following reply:

"No, these seven unfortunate Jews, I need them in order to save ninety-three of their co-religionists!"

Oh yes, if there had been a German demand, then Touvier would not have failed to answer in such a way in order to justify his order to Reynaud and also not to look like an assassin. And if he had answered in such a way, the Milice members interrogated after the war would not have failed to give this information to the instructing judges who interrogated them about the massacre of Rillieux, so as to attenuate their own responsibility.

Because you will know that it is a less serious matter to kill seven Jews when one hundred have been demanded, than to kill seven when none has been demanded.

But the problem is that Touvier did not say: "Reynaud, go and request the presence of seven unfortunate Jews here at the Impasse Cathelin." No! No! He said: "Reynaud, go and find me seven bits of Jew garbage." This is how Touvier describe them in his writings after the war.

That is what has been said. Because there never was the slightest order or even the slightest demand from the Germans. But did I not omit here another demonstrative? Did he not say: "Go and find me *these* seven pieces of Jew garbage," suiting the action to the word in holding for Reynaud or somebody else a list of names of Jews to be arrested?

61

Certainly. Otherwise, how can one explain the long time—almost ten hours—that were necessary to find seven Jews in a city where dwelt at least fifteen thousand? In fact, it was not seven, but five Jews that were necessary, because two Jews were already in the jail of the impasse Cathelin.

What, ten hours for five indeterminate Jews? That's indeed slow for a Milice member as trained as was Paul Touvier. It's indeed slow for a service that had a card file of Jews! But all this can find an explanation if these were particular Jews for whom they were searching.

In fact, exactly like at Mâcon there was a list, but while at Mâcon the names mentioned on the list were there by virtue of their sympathy with the Resistance, Paul Touvier had made out the list at Rillieux because they were Jews. The birth certificate of these seven Jews was for them a death certificate.

The version supported by this argument was also corroborated by the testimony of Max Roxencwaig, a Jewish barber who was arrested at about 3 a.m. on June 29, but who did not arrive at the Impasse Cathelin until about fifteen minutes after the truck carrying the other seven had left, and so was spared.

The argument resumes: "Because they were Jews, of course, but also because Paul Touvier knew that he could achieve pecuniary gain. A gain for the Milice, but also for himself. To the crime against humanity is added the common law crime. That, for sure, is barred by the statute of limitations. . . ."

Touvier's actions were also documented in a 1970 government report, authored by investigator Jacques Delarue:

On June 28, the death of Philippe Henriot—struck down by the Resistance—having been announced, Touvier decided to avenge his death by instituting a set of reprisals. A "hunt for Jews" was immediately undertaken by the Second Service; this involved rounding up seven shopkeepers who had not already been arrested. On the 29th of June at daybreak, they were brought to Rillieux (a suburb of Lyon), lined up along the wall of the cemetery and struck down. During the course of that day, their stores were completely pillaged.

Delarue later took inconsistent positions in various judicial proceedings, at one time testifying that "The Germans simply didn't care about Philippe Henriot at that time, because they had other preoccupations," and at another time supporting the idea that the Rillieux assassinations were the result of a German initiative.

The German officer Knab's supposed vehemence to avenge the death of Henriot was not reflected in any contemporary documents, including a detailed report of a dinner hosted by Knab on·the evening of Henriot's death. As Arno Klarsfeld put it in his summation:

Ah yes, in this report there is not a single word about the death of Philippe Henriot. How is it that someone like Knab, who several hours before, wanted to massacre one hundred Jews by way of reprisals after the death of Philippe Henriot, had by that same night forgotten everything?

The theme of this dinner and its raison d'être were above all the political situation in France.

Moreover, in the Knab dossier that my opponent knows very well, because he has devoted many mornings to it, there is a telegram in which Knab imparts to Oberg, the chief of SIPO-SD in France, his displeasure that Henriot did not submit to the Germans the text of a speech the latter made after the attack at the Glière plateau. This same Oberg, interrogated in 1946 concerning Henriot, affirmed: "I met Philippe Henriot at the German embassy where he was present at a reception following his return from the Reich. I saw him again once or twice in various public gatherings, notably some time before his death. *I never had any sort of dealings with him, he never visited my home, and I never visited his.*"

It appears from these documents that Knab, chief of the SIPO-SD of Lyon, not only failed to evoke the name of Philippe Henriot the same day of the latter's execution, but also that during the dinner the discussion mostly centered on the situation in France, and finally that the latter had irritated him by not submitting the text of his speech to the occupying power.

As for Oberg, Knab's superior, Henriot was treated with indifference. As a crime of passion, this court of assizes has already seen better!

In contrast, Klarsfeld also documented the Milice reaction to Henriot's death, further bolstering the claim that Touvier and his Milice associates were prime movers in the reprisals:

We set the scene with the help of a report from the Commissioner of the Interior: "Shades of black were spread in the hall of the *Progrès*[55] [the new headquarters of the information service of the Milice in Lyon] in memory of Henriot; a coffin, a flame, guarded by Milice members, stood at the center. Men who had forgotten to remove their hats, or who perhaps were observed to have a slight smile in seeing all of this, were forced by the Milice members to remain for hours on their knees in front of the coffin (and certain of them were required to hold their hands behind their backs)."

Francis Bout de l'An wrote in the Milice journal, *Combats*:[56] "The Milice member Philippe Henriot is dead and it is our responsibility to safeguard his memory, to strike at those who, from nearby or by far, prepared the crime. I know that he did not like blood shed, I know that he did not like to see us multiply vengeance or reprisals, but I know also that he would not understand a curiously indulgent society that simply gives a few years of imprisonment to such criminals."

Indeed, even the reprisal execution of Georges Mandel was probably the work of the Milice and not of the Germans. There is evidence that even senior Vichy government officials thought the Milice had gotten out of hand in killing Mandel.

Touvier could not credibly deny his part in the killings, but he added to his claim that he had spared lives. He said:

> The dead of Rillieux were not simply hostages chosen among the population because they were Israelite, but because of their "anti-national activities," in accordance with the laws of that time . . . It is even more scandalous to accuse me, considering that I did everything I could to save human lives, and that in taking very grave risks.

* * *

> I have already said and I will say it again: a hunt against Jews was never unleashed after the assassination of Philippe Henriot. Moreover, I recall that the dossier establishes that some of the Jewish victims had already been arrested several days before.

In the context of Touvier's trial, two questions emerge from the evidence: First, who gave the initial order for the killings? It seems clear that there was no German order of the kind Touvier described. Thus, his claim that by some grim utilitarian calculus he had saved lives could not be sustained. Even if the existence of a German order had been proved, the presiding judge had expressed skepticism at such a claim, asking why Touvier could not have sought help from the Vichy government itself or simply refused to carry out the orders. In any event, a defense of "superior orders" is not available in crimes against humanity prosecutions, save as it may be considered in mitigation of punishment.

64

The second question was more difficult. In the context of June 1944, was there a sufficient relationship between Touvier's actions and a government to satisfy any "hegemonic" state actor requirement that might be found to exist? The Cour de Cassation judgment was controversial. It had no doubt prompted relief among those who wanted to preserve a certain image of the Vichy government, as well as among those who do not want to see the crime against humanity expanded in ways that could lead to prosecutions of French officials for their conduct in France's colonial wars. However a future court might interpret the statute, Touvier could not be convicted at his trial without proof that he was a Nazi accomplice.

Here was a puzzle. The Cour de Cassation had said that the Vichy government was not itself an arm of the Axis powers. Therefore, Touvier could not be guilty solely by virtue of this elevated position within the Vichy police hierarchy. He could not be guilty based on an order from the Nazi Knab if there was no such order.

However, there was a third possibility. Touvier could be guilty if he carried out his plan to serve the Nazi interest and to forestall the impending Nazi collapse. Under familiar principles of criminal law, one can be an accomplice without prior agreement. In systems that punish conspiracy, the crime consists essentially of an agreement to commit an offense. If an offense is actually committed, it is by prearrangement. One may become an accomplice to crime by a voluntary action to aid the principal offender, without the command or even the consent of the principal. For example, if A sees B in the act of robbing X, and helps out in hope or expectation of gaining part of the loot, A is B's accomplice regardless of whether B agrees to A's participation. It is even possible to imagine a scenario in which B is unaware of A's help, as where A keeps a lookout for any approaching police and is ready to sound the alarm, provided of course that A has the proscribed intent.

During the long campaign to have Touvier prosecuted, many had based their condemnation of him on his having served the Vichy France cause in ordering Jews to be killed. By the time of his trial, those who had advanced that theory, including Arno Klarsfeld, had to adjust their advocacy to fit the limitations imposed by the Cour de Cassation.

Touvier was convicted on the theory that he was in fact aiding Nazi German interests by his crime, and intended to do so. Whatever moderation—and it was little—Vichy had shown in carrying out Nazi wishes, Touvier in particular and the Milice in general were fully imbued with Nazi ideology.

As for the Milice, advocates at the trial traced their increasing influence with the Vichy government. The complicity of the Milice with the Gestapo in the concerted plan called the "Final Solution of the Jewish Question" is obvious:

When, in response to the German pressure on the Vichy government, as recalled by all the historians who gave evidence before you, Joseph Darnand seized the levers of power of the State police in becoming Secretary General of the Maintien de l'Ordre [paramilitary police organization], Jews of French nationality were already prone to massive arrests by the police. Bousquet, Laval and Pétain had already loaned the services of the French police to the Germans in order to arrest Jewish aliens and their children; but they had refused to turn over French Jews.

On November 29, 1943, Colonel Knochen wrote to Bousquet: "The security police and the SD at Limoges have asked the Prefect of this region to examine the list of Israelites established by himself. He refused to accede to this demand. He presented this refusal in declaring that, according to information given by the competent French authorities, the German authorities could only look at the list of foreigners, and not the list of French Israelites, this in conformity with an agreement concluded between the General Secretary of the French Police and the commander in chief of the SS and the German police officials."

On November 22, Bousquet responded to Colonel Knochen: "On November 12, 1943, I received a communication from the regional Prefect of Limoges telling me that the regional Chief of the Security Police-SD asked him for the authorization to check the lists set up in the prefectures concerning the Israelites. I indicated to him that it would be impossible to satisfy his demand. Again, recently, the same demand having been presented at the request of the German authorities to the chief of government by the General Commissioner on the Jewish Question, I was required to clarify again the point of view of my administration that has been formally approved by the French government. As far as the French police and administration are concerned, the fact of being an Israelite does not constitute a presumption of responsibility, neither in a political sense nor as a matter of law. So, it would not constitute an aggravation of such responsibility if a Jew is prosecuted for a crime or tort punished by our penal legislation. Moreover, the German laws are applicable only in the occupied zone. In consequence, the attitude of the

French administration cannot change, and there is no way to modify the instructions that I have sent and given in order to assure compliance with our legislation. I am sure that you will have the good grace to transmit to your services all instructions that may be necessary to avoid similar requests to the French authorities which are simply unable to honor them."

On December 4, 1943, Hitler demanded of Marshal Pétain that "Laval be ordered to reorganize without delay the French cabinet in an acceptable manner for the German government and that he will guarantee their collaboration. This cabinet will operate under the complete support of the Head of State."

That is the reason why Darnand and Henriot came into the Vichy government. On January 10, 1944, when the Gestapo of Bordeaux demanded that the Prefecture of Bordeaux begin the arrest of French Jews in this region, the regional Prefect responded "Without some contrary indications from the Vichy government, the operation could only be executed by the German police itself." The Bordeaux Gestapo then alleged that Darnand had already given his approval to the operation; the Prefect declared that "He will stick to the decision taken by the head of the Vichy government." At the end of the evening, Darnand called the Prefect on Laval's behalf, and informed him "that it is advisable not to delay any longer the execution of this operation. "

The operation took place during the night and brought to Drancy, and then to Auschwitz, more than two hundred Jews of the Bordeaux region. July 2, 1942, had marked the abandonment by Bousquet and Vichy of the foreign Jews, arrested from then on by the French police; January 10, 1944, marks the abandonment by Darnand and Vichy of the French Jews, arrested thereafter en masse by the Vichy police, as well as by the Gestapo, thanks to the lists coming from Prefectures and to indications given by the Milice.

On January 25, 1944, the general director of the National Police informed the Milice member Knipping, who had become the representative in the north zone of the General Secretary of the MO, that, "by a note of the 20th of November 1943, that has just come to my attention [this was a reference to the Knochen note that I already cited and to which Bousquet had replied by the negative, which response I have also mentioned], the commandant of the Security Police and of the SD has just demanded that I give instructions to the Prefects in the southern zone allowing the German police services to have access to information at the headquarters of each prefecture in order to know the names of French and alien Isra-elites. I have the honor [sic] to let you know that I have just sent instructions to all of the regional Prefects."

Therefore, by the intervention of Darnand, the Germans obtained that which they sought and to which even Bousquet had refused to give his consent.

The seizure of control of the State Police by the Chief of the Milice and his crew opened a new phase of persecution: first, the massive arrest of Jews of French nationality by the French police forces conducted by Darnand for the benefit of the Germans; and second, the participation of the Milice in the summary execution of Jews. Up to that point, Vichy had always caused or allowed the deaths by physical misery of Jews interned in the camps of the Free Zone [Vichy France], such as those at Gurs, Noé or Rivesaltes. Up to that point, Vichy had delivered to the Germans Jewish Resist-ance members that the Germans executed by firing squad as hos-tages. But up to that time Vichy had not gone as far as the summary execution of Jews.

This was the work of the Milice, an organ which, we must recall, was created and promoted by the Germans in 1944, the iron lance of the police forces of Vichy, forged to strengthen the defenses of this collaborationist government that it served so well.

The Gestapo wanted the arrest of a large number of French Jews. The Vichy of the Milice, the Vichy of 1944, agreed to accomplish that which the Vichy of 1942 and of 1943 had refused.

In 1944, notably after the Normandy invasion, the Gestapo, impelled by rage, fear and hatred, began the summary execution of Jews and Resistance members. The Milice, its accomplice, servilely followed its example.

Like their chief, Joseph Darnand, all the Milice members were united by oath to Hitler and in their heart were wearing German uniforms: they were indeed seen as such by their compatriots, who saw in them French Hitlerites matching entirely with the Nazi ideology.

A French Hitlerite: that is what Touvier was when he brought about the massacre of seven Jews at Rillieux-la-Pape.

By focusing on a roundup of Jews in Bordeaux, this bit of advocacy directly implicated Maurice Papon whose case was to be tried several years later.

Turning to Touvier individually, his efforts to portray himself as moti-vated by a desire to see the law respected, and his denial of anti-Semitic animus, failed for want of evidence. Touvier had kept a diary during his years of exile, which contained more than his sympathetic regard for Barbie's fate in Lyon.

In his diary, Touvier referred to a French female newscaster and her interview subject as "Jewish garbage," the old Milice slogan. A French intellectual was called "a dreadful Jewish shopkeeper." Mengele, on the other hand, was "a victim of hatred." Touvier's diaries contained many similar utterances. Touvier was convicted, and sentenced to life imprisonment.

The procedure in the Touvier case may give us pause. He was prosecuted thirty years after the events. Many witnesses had died. Records of their interviews with police officials survived and, in some instances, statements under oath to an investigating magistrate. Under American constitutional law, this testimonial hearsay would not be admissible in a criminal trial. Civil law procedure permits it to be received, subject to safeguards. Of course, in American law there is no statute of limitation for murder in most jurisdictions, but whenever the trial is held it must be conducted with sixth amendment guarantees of confrontation. One must note that the procedure in Touvier's trial did not differ from those in any French criminal case: he was entitled to no more, nor less, of the protections against witness error, bias, and mendacity than any defendant. In any system for prosecuting and punishing state-sponsored terrorism, one must account for the unusual difficulties that prosecutors and defenders will have, many years after the alleged events.

8. Maurice Papon and the Confession of Collaboration[57]

Some of my students and I wrote an article, on which most of this essay is based, about the Touvier case in 1994; the article appeared in 1995. We thought it unlikely that any more World War II cases would be tried, given the age of the alleged perpetrators and the political resistance to such trials. Then, in January 1997, the French Cour de Cassation rejected an interlocutory appeal by Maurice Papon and it appeared that this high-ranking government official would be tried for his World War II conduct.

The Papon case became far more significant than those of Touvier or Barbie. When I first began to lecture in France on crimes against humanity and the French trials, some of my French colleagues reproached me, and the French legal system, for digging up the past in this way. "Law and history do not make good bedfellows," one French law professor declaimed. I thought him wrong in general and specifically. Law and history are, or ought to be, well acquainted, and even intimate friends.

One principal theme of this book is that ignoring the lessons of history inflicts a great social price.

The Papon case dredged up enough history, even fairly recent history, that it provoked a shift in attitudes. The January 1997 Cour de Cassation opinion signaled a different judicial attitude towards the Vichy government. The trial itself caused a change in the attitudes of many people who had been holding on to old illusions. I recall that after giving a lecture on the crime against humanity shortly after the trial court judgment against Papon in early 1998, one of my French colleagues took the podium to say, "J'aveu. La France, elle etait collaboratrice. [I confess. France was a collaborator.]"

Papon had a distinguished law school record and, in the 1930s, had read Hitler's works and understood their meaning and menace. During World War II, he joined the Vichy France government and was an official in its Ministry of the Interior. In February 1941, he became sub-prefect of the Gironde, based in Bordeaux, which was part of Vichy France. As part of his official responsibilities, he assumed the position of Secretary for Jewish Questions, and was in charge of the police, gendarmerie, and detention facilities.

At some point during the war, Papon also assisted the French Resistance while still serving in his official positions. This limited assistance was to become one theme of his defense. After the war, his political career continued. He became a mayor, a prefect of police in Paris, and then a minister in the conservative government of President Valéry Giscard d'Estaing. Powerful figures in French politics tried to derail any potential prosecution. On the side of prosecuting, however, were ranged the powerful voices of deportee organizations—the same ones that had lobbied for passage of the 1964 amendments to the French Penal Code and the Touvier prosecution.

On October 17, 1961, then-prefect of police Papon ordered suppression of a mass demonstration being held by people agitating for Algerian independence from France. This was in the final months of the French occupation of Algeria, and the Algerians were to win independence early in 1962. Acting on Papon's orders, the police rounded up thousands of demonstrators who were then held in deplorable conditions. Additionally, the police opened fire and killed between one hundred and three hundred demonstrators. After the event, Papon was instrumental in covering up the facts. However, he was not prosecuted for any of the 1961 events, although the vivid memory of those events lent fuel to the demands that he be prosecuted for his role in World War II events.

In 1981, the French presidential election pitted Giscard d'Estaing, who was seeking a second seven-year term, against François Mitterand, the Socialist candidate. During the campaign, a French newspaper published an expose of Papon's wartime role in signing orders sending Jews to concentration camps.[58] The publicity is said to have rallied some voters to candidate Mitterand who won the second round of voting with 53 percent of the vote. From that point, the prospect of Papon being tried for crimes against humanity was often debated in the press and in political councils. However, the official investigation of his role proceeded fitfully. There is some evidence that Mitterand himself was opposed to pursuing Papon, lest there be a raft of cases examining the wartime activities of many high-ranking French politicians of all political parties. Again, we see the many pressures that arise within a national context when the idea of redressing past terrorism is raised.

Finally, in September 1996, a set of charges of complicity in crimes against humanity was filed in Bordeaux, in the prefecture of the Gironde, based on a detailed set of factual allegations. These allegations focused on the arrest and deportation of hundreds of Jews and other Nazi targets, and were based on a lengthy investigation phase conducted under the supervision of magistrates. The indictment charged Papon with crimes against humanity committed between July 1942 and May 1944, during his service as sub-prefect of the Gironde.[59]

Papon challenged the charges in the Cour de Cassation, which rejected all his legal claims. That court noted that crimes against humanity are not subject to any statute of limitation, and it rejected Papon's claim of excessive delay in bringing the case. Turning to the merits, the court held that the prosecution would have to prove that somebody responsible for the deportations and deaths was acting as agent of a hegemonic regime. This element was clearly satisfied by the proposed proofs because of the involvement of German Nazi police officials in designating who was to be rounded up, when, and where. However, in order to be complicit in the crimes of such people, Papon did not have to share their ideology or their direct subservience to that regime. He did not have to be a member of the unlawful organization.

The Germans demanded roundups of Jews. Papon was in charge of a list of Jews drawn up under Vichy government guidelines as that government brought its policies in line with Nazi wishes. He signed orders for searches, seizures, and detentions of Jews. He, therefore, became an accomplice of the Nazi regime and its ideology. This legal theory echoed the argument quoted above from the Touvier case.

Papon acted with knowledge of the Nazis' actions and motivations. Therefore, he could be an accomplice even though he did not share the Nazi ideology and was not a member of any Nazi organization. This holding did not differ greatly from the analysis used in Touvier's case and is consistent with accomplice law in most legal systems.

However, there was a second conclusion that followed from applying this accomplice analysis to Papon's conduct and position. Touvier was a foot soldier, a murderer, a petty thief, and a Gestapo wannabe. He spent his postwar life on the run, sheltered by far-right clerics. He was charged with a single act: rounding up seven Jews to serve a distinct Nazi purpose towards the end of the war.

Papon acted from a position of authority in the Vichy government, and over nearly two years. The Cour de Cassation opinion cast significant doubt on the claim that Vichy France was truly an independent state. It used evidence of Papon's power and influence, and of his continuing contact with Nazi agents and officials, as central to its argument that the indictment charged an offense. If a man who systematically ordered deportations of Jews served as Vichy interior minister and as a prefectural official, the Touvier case description of the Vichy France as disorganized, somewhat well-intentioned, and pragmatic hardly bore examination. In setting the stage for Touvier's prosecution, the Cour de Cassation insisted on proof that he served the Nazi cause, and dismissed all efforts to characterize the Vichy government in any particular way. The judges who decided Papon's case did not forthrightly declare themselves. However, they cast doubt on Papon's claim of innocent intent by saying that, given his service in the Vichy France Interior Ministry, he surely knew of the Vichy government's "anti-Jewish policy," and his acceptance of a job entitled "Jewish Questions" added more proof of his culpable mental state. These references characterize the explicit policy of the Vichy government as pro-Nazi and collaborationist in a way that the Touvier court did not.

Papon was convicted of complicity in the deportations, but acquitted of complicity in the eventual deaths of the detainees in concentration camps. He was sentenced to ten years in prison. While his appeal was pending, he left France for Switzerland and lived there under an assumed name. The French courts dismissed his appeal because of a French law that deprives a fugitive of the right to appeal. The European Court of Human Rights in Strasbourg held that dismissal of the appeal is too harsh a sanction. The French courts then reviewed the merits and affirmed.

In the meantime, influential French politicians secured passage of a law that allowed an aged and infirm person to be set free from prison. Papon, who was at that time over ninety years old and in ill health, was liberated.

What do the Touvier and Papon cases tell us about national courts applying transnational law to punish state-sponsored terrorists? It is a mixed lesson and provides little cause for optimism. The amendments to the French penal code that permitted prosecutions for crimes against humanity were not added until 1964, nearly two decades after the end of World War II. A broad-based political campaign was necessary to secure this change. Once the penal code permitted prosecutions, it was 1983 before Barbie was brought to trial, and almost ten more years before Touvier's trial began. French officials' reluctance to confront the widespread complicity with the Nazis was the principal reason for the delay.

There has never been a prosecution under French law for crimes against humanity committed by French soldiers or commanders for actions in Indochina, Algeria, Tunisia, and other empire outposts, nor for brutal police actions such as the 1961 killings in Paris when Papon was prefect of police. Such prosecutions would be deterrent and educational, just as were the Papon and Touvier cases. However, there is a significant right-wing element in French politics whose power is sufficient to deter authorities from pursuing any such cases. This element organizes around racial and ethnic issues, including the alleged surrenders in Algeria and Indochina.[60] The uprisings in French Muslim communities in late 2005, and the public and political reaction to them, show that racism and ethnic prejudice run deep in French society. This fact is both an explanation of why politicians do not care to examine the history of French colonial power and, in some measure, a result of the state not having addressed the issue.

From this recitation, one can well conclude that national tribunals approach prosecution and punishment of high public officials involved in serious wrongdoing fitfully, inconsistently, and belatedly, if at all. The Barbie, Touvier, and Papon prosecutions did not come about because there was a general understanding that complicity in genocide was wrong and should be punished. That general understanding had been reached and was enforced in the Nuremberg trials and judgments. However, none of the victorious Allied powers took the opportunity to review the conduct of their own officials. As I have noted, the United States welcomed many former Nazis into positions of responsibility; there were denaturalizations of Nazi collaborators who had become U.S. citizens, but these few cases underscored the selective nature of the enforcement process.

In France, a vocal and effective public outcry resulted first in passage of legislation and then in the three prosecutions, but even that broad-based political support was devoted almost exclusively to the plight of French people who had suffered during the war. In metropolitan France, there has not been a significant political movement, let alone a consensus, that state power should be exercised to address French colonial atrocities. Systems of state power tend to act self-referentially. We have seen the resistance of nation-states to accepting and applying the newly developed rules of official responsibility for state-sponsored terrorism—rules that originate from outside any particular national system.

To see the matter from a different perspective, it is possible to commit the offenses defined as crimes against humanity, such as genocide, and related offenses such as torture, without that conduct being part of a pattern of state-sponsored terrorism within the meaning of my suggested definition: systematic state-sponsored violence, conducted against political enemies, and in disregard of historically determined fair substantive and procedural standards. For the commission of such offenses to descend to the level of terrorism, the conduct must have been systematic and in furtherance of a national policy. The French courts' judicial narrowing of the Penal Code brings that definition more into line with that of terrorism, given the insistence that the prosecution prove that the unlawful conduct was undertaken in furtherance of a policy of hegemony. For this reason alone, discussion of the Barbie, Touvier, and Papon cases belongs in this discussion.

However, the French courts' definition also narrows the statutory language to exclude cases involving systematic state-sponsored violence with the evident purpose of evading a confrontation with France's Vichy past and its colonial experiences. This narrowing illustrates a consistent problem with asking national tribunals to address official conduct in their own country.

The French experience with a national tribunal addressing state-sponsored terrorism stands, therefore, in contrast with experiences in South Africa and Chile, discussed elsewhere in this book.

F. Reconciliation, Amnesty, Truth—South Africa, Chile, and Elsewhere

In both South Africa and Chile, 1990 was a significant year. In that year, Nelson Mandela was released from prison and Augusto Pinochet stepped down as President. These were significant transitional moments in each country. If we take a historical survey, we will see that such moments are often the occasion for examination and accountability of the outgoing regime's acts. In prior centuries, we can recall the unedifying spectacle of the new regime killing the leaders of the old one in proceedings marked by unfairness and without advancing any coherent articulation of standards of conduct. In other transitions, the old leadership gathers up the product of its plundering and settles in a country where it can spend the money free from vexation.

The South African apartheid regime and the Chilean military junta ruled with state-sponsored terror. The rather different experiences of the two countries in addressing issues of accountability engage our attention. In South Africa, under 1995 legislation—five years after Nelson Mandela's release from prison, a Truth and Reconciliation Commission heard testimony from victims and perpetrators of terrorism during the apartheid period. Those who came forward were given amnesty. In Chile, a commission of inquiry established in the wake of the military junta's leaving power gave widespread amnesty. The South African commission has mostly been praised for its work. The Chilean amnesties have been undone by Chilean courts, and are generally seen as improper concessions wrung by the departing military leaders as a condition of consenting to democratic elections. There are many other examples of amnesties in various forms as responses to regimes that practiced terrorism as an instrument of governance.

Some see the amnesty process as inherently suspect. Professor Jeffrie Murphy has written:

> I am getting so old that I can still remember when most of the skits on Saturday Night Live were very funny. One of my favorites from those days involved Steve Martin in situations in which he played a person who had done something truly unspeakable, quite beyond the pale, and who tried to deal with his iniquity with the very worst sort of apology. In one of these skits, if I recall correctly, he played a surgeon who had removed a child's brain instead of the scheduled appendix. He faces the distraught and angry parents and, after impatiently listening to them carry on for a bit, simply says to them "Well excuse me!"
>
> Humor, of course, is no laughing matter, and so let me be tedious for a moment and inquire into why many people find this scenario funny. I think it is because most people find the absurd funny, and absurdity is found where there is a radical tension or disconnect between the reality of a situation and a particular response to that situation. What this surgeon has done is so vile that it is ludicrous

that his primary response to it is a mere apology, and particularly ludicrous when the apology is so obviously and contemptuously insincere. . . .

Some people, of course, find the growing culture of apology a very good thing, whereas others—and I count myself among them—fear that it may be little more than a sign of what theologians have called "cheap grace." Those who defend the development will typically see it as advancing general social utility and progress, goals that will be retarded if we remain stuck in the past. "'Let bygones be bygones' says Wernher von Braun" as the old Tom Lehrer song has it.[61]

Professor Leila Nadya Sadat, in her magnificent 2006 *Notre Dame Law Journal* article, argues persuasively that most amnesties are a form of impunity that will simply encourage practitioners of state-sponsored terrorism to continue their unlawful ways in the certainty that no temporal punishment awaits them.[62] Professor Sadat's article points up a theme that emerges from study of the Letelier case, the Pinochet cases, the Kissinger litigation, and the experiences of Chile and South Africa. In the introduction, I spoke of lawyers' role in remembering for the beneficent purpose of helping us to avoid repeating bad events. Sometimes, remembering logically goes along with forgiveness or redemption as a way of helping victims, wrongdoers, and societies to move forward. No less a philosopher than country legend Willie Nelson knows that forgiving is different from forgetting:

"Forgiving you is easy,
But forgetting takes the longest time."[63]

The South African Truth and Reconciliation Commission was founded on the idea of creating a reliable historical record to assist in avoiding repetition of crimes against humanity that had been committed during the apartheid period. That same idea lay behind the Nuremburg trials, and the French trials of Barbie, Touvier, and especially, Papon. One wanted to put beyond the reach of all responsible criticism the true history of certain events. Trials of historic events should be fair and open. Trials that do not meet that standard do not have reliable outcomes on a case-by-case basis. They also create suspicion and hostility, and do not truly resolve the issues they purport to decide.

The South African commission was also endowed with the force of state power. Those who did not come forward could and would be prosecuted. The Chilean commission, by contrast, was dominated by the political elements associated with the junta, and its conclusions were inherently suspect. The various amnesties and immunities that were granted during the transition to civilian rule were imposed on the new government and were rightly invalidated in later years. I dare to see an analogy to the Kissinger litigation in the United States, and to the 2006 legislation of immunity for American officials relating to detainees.

Domestic tribunals are the first line of action against illegality. They have the undoubted power to judge the actions of domestic officials and to provide remedies to victims. In the United States, there has appeared a curious duality of judicial reasoning concerning state-sponsored terrorist behavior. On the one hand, U.S. courts have assisted victims of terrorism by holding foreign states and sovereigns liable for conduct that takes place within the territorial jurisdiction of the United States or that affects U.S. nationals. When the Chilean government claimed that involvement in the assassination of Orlando Letelier would be an unreviewable sovereign discretionary act, Judge Joyce Hens Green rejected the claim outright. Yet, U.S. courts have bowed to executive will and largely immunized U.S. officials from liability for equivalent conduct. The Congress has acquiesced in giving virtual immunity to executive branch agents who have committed torture.

The executive branch shares responsibility for nonenforcement of norms. When reliable reports show that criminal behavior—including extraordinary renditions, torture, violation of the laws of war, and violation of the Geneva Conventions—is pandemic, prosecutors have failed to act. All of us have seen, even in our own communities, how such scandals as public corruption long go unprosecuted and unpunished. Discretion not to prosecute, as well as the choice of defendants, is well-nigh unreviewable in the American system.[64]

Responsible lawyers, singly and in associations devoted to legality, have an opportunity and, I would say, a duty to speak up against executive and judicial retreat from the obligation to enforce norms of behavior.

The reticence to find liability, while disappointing, is not wholly unexpected, either in American history or transnationally. As I have noted, accountability for serious governmental wrong must often await the passage of time. As Professor Sadat and others have chronicled, immunities, exiles, and amnesties have been a common feature when a repressive regime is replaced. Prosecuting and judging are functions of state power. State power justifies itself by a claim of neutrality to stand indifferent between the sovereign and the people. Many essays in this book show how that mask has come off in prosecuting and punishing alleged terrorists and terrorist groups.[65] That is, the executive branch does not follow the law when seeking targets of prosecution. In the context we are now considering, we see an analogous inconsistency. Just as with the authors of French revolutionary terror, the state relentlessly pursues its claimed enemies, and recognizes no limits on its own behavior.

In such a circumstance, what must be done if one does not wish to await the belated and uncertain judgment of fickle history? People are dying out there, and one is reminded of Robespierre's words in opposition to capital punishment, later withdrawn and perhaps even later recalled: "Of what use are sterile regrets, the illusory reparations we may accord to vain shadows and insensible ash."[66]

The South African Truth and Reconciliation Commission has been criticized for assertedly going easy on African National Congress violence, and for bestowing amnesty too easily and thereby trivializing serious criminal conduct. On balance, I think it was a necessary part of the transition away from apartheid. The African National Congress faced many challenges as it assumed state power. It had to put in place structures to address the social needs of millions of people who had been systematically deprived by the apartheid regime. For example, Kadar Asmal, the first Minister of Forestry and Water Affairs in the Mandela government in 1994, faced a situation in which more than half of black South Africans had no access to potable water. Within a few years, he had organized and directed a system that brought water to millions. This was just one area where immediate and expensive attention had to be paid. From another direction, private interests from major corporations to the organized bar were expending money and energy to preserve their prerogatives and prevent the new government from accomplishing its announced goals.

Lawyers and litigants know a simple truth: litigation represents an investment decision. If you are poor and without access to a lawyer, the investment decision is made for you. If you are able to find a lawyer and to have access to the courts, the process will be costly. Somebody has to pay that bill. Trying all, or a representative sample, of those who perpetrated violence in support of apartheid would have been very expensive if the regime were to keep its promise to make the criminal justice system fair by providing procedural rights. The new state chose not to make that investment decision but rather to create the TRC in the hope of accomplishing the same results more quickly and efficiently. The hoped-for results were to vindicate the power of the new regime, validate norms of conduct, and contribute to social unification. These are the same goals that a punitive model of criminal justice seeks to obtain.

Seen in this light, one can readily see the flaws in the Chilean reconciliation process, which proceeded from weakness rather than strength to a preordained conclusion that bolstered impunity rather than accountability.

G. International Criminal Tribunals—Jurisdiction, Procedure, Fairness, Limits

The movement to create an international criminal court is welcome. Given the structure of the United Nations, the tribunal will be influenced greatly by states that are not great powers. It will be able to receive, interpret, and apply the body of international human rights law that has developed in the past one hundred years—the existence and tenor of which I discuss elsewhere in this book. However, there is another type of international tribunal somewhere between the domestic courts and the ICC. That is the ad hoc court established to try cases arising in a particular area. The Nuremburg court was such a tribunal, as are the International Criminal Tribunals for Yugoslavia and Rwanda.

The Nuremburg trial process had great advantages over alternative means of dealing with Nazi leaders. Its founding charter and its rulings advanced the cause of transnational criminal law. It has rightly been criticized for unfairness to defendants,[67] but its judgments fulfilled the historic purpose of establishing not only norms but a historical record of Nazi atrocities.

The International Criminal Tribunal for Yugoslavia has been praised as an efficient and effective instrument for trying and punishing human rights violations that occurred during the ethnic strife in the republics of the former Yugoslavia. The tribunal was established by the United Nations Security Council. A detailed statute, setting out its powers and duties, was passed by the General Assembly on May 25, 1993, and amended several times.[68]

The tribunal sits in The Hague, and consists of trial courts, an appellate court, a prosecutor's office and a registry, which fulfills the function of a court clerk's office. Trials are held before panels of three judges, and procedure is an amalgam of common law and civil law rules. The Security Council created the International Criminal Tribunal for Rwanda (ICTR) in 1994 to prosecute perpetrators of the 1994 Rwandan genocide. That tribunal, organized like the ICTY, sits in Tanzania. The prosecutor's office is in Kigah, Rwanda. These tribunals apply substantive criminal law principles drawn from treaties, customary international law, and

79

norms of international law that have become peremptory or *jus cogens*. Here is a representative list of criminal offenses:

- Grave breaches of the Geneva Conventions of 1949, including willful killing; torture or inhuman treatment, including biological experiments; willfully causing great suffering or serious injury to body or health; willfully depriving a prisoner of war or a civilian of the rights of fair and regular trial; unlawful deportation or transfer or unlawful confinement of a civilian; taking civilians as hostages.
- Violations of the laws or customs of war, including employment of poisonous weapons or other weapons calculated to cause unnecessary suffering; wanton destruction of cities, towns or villages, or devastation not justified by military necessity; attack, or bombardment, by whatever means, of undefended towns, villages, dwellings, or buildings; seizure of, destruction or willful damage done to institutions dedicated to religion, charity and education, the arts and sciences, historic monuments and works of art and science.
- Genocide, including not only direct violence but incitement to commit genocide.
- Crimes against humanity, when committed in armed conflict, whether international or internal in character, and directed against any civilian population, including murder, extermination, enslavement, deportation, imprisonment, torture, rape, and persecutions on political, racial and religious grounds.

The Yugoslavia tribunal (ICTY) was fortunate in having a distinguished group of judges from its inception. Its most fortunate circumstance was Justice Richard Goldstone's willingness to serve as its first Chief Prosecutor. Justice Goldstone had served in the courts of South Africa during the apartheid period and earned a reputation as a courageous foe of apartheid. When Nelson Mandela was released from prison, Goldstone headed up an inquiry into state-sponsored terrorism and related violence committed with the connivance of South African security forces against freedom fighters. President Mandela appointed him as a Justice of the newly created Constitutional Court of South Africa, but allowed him to take up the position in The Hague as well. Goldstone organized the prosecutor's office and its investigative work efficiently and effectively and ensured that the trial chambers had work to do with potential defendants.

Both ICTY and ICTR have a regular staff of defense lawyers. In addition, the tribunals appoint counsel for individual cases who are compensated for their work. These lawyers are drawn from many countries, with preference being given to lawyers with international criminal justice experience.

Within the adversary system created by the UN resolutions, the ICTY and ICTR have developed a significant body of law concerning the definition of offenses and the liability of perpetrators. No person is immune from punishment by virtue of his or her governmental position. No person is exonerated because he or she was ordered to and did commit unlawful conduct, though obedience to such orders may be considered in mitigation of punishment.

The ICTR faces a significant resources problem in that tens of thousands of people were culpably involved in the genocide committed against Tutsi people and the ensuing forcible relocations and mistreatment of refugee populations.[69] However, it has issued judgments in significant cases, apparently chosen by prosecutors in order to show historically and socially significant aspects of the genocide and terror. For example, in December 2006, the tribunal convicted Father Seromba, a Catholic priest charged with committing and masterminding genocide. Three Catholic nuns had earlier been convicted of similar offenses. The following was among the charges: Father Seromba directed that the militia pour fuel into a church and set it ablaze with 2,000 people inside it. When all were not killed, he ordered the Church demolished.

The ICTY has focused its prosecutorial attention on atrocities committed by Serbian forces against Kosovar partisans and civilians who were seeking either autonomy from Serbia or alliance with Albania, and against other groups seeking independence from Serbia, such as the Bosnians. Among its most dramatic cases are those arising from the Serbian forces massacre at Srebrenica. There is spirited debate over whether the tribunal's focus on Serbian conduct, and its relative lack of interest in Croatian atrocities against Serbs, is a legitimate exercise of prosecutorial discretion or in fact reflects the foreign and military policy goals of the United States and Great Britain.[70] Critics and chroniclers of NATO intervention in the former Yugoslavia have pointed out that the military action could not really be said to be a United Nations operation, and was in fact carried out by a few members of NATO led by the United States and the United Kingdom. Unquestionably, the military action led to thousands of civilian casualties. Its occurrence has later been cited by leaders of other states as a justification for their own deadly military incursions.[71] Additionally, it was the military incursion that put forces on the ground to arrest potential defendants for trial before the ICTY.

Richard Goldstone, in his exciting book *For Humanity: Reflections of a War Crimes Investigator*, describes his own work and that of his team. He describes his desire to make prosecutorial decisions independent of political and diplomatic pressures.

Americans who study the judicial system are familiar with the problem of prosecutorial discretion. Prosecuting agencies cannot possibly bring to court every case of plausibly unlawful conduct. Choice is inevitable. For example, prosecutions for criminal tax evasion probably represent a small fraction of intentional tax cheating. Prosecutors choose the most serious cases, and let the civil enforcement system handle the others. If, for example, the government perceives that in a particular area doctors are not reporting cash fees, it may bring a criminal case against a physician to send a message. Prosecutorial discretion is inevitably underinclusive, in that it attacks only a fraction of potentially punishable behavior. Prosecutors and police have limited resources. More importantly, increasing police and prosecutorial activity can and often does lead to curtailment of essential freedoms.

In addition to legitimate exercise of discretion in this area, there are many documented cases of tax audits and eventual prosecution being used against political enemies of a current administration, or as a way of getting at somebody against whom there is suspicion but not solid evidence of other kinds of wrongdoing. In the administration of capital punishment, there is extensive evidence that a person of color who kills a white person is far more likely to be prosecuted for capital murder than a white person who kills a person of color.[72] When choosing a prosecution strategy to deter prostitution, does the prosecutor bring charges only against providers of sexual services or seek a broader swath of deterrence by targeting customers?

The fact of prosecutorial discretion is obvious and inevitable. The ICTY dispute provides an opportunity to address the institutional controls on discretion and the basis for exercising discretion in combating state-sponsored terrorism. The goal is clear and includes the same elements that one finds in all efficient criminal justice systems: deterring state actors from engaging in terrorist behavior, giving victims a sense that justice is being done, increasing potential victims' sense of security, imposing just punishment for harmful actions, and visibly respecting fair norms regarding selection of defendants.

The institutional setting of prosecutor discretion is an important and sometimes overlooked aspect of the problem. In the United States, most local prosecutorial decisions are made by elected district attorneys. Some state attorneys general have the power to prosecute for particular offenses, such as securities fraud and public corruption. The federal prosecutorial establishment is a small fraction of that which exists in the states. Prosecutorial policy is set by the Justice Department in Washington, D.C., but in practice United States Attorneys have a great deal of discretion in running their offices. Justice Department lawyers may also be sent to particular judicial districts to prosecute given types of offenses or particular high-profile offenders.

The ICTY statute provides:

1. The Prosecutor shall be responsible for the investigation and prosecution of persons responsible for serious violations of international humanitarian law committed in the territory of the former Yugoslavia since 1 January 1991.
2. The Prosecutor shall act independently as a separate organ of the International Tribunal. He or she shall not seek or receive instructions from any Government or from any other source.
3. The Office of the Prosecutor shall be composed of a Prosecutor and such other qualified staff as may be required.
4. The Prosecutor shall be appointed by the Security Council on nomination by the Secretary-General. He or she shall be of high moral character and possess the highest level of competence and experience in the conduct of investigations and prosecutions of criminal cases. The Prosecutor shall serve for a four-year term and be eligible for reappointment. The terms and conditions of service of the Prosecutor shall be those of an Under-Secretary-General of the United Nations.
5. The staff of the Office of the Prosecutor shall be appointed by the Secretary-General on the recommendation of the Prosecutor.

Thus, the ICTY prosecutor is institutionally independent. The Secretary-General could seek to influence him or her by affecting staff appointments but would be subject to countervailing pressure from the General Assembly and the Security Council. Goldstone proved to be an able advocate for his own and his staff's independence. His conduct of the office is popularly credited as the reason why the International Criminal Court prosecutor was accorded a similar degree of autonomy in the Rome Statute that established the ICC.

The situation might have been otherwise. Goldstone's appointment as prosecutor followed months of stalemate as some candidates declined the post and the Security Council could not agree on others.[73] Goldstone emerged as the perfect candidate because of his involvement in the South African liberation struggle, which had seen the initial success of Mandela's release from prison in 1990.

For his part, Goldstone denies being concerned about the political impact of his prosecutorial decisions. He instituted proceedings against Serb leaders Mladic and Karadzic, though he must have known that this would affect the political efforts to bring an end to conflict in the region. Indeed, he reveals that UN Secretary-General Boutros-Ghali lamented that Goldstone did not consult him on the timing of these investigations.

In 1998, a diplomatic conference reached agreement on the Rome Statute, calling for creation of an international criminal court that would have jurisdiction over human rights violations as well as other crimes. By June 2002, when sixty nations had ratified the treaty embodying the statute, the ICC could begin work. It was formally inaugurated at The Hague on March 11, 2003. Although U.S. representatives had participated in drafting the Rome Statute, the United States has not ratified the treaty. Indeed, the United States has actively discouraged other nations from ratifying it. The Bush administration has expressed fear that Americans who participate in tortures, extraordinary renditions, and other offenses would be subjected to trial before the ICC. Once again, this objection is based on fears about the wrongful exercise of prosecutorial discretion, given that these acts would be crimes under American law if committed by U.S. nationals. In January 2007, it was reported that there was resistance to a UN force in Somalia because some perpetrators of human rights abuses feared that the UN forces would arrest potential defendants to be tried before the ICC.[74]

In the 1980s, the American Bar Association assembled a committee to work on a potential international criminal court. Benjamin Civiletti, former U.S. Attorney General and Chair of the Litigation Section, headed up the committee. George H. W. Bush's administration was actively hostile to the entire idea, largely on the grounds that the George W. Bush administration continues to assert. The ABA position was that transnational institutions were best equipped to deal with transnational challenges to public order. This concern did not arise solely or even principally from human rights concerns. Environmental pollution, violation of labor rights, financial wrongdoing, anticompetitive behavior, and many other ordinary crimes are committed by individuals and entities whose activity, power, and influence make them more or less beyond the reach of any national sovereign power.

To be sure, a transnational body may excite suspicion and controversy, but its decisions are likely to enjoy more credibility than those of a particular state or even of a group of states. The criticism directed at the ICTY is not based on its character as a transnational institution but on allegations that, in its origins and actions, it in fact followed the agenda of a small group of great powers. In a related context, recall the controversy over the prosecution of Augusto Pinochet. The charges were brought by Spain. Some Chileans derided the prosecutorial effort on the grounds that Spain had been colonial master of Chile in past times, and that any prosecuting should be done by Chilean officials. Of course, the real prosecutorial activity in Chile did not begin until the British proceedings had not only exposed Pinochet's crimes to the world but had shown that he could and should be held accountable.

Throughout this book, I have sought to draw lessons from past conflicts. Let us revert to some basic ideas. First, principles of criminal liability are worth nothing unless some sovereign state power exists and has the political will to enforce them. Criminal law is not what it says but what it does.[75] Norms, principles, and laws that condemn human rights violations came into being based on social struggle and will be applied or not applied based on the relative strengths of potential defendants and likely sovereigns.

Where will one find sovereigns with the power and the will? National tribunals are the first line of defense. They have the longest history and the most organized mechanisms of enforcement. Therefore, the question of power hardly arises, at least with respect to prosecuting conduct historically within the lawful power of a national sovereign. As we have seen, that historic power extends to conduct on the national territory, as expanded by national emplacements such as embassy premises, military bases, and ships flying the national flag. Additionally, a sovereign may prosecute conduct outside its borders undertaken with the expectation and realistic prospect of having some impact in the territory. For example, narcotics dealers aiming their product at the United States, or price fixers seeking an impact on U.S. markets, find themselves subject to prosecution. Next, a sovereign may impose its laws on its own nationals' conduct, done anywhere in the world; the United States does not make much use of this basis of power. A sovereign may prosecute those who commit crimes against its nationals or premises, regardless of place. Finally, there are crimes as to which there is universal jurisdiction, no matter the defendant's nationality or where the conduct occurred. As to these offenses, the sovereign who has the defendant's body must prosecute or extradite to a sovereign who will do so: *aut daedaere, aut judicare* in the law Latin.

So, the issue is not power but political will. In France, Chile, and the United States—to take three examples discussed in this book—it has been difficult to engage the legislative, executive, and judicial branches in defining, prosecuting, and judging human rights violations. In France, it was nearly two decades after World War II that the Penal Code was finally amended to authorize prosecution of Nazi collaborators. Then, it was years longer before the first prosecution of an avowed Gestapo agent and more years until French collaborators were brought to trial. In those trials, the courts were careful to close off any prospect that French citizens could be tried for atrocities committed by French forces in Asian and North African colonies.

In Chile, as I have said, when Pinochet stepped down as President, the junta left in place constitutional provisions that ensured the military's continuing influence over national politics. Former governmental officials were granted amnesty for human rights violations. Democratic forces in Chile were not sufficiently empowered or bold to strip Pinochet and others of amnesty and conduct a determined campaign against abuses of the junta regime until after the Spanish and UK proceedings. These latter proceedings showed the way by mapping legal and factual theories. The fact that they occurred without the military having the power or will in Chile to create serious disturbance gave a sense of confidence to those in Chile who wanted to press ahead in domestic tribunals.

Although Pinochet left the presidency in 1990, it required more than a decade of political struggle for the Chilean response to gather strength. The flowering of that response, when it came, encouraged Chileans to support the goals of the ICC even against American opposition, and helped Michelle Bachelet to build the alliance that carried her to the Presidency of Chile. President Bachelet had herself been a victim of torture under the Pinochet regime.

In the United States, domestic tribunals have been reluctant to provide relief to victims of human rights abuses. There has been judicial re-examination of the Japanese relocation, but civil cases involving American complicity in tortures, disappearances, and assassinations have not met with success. There has been no activity on the criminal side of the docket. In 2000, when the Executive Branch responded to Congressional legislation and admitted complicity in the human rights crimes of the Pinochet regime, those admissions were accompanied by release of declassified documents but by no other official action of consequence. Power there was, but not political will.

The power of domestic tribunals to address human rights violations will vary depending on local law. In France, the President of
the Republic enjoys special rights concerning when and under what
conditions he or she may be charged with offenses. In 2007, the President in Israel was prosecuted for rape, although formal criminal
proceedings could not begin until he left office. His predecessor was
forced to resign under threat of prosecution for financial irregulari-
ties. In the United States, President William Clinton was impeached
by the House of Representatives and tried—and acquitted—in the
Senate for alleged lying and obstruction of justice. President Richard
Nixon resigned rather than face impeachment for serious abuses of
official power. However, there has been little Congressional support
for an investigation of executive responsibility for torture, unlawful
detentions, and unlawful killing connected with the incursions into
Afghanistan and Iraq.

Domestic, or national, tribunals have been more receptive to cases
involving crimes committed by citizens of foreign countries. The Pinochet case is an example, in which Spanish and British courts swept aside
barriers to prosecution—the defendant being spared only by a finding of
ill health. However, it is important to note that a domestic tribunal will
assert less authority to hear a civil than a criminal case. For example,
in the United Kingdom, the House of Lords upheld dismissal of a suit
brought by people who claimed to have been tortured in Saudi Arabia by
agents of the Saudi government. In the United States, the Foreign Sovereign Immunities Act, under which the *Letelier-Moffitt* case was brought,
does not confer jurisdiction over a foreign country with respect to events
that occurred outside the United States.

Even where a domestic tribunal is willing to act, its power may be limited by international law rules concerning immunity. In 1998, Abdoulaye
Yerodia, the foreign minister of the Democratic Republic of the Congo,
publicly urged citizens to kill opponents of the government who were
mostly ethnic Tutsis. At that time, Belgian law asserted universal jurisdiction over genocide and crimes against humanity, and a Belgian court
issued an arrest warrant for Yerodia. The Democratic Republic of the
Congo sued Belgium in the International Court of Justice in The Hague,
claiming that under international law a serving foreign minister was
immune from the criminal judicial jurisdiction of a foreign country. On
February 14, 2002, the ICJ ruled in the Congo's favor and ordered the
arrest warrant withdrawn. There was disagreement among the ICJ justices, three of whom dissented on the immunity question, and six on the
question of remedy.

The ICJ decision can be regarded as a setback for the idea of universal jurisdiction. Before joining any such chorus, one should read the opinion written by Judge Bula-Bula, the Congolese member of the tribunal. Under ICJ procedures, one judge each from the Congo and Belgium sat as ad hoc members of the Court. Judge Bula-Bula's opinion can be characterized as exclaiming: "What! Belgium is to give lessons on humanitarianism to the Congo?" The ICJ ruling means that as a practical matter, Minister Yerodia will never be tried anywhere for his actions, unless the new International Criminal Court takes up his case.

The result might well have been different if Yerodia was no longer in a governmental position, because the Court based its decision on his position as an incumbent minister exempt from criminal process, and not upon a broader ground of exemption from criminal jurisdiction. Some judges expressed the wish that the court had gone on to discuss these broader issues but they were a minority. Therefore, the idea of a core national power to try people for committing crimes against humanity, regardless of victim and defendant nationality and venue, remains viable. Sovereign states hesitate to exercise such power, however, for fear of jeopardizing their own foreign relations concerns.

The next step up the ladder of power is the ad hoc tribunal, such as those for Yugoslavia and Rwanda. Under the statutes of those courts, officials have no immunity from arrest, criminal liability, and judgment. Although a potential defendant who is an ambassador or other diplomatic representative may be immune from arrest while performing certain functions, no such person is immune from prosecution and punishment. Thus, the ICJ in the Congo-Belgium case could legitimately note that its resolution of the issues before it did not foredoom efforts to hold high officials accountable for state-sponsored terrorism.

Of course, ad hoc international tribunals carry inherent problems of legitimacy. Michael Bohlander, Roman Boed, and Richard Wilson's magnificent book, *Defense in International Criminal Proceedings*, contains a detailed discussion of the procedures before the ICTY, ICTY, and ICC. Professor Wilson's chapter on the right to counsel and other procedural safeguards is a valuable resource. He points out that defendants at Nuremberg and in the Tokyo tribunals did not have the effective assistance of competent counsel at all relevant procedural hours. Even in these latter days, before the ICTY and ICTR, Wilson voices legitimate concern about the mechanism for selecting counsel.

It bears reiteration that trials in state-sponsored terrorism cases are didactic in several senses. They ought to command respect for having established, by competent evidence, important historical truth. They ought to teach potential defendants and potential victims that justice worthy of that name has been done and might be done again to other perpetrators. We know by now that a fair trial requires that the adversaries have equal access to sources of potential evidence and equal ability to present their versions of events to an impartial tribunal. These guarantees stand alongside a requirement that defendants be fairly selected, without unfair discrimination, as measures of perceived legitimacy.

Professor Wilson makes this point in discussing Jacques Vergès, who represented Klaus Barbie and Saddam Hussein:[76]

> Verges himself, when asked why he took on the case of Saddam Hussein, responded, "I am against lynching and lynching is the tendency of the people. And my pride is when a lynching is in preparation, to stand between the so-called criminals and the lynchers." Professor Michael Tigar, no stranger to controversial clients himself, states that "I find comments that begin 'how could you possibly represent' to be offensive and (quite literally) impertinent, at least if lawyers make them." While he examines the case of Verges and concludes that he would not himself represent a Nazi, he agrees to struggle with the question. His answer is simple, elegant and appropriate as an ending to this chapter, "Once you make the choice to take any case . . . the task is set: Figure out how to win. . . . When we think of crimes against humanity, we must remember that governments and government groups are the most dangerous criminals. They have the most power to inflict harm, and they are the most likely to be recidivists. State-sponsored terrorism is the most dangerous brand, especially when it masquerades as justice.

Both the ICTY and the ICTR have jurisdiction to prosecute offenses by non-state actors. Typically, the defendants acted in concert with or at the direction of state actors. The cooperation between officials and terrorists who show up and help is familiar in American law. For example, in *United States v. Guest* and *United States v. Price*,[77] the Supreme Court broadly construed the civil rights laws to criminalize conduct by non-state actors who were "under color of law" in the sense that they knowingly acted in concert with state actors. However, given that many terrorist acts take place in the context of armed conflict, and not simply as isolated acts, and that such acts often are transnational in character, the jurisdiction of transnational tribunals is implicated. Creating tribunals to try cases of alleged terrorism, or recognizing the jurisdiction of the permanent ICC, would be one way to solve problems of discriminatory prosecution and national bias. In other parts of this book, I have pointed to cases in which the goals and values of prosecuting alleged terrorists in American courts have been muddled, discriminatory, or beset with procedural unfairness. A transnational tribunal might well bring a perspective to non-state sponsored terrorism cases that reflected concern for fairness and even-handedness as well as the need for enforcement.

H. From the Table of Free Voices: Terrorism, Liberty, Security, Profit

If we are to have a more peaceful and just world, we must listen to voices that speak many languages other than our own. I hope that is one conclusion from what I have written above. "Languages" means more than the words we use to describe a condition, item, or action. It takes in the entire idea of points of view and of reference.

On September 9, 2006, 112 people sat down at the Table of Free Voices in Berlin's Bebelplatz. The plaza is flanked by Humboldt University, St. Hedwig's cathedral, and the state opera building. It is named for August Bebel, founder of the German Social Democratic Party. On May 10, 1933, Nazi thugs burned some 20,000 books at this site. There is an impressive monument to this event.

The 112 people at the Table of Free Voices were selected from many countries, professions, and perspectives. The multinational sponsoring organization, droppingknowledge.org, sifted through thousands of names before sending out invitations. For more than a year, droppingknowledge staff members had gathered questions from contributors around the world. From these Internet submissions, they selected one hundred questions in fields of economics, social responsibility, conflict, justice, science, governance, and ecology. The moderators, actor Willem Dafoe and Nigerian activist Hafsat Abiola, read out the questions one by one. At each participant's place was a small video camera and a microphone. The participants had about two minutes to answer each question to which they wished to provide an answer. The organizers are uploading the answers to their Web site. The event was supported by an array of business and nonprofit groups representing many political tendencies. All this material is copyleft—in the public domain.

I was invited to be one of the voices, honored to be with people engaged in struggles for justice in their own countries and transnationally. In some areas of discussion, views diverged, and at the level of specific policy choices, there were great differences of approach. However, with respect to fundamental questions that have us thinking about terror, there was a surprising confluence of views. I set out some of the responses for the same reason that I have included so many different perspectives in different parts of this book: No country or people can long follow a policy that ignores the views of the rest of the world. The interpenetration of ideas and ideologies from different social systems has strengthened the cause of social justice. Bluntly put, we need to listen to these voices. In too much of the political discussion in the United States, we are simply talking to ourselves.

The answers, some of which I have excerpted below, dealt with both state-sponsored and non-state-sponsored terrorism. The latter variety is the subject of later essays in this book, but these comments provide a challenging introduction to that later discussion. The speakers give us valuable insights into questions of national complicity in state-sponsored terrorism, accountability for terrorism, and the procedural framework within which any attack on or condemnation of terrorism must operate in order to be effective, credible, and legitimate.

Two of the one hundred questions were: "Who is profiting from terrorism?" and "How much of our liberty are we going to offer for our supposed security?" The first of these was from the 2004 Barcelona Forum, a significant gathering that was in some ways a precursor of the Table of Free Voices. The second one was contributed by Florian Grosse, of Starnberg, Germany.

The "who is profiting" question evoked answers that were remarkably consistent in approach, though based on many different experiences. The responders who sought to define the term terrorism were consistent in their descriptions. A majority of respondents identified arms manufacturers and suppliers as principal beneficiaries of terrorism, along with the political and military structures that support them. Given that the Iraq military adventure had, by 2006, become unpopular with a majority of Americans, it was not surprising to hear criticism of George W. Bush. The vehemence of some of this criticism, and the way in which participants drew parallels to situations in their own experience, was instructive.

Here are some of the voices:

Martin Almada is a courageous Paraguayan lawyer who spent seven years in prison for his opposition to the Stroessner regime in that country. He was repeatedly tortured during his confinement. I met him at breakfast one morning in Berlin. Because he and I had both worked on legal issues concerning the Pinochet regime, we were quickly engaged in animated discussion. He is pursuing legal remedies against the Stroessner regime on behalf of its many victims. His answer reflected the priorities

91

established by his own and his country's experiences (translated from Spanish):

> When a terrorist is a state itself, a whole industry chain and building companies, alongside with the military industry, gain big profits and good capital. A war produces numerous deals with great profits under extraordinary conditions. Nowadays not only arms industry gains from a war, but big real estate companies ready to rebuild cities, companies ready to provide medicine, equipment, medical help, education, communication. Everything that is destroyed in two days provides very good deals that will last more than twenty years, as it was the case during the Lebanon war in the 80s.

Yassin Adnan is a journalist, literary correspondent of the London-based Arabic language newspaper *Al-Hayat*. He is Moroccan. He began by noting that because of his name and evident ethnic heritage he had difficult airport security problems coming to the Berlin conference. He added:

> We in Morocco know how it is to be the victim of the terrorism. In the May 16 in Casablanca two years ago there were terror attacks. However it is also certain that we are the biggest victims of this phenomenon. Our reputation and the value of freedom are suffering because we come from an Arab-Islamic country.

Udi Aloni's 2006 film *Forgiveness* is set in a psychiatric institution built upon the ruins of a destroyed Palestinian village. He is a native of Israel and profoundly interested in the semiotics of terrorism as an evocative epithet. He acknowledged the widely held view that forces in the West benefit from terrorism, but wants to explore a different side of the issue:

> I know old answer how America and the West and everyone gain from it. But, there is something there that we have to speak. The power of mythology also gains from it. We are all fascinated by it. We all—its give us a feeling of living and we saw it in different movies how it act this fantasy. I think we can speak about [the film] Fight Club. . . . It's this place we love to play. It's this death we like to feel in order to feel the life. And, we should begin to speak with those psychoanalysis terminologies sometimes to understand why we are so fucked up because all the time we think we're saying, the truth is so simple and it never happened like that. So, there is the economy profit. But, there is also the profit of our twisted mind, and let's not forget it. We love to see those movies, we love the images. . . . My friend said who is a terrorist? You are the terrorist. How can I be a terrorist when I live in my own land? Who is the terrorist? You

are the terrorist. You killed my fathers, you stole my land. So, who is the terrorist? You are the terrorist. This is a free translation from DAM, Palestinian rappers, that remind us who is the terrorist.

This answer, and several in the same vein, invite everyone who lives in a country that is making war, or where armaments are produced, to ask a question about his or her own responsibility. As I read these answers, I am reminded of the Papon case in France, and the eventual and reluctant admission that many French people were in some measure complicit in the Nazi horrors. Some gave their silent consent but others were more active participants, often by the simple process of doing their jobs or following orders.

Antoschka, also known as Ekaterina Moshaeva, is a clown—the "queen of Russian clowns." Around the table at breaks in the action, and at other gatherings, she would confront participants with small clown routines in mime. Her answer evokes part of the universal language of clowning: seeing irony in events. She began by referring to the fact that the CIA funded and armed Islam extremists in Afghanistan to oppose the Soviet forces there, and now confronts those same groups:

> It is very interesting. America is the first creator of the terror groups, and then they became problems with terror groups of Al-Qaeda which were fighting on the other side then. Then there is one more problem. People should think before they start aggression, because every stick has two ends. And the next time you can get it beating your own head. . . . Yet the problem of masses is that they are passive. They do not feel. They are not strong enough to realize, that everybody is able to act. Even a butterfly, which with a single beat of wings can change the climate and cause a storm on the other side of the planet, can do something. Everybody can do something.

Mohammed Arkoun is a professor of Islamic Studies at the Sorbonne. For decades, he has been a student of Islamic liberation movements and a voice for creating and enforcing transnational human rights norms. His answer reflected his experience in the Algerian independence struggle, which was marked on both sides by conduct that fits the definitions of terrorism developed in this book. He also contrasts the consequences of great power military action with insurgent actions that sometimes merit the label terrorist.

> Nobody can make a profit from terrorism. Because terrorism takes place within societies. . . . [In Algeria], there was a murderous and atrocious civil war and this war did not benefit to those who led it

with terrorism, neither to the Algerian society itself, nor even less, to the governments. And this is only an example. There are civil wars everywhere, in Ivory Coast, in Sri Lanka, in a lot of African and Asian societies and therefore terrorism is nowadays the expression of the imposed unequal war. Since there is a war and one side has the means to do war without losing a human life, this is the ideal American war. They are even called clean wars, and to wage war without loss, to achieve a total victory by completely subduing a people or people even to a situation that is opposite to the elementary rights and the elementary ethics and well that creates an accumulation of hate, an accumulation of resentments, an accumulation of revolt aiming to express itself somehow and the fact of resorting to terrorism whereas those exercising terrorism don't have a political program at all to give at least a hope of liberation and end of inequalities through terrorism, the end of injustices and oppressions and well terrorism is limited to this eruption of violence by an accumulation, I repeat it, of revolts that make life difficult to bear as well to the consideration of leaders inside as to the consideration of a world system confirming the state of structural violence imposed to those living under totalitarian political systems.

Jwan M. Aziz is an Iraqi engineer and head of a new nonprofit organization in Iraq that addresses the status of women in that country. She had obviously come directly from a war zone in which actions labeled terrorist were being committed by governments and non-state actors. Her reply spared no one:

> It is a very nice question. If we agree that the terrorism is killing civilians, occupying the territory, destruction of the dignity [of people], and it is one of the [methods of] war. So, the several gangs, the mafia, the false politic, and the military superpowers are profiting from the terrorism.

Many respondents argued that terrorism and a war on terrorism serve the interests of arms manufacturers, arms merchants, and military contractors. An insurgent group may begin by capturing weapons from a state actor, or even by purchasing them directly from a manufacturer in violation of domestic and international law. Sometimes, it forms an alliance with the state actor and gets money and more sophisticated weaponry. This was the case with the Taliban in Afghanistan, which the United States armed and financed as a counterweight to the Soviet occupying forces in the 1980s. As sovereign states move against insurgent groups, the arms manufacturers profit.

When Israel retaliated against the country of Lebanon in 2006, responding to a relatively minor border skirmish with a non-state actor, the Shiite Muslim group Hezbollah, it did so with armaments provided by the United States, including weapons that were formally interdicted for aggressive use. In turn, Hezbollah was armed by Iran and Syria. The arms trade thus permitted an existing conflict to be escalated to the extent that thousands were killed and hundreds of thousands left homeless.

There is an extensive secondary market in armaments, including those directly purchased from manufacturers in violation of local laws and international conventions, and those stolen or otherwise appropriated from military stockpiles. The respondents who focused on this issue tended to liken the situation to that in a country, such as the United States, where gun violence thrives in an atmosphere where getting a gun is easy.

Roland Berger, a leading figure in German finance and a consultant to German governments, said:

> To stop this arms trade should be the aim of the mighty democracies in our world. On the other hand we also have to do something against the origins of terrorism namely poverty, underprivileged people, humiliation of persons and peoples who don't see any other possibility to defend themselves and their interests but to draw attention to their problems by making terrorist attacks. The problem is that by drawing attention to their problems by means of terrorism they also disavow and make illegal their cause and they lose the support of the people.

Philippine indigenous leader Donato Bayu Bay Bumacas said, "Only two sets of people are benefiting from terrorism: the mastermind and the weapon manufacturers."

German physicist Hans-Peter Durr worked with Edward Teller on development of the hydrogen bomb and became horrified at the potential consequences of nuclear weapons. He is the former director of the Max-Planck Institute for Physics: "When we have a warlike conflict of such extent and such violence we say: 'Where are all these weapons actually coming?' And we know that all the industrial states are involved into this production. Why cannot we stop it?"

Jonathan Granoff, an American lawyer and American Bar Association activist in the field of international law, analyzed the issue at some length and concluded: "I guess you would say at the end of the day that the only people that are profiting from terrorism are people who are—who use military means of addressing social issues. It's terrible."

Paul D. Miller is also known as DJ Spooky, an important figure in contemporary music. He sounded the same note as Jonathan Granoff: "Well, who is profiting from terrorism? The military industrial complex is all about continuing the idea of permanent war. So you have to understand that permanent war implies an ideology of continuous output, continuous input."

Inuit teacher Angaangaq Lyberth spoke in the same vein: "Those who produce and sell any killing machines are profiting from terrorism. Do you know how much money is being spent on killing machines? Enormous amounts of money are being spent to be able to kill."

All those who spoke of terrorist acts condemned them. No speaker, from any country or point of view, believed that large-scale military violence was a proper response. German film director Wim Wenders said:

> Fanatics and fundamentalists on all sides profit the most. They have a win-win situation. They attract and recruit new forces on both sides. Oil companies profit if the prices go up as a consequence of terrorist acts. Contractors profit if they can rebuild what's been damaged, especially if they have those deals in place before the damage is done. Politicians profit if they find a profile that they otherwise would not have gained. The military profits as they have new arguments to build up their weapons arsenal. So it's a win-win situation against us. We are in the lose-lose position, we the people, except if we are able to implant non-violence as a reaction. It's our only weapon to firmly and deeply implant that idea into more and more peoples' head there is no other chance. That even in the war against terrorism that unspeakable expression, that ridiculous expression, that even in that and I say it with quotation marks, "non-violence is the only answer because it excludes profit."

Famed Argentinian filmmaker Fernando Solanas was more blunt:

> Those who benefit from the so-called terrorism are without the slightest doubt the United States. They have usurped Iraq and they are advancing to usurp the oil reserves of the whole world. Those who benefit from these pre-emptive wars are the powers that are starting them. From the people's point of view, the people benefit from no type of terrorism at all. I am an opponent of all forms of terrorism. You have to distinguish between different types of exertion of violence. Why? When the marquess of France or the resistance fighters of Algeria used forms of terrorism, it was one of the

96

few possibilities they had to bring to bear their resistance against the occupation by a foreign power. So, just wars are wars of resistance carried out by the people in the face of an invasion of aggression by foreign powers.

Many speakers also noted the connection between military responses to terrorism and domestic repression. Social activist Arundatha Mittal made this connection:

> Well, I would say terrorists are benefiting from terrorism. By that I mean it includes governments of United States, for example, the Bush administration who is benefiting from terrorism. I would say corporations such as Bechtel or Lockheed Martin are the ones who are benefiting from terrorism. And, of course, it's the people who are in power, they are benefiting from terrorism because that has become a way of colonizing our minds, of creating this culture of fear when you can put people in fear so they would be willing to give away the basic rights, their civil liberties, that they would agree to the kind of intervention we have in our lives of why attacking and everything. So those hard won rights that have been removed just because in the name of fighting terrorism, we know who's winning: it's the terrorists. This is not about you and me. This is really about the corporations, this is about the powerful politicians, this is about some fundamentalists who are benefiting from it; but it is definitely not the humanity.

Valentina Melnikova is a Russian social activist who confronts the human rights abuses of the Putin regime:

> Unfortunately terrorism has become a branch of industry, a branch of politics. Unfortunately many people make their profits on it: those who use terrorism to achieve their goals, to impose their own religious and ideological dominance, and also those governments for which war against terrorism is a justification of reducing democracy in their countries. Awful events as destruction of Twin Towers in New York and the awful death of children in Beslan were misused by American and Russian governments for attacking human rights, violation of fundamental human rights and liberty.

Many also recognized the connection between inequality and terrorism. Recognizing this connection is not a means to excuse or justify terrorist acts by state or non-state actors. Rather, one can see that military force can contribute to higher levels of violence and that often interventions in the name of anti-terrorism are, in fact, a cover for maintaining unjust systems. Pico Iyer, a British-born international journalist, said:

> I was staying in Dharamsala, a home of exiled Tibetan of the Dalai Lama last year and I had a militant Tibetan in exile expand what he called the mosquito theory and that theory is simply that a mosquito can get the better of a bear or a dragon, it can never defeat the dragon, but it can so pester and possess the dragon that the dragon is distracted and unable to go about its business. And this gentleman who speaks on behalf of violence from the Tibetan community against the Chinese in Tibet was essentially saying that the mosquito through its peskiness can redress the imbalance of power against the dragon. And I think terrorism ever since its origins arguably among the assassins in the 11th century in the Middle East has been essentially about placing fear within individuals, and so long as we respond with fear, the terrorists have won. In 21st century America, I feel that each convulsion and each new explosion of paranoia and red alert systems in America allows the terrorists to claim another victory, of these enemies of America to claim another victory. And so, insofar as terrorism is an attempt to disseminate fear, we can only respond to it by disseminating hope or disseminating a larger perspective and not allowing ourselves to be unsettled by its diabolically cunning logic. It is easy to say that terrorism is a situation in which nobody wins, but really it is a way in which—a situation in which those who have very little feel that they can redress the balance as the mosquito against the dragon, against those who have very much.

Mohau Pheko, a South African economist who specializes in development issues and a leader of feminist political forces in South Africa, said:

> I think when one builds or maps where terrorism is happening in the world today and I think that there are many sorts of terrorisms there, there is economic terrorism and I think that's the terrorism I really want to focus on. When I look at and map economic terrorism, it is happening in countries with the largest amount of natural resources. For example, when you look at Congo where there is coal bed, where there are water diamonds, where there are natural diamonds. You look at Sierra Leone, for example, where there are natural resources, wherever there are natural resources and

you look at the corporate powers behind these natural resources and their desire to actually claim those natural resources without domestic regulations in place, without accounting to anybody, without transparency in terms of how you get those resources out of certain countries into other countries and use them as raw materials to build Nokia cell phones, for example. It is quite clear to me that those who benefit from economic terrorism are certainly the huge corporations. When you look at the Congo and you look at the corporations that are involved behind the scenes, it's always the huge mining sectors, the Canadian mining sectors, even the South African mining sectors there, and the level of corruption that is there and ensuring that the rebels get a certain portion of that money in order for those resources to be [pulled]. So, I think that we have to map where the natural resources are in the world to really understand why there is such a large and high level of economic terrorism in the world today and why it remains beneficial for both those who want to disrupt authentic democracy in these countries as well as those who want to access those natural resources for their own personal profits. So, I think that at one level, we have to fight the profiteer—those who profit from these natural resources as well as those who want to obstruct the democratic processes in these countries. And I think the Congo is a point in case. So, I think that we have to focus on the sorts of terrorism that we are talking about because terrorism also has come to mean different things to different people. So, for me, in this case, my response to this question is really around economic terrorism as a concept that we really need to confront and interrogate fundamentally.

Sanar Yurdatapan is a courageous Turkish journalist who has exposed the crimes of Turkish regimes and has suffered for his candor. He has direct experience with the suppression of Kurdish forces by the Turkish government. He draws an interesting parallel:

How could Mr. Bush, Mr. Blair and some Iraqis be so aggressive if they did not—if they were not able to use the fear of the people on the street in their countries? The same thing in my country too. The military in Turkey has used us too much; they're still using—on the days with the war against PKK, we were complaining about the human rights violations made by the military and today it's still going on unfortunately. But they say that "No we are fighting against terrorism." After 9/11 and they were very happy, I said, "Look, now the whole world understood about us." Unfortunately not the whole world, but Bush and Blair used this to eliminate many rights of the people who were opposing them and their aggressive policies. Simply, yes, those aggressive policies benefit from that this way.

Yurdatapan's view is a kind of bridge to the second set of responses, directly addressing the liberty-security connection. The question, "How much of our liberty are we going to offer for our supposed security?," is of course loaded with the word supposed. The questioner expresses a point of view. Beyond that, however, the most challenging answers were from respondents who do not live in Occidental countries. For Americans, the security-liberty debate is rooted in constitutional theory and history, as well as in the collective American experience. We are, as a people, secure in our consumption of a quarter of the world's resources, living in a society with an enormous military budget, and domestically with an incarceration rate five to seven times that of Western European countries. We sit astride the largest stockpile of weaponry in the world. Our police forces are the most highly trained and best-armed. Yet, many speak of dangers to security that they argue are a reason to empower the executive branch to curtail liberty.

However, most of the world lives very differently from those in the first world. For a majority of the world's people, security and liberty have to do with obtaining the basic necessities of life. Many respondents expressed this view.

Lebanese poet Abbas Beydoun:

The person who asked this question must be European. This question is strongly posed in the societies where there is liberty, so security could damage liberty in these societies. In other societies where there is neither security nor liberty we do not know which worry we should have. Should we worry about liberty? Or should we worry about security? In these societies both cases cooperate with each other where people live without liberty and security. Generally in these societies it is said to people that dictatorships can guarantee the stability but without liberty.

Chinese artist Lijun Fang:

It depends on the standard and definition of security. For instance, are people in Iraq, Afghanistan or Palestine safe? How can they still offer their liberty to defend their security, if they do not have basic security?

Mohammed Arkoun:

This question is addressed to the occidental countries, to the occidental democracies. These democracies are facing a drama we all witnessed, the drama of terrorism protesting against a worldwide situation, against the design of the world map, a map of force and prosperity and the map of rejection. . . . There is the Occident and the rest of the world, the world's waste product. And as there are countries who are treated like the waste product of an ancient archaism who are official called terrorists, Islamic fascists there is a terrifyingly division of people living on our planet. That's not about justifying the murderous terrorism but about listening to the human suffering originating from prisons where whole peoples are living in.

These thinkers are inviting us to think outside the debate that is framed in the United States and other Western countries and, perhaps in that way, to find answers to the problems that make us ask the question in the first place. In many countries, the view is widely shared that economic security, security from torture and other inhumane treatment, education, housing, health care, and other social rights ought to be guaranteed. A number of United Nations documents enshrine these rights and they are included in the constitutions of many countries, including Namibia and South Africa. These rights were initially defined, and their recognition obtained, through social struggles. Thus, one can see a relationship between the liberty to engage in political action and obtaining a certain level of security. Sometimes, as with the South African liberation movement, there was no formal right to engage in political action; rather, the right was assumed and acted upon.

There is a saying in the Chicano activist community: "sin justicia no hay paz [no justice, no peace]." Justice means freedom from the arbitrary action of governments and from economic injustice as well. Peace means social order, which is a principal ingredient of security. Some Table of Free Voices respondents drew on their experiences to talk about a relationship between liberty and security.

Udi Aloni:

We should understand that our security is our freedom, and again the way we build it is all the time—sometimes we really have doubt, is really freedom is an option for us to sacrifice for our security, or the whole system built by that will take our freedom—will be taken from us anytime what we call security appear. So, as I repeat, in

101

many question here I see that the question themselves that come in good faith, already have inside the terminology of the Western discourse. So, we have to rethink of the question ourselves. So here I repeat, how much freedom we should need more to enhance in order to increase our security.

Thai Buddhist philosopher Sulak Sivaraksa:

The so called security in fact is a trick by most government. And the more they mention security, the more they want to take our liberty away. I don't think security should be separate from liberty. Liberty and security should go together. If one feels secure, one would feel free; one would feel free to express oneself positively, constructively. And, of course, one could also criticize the government. On the whole, most government do not work for the benefit of their people, they work for the benefit of themselves and international corporations which link to them. I think every citizen has a right to challenge the government.

Several speakers in positions of power in first world countries argued that the threat to security today justifies, perhaps requires, security measures that inevitably cut back on personal and political liberty.

Roland Berger spoke of "a balanced mix of freedom and order." Pico Iyer said, "The sad truth is, in our current world, we are probably going to have to give up a fair amount of our liberty in exchange for supposed security." Former Mitsubishi Electric Managing Director Takashi Kiuchi was even more emphatic: "A lot. A lot. The security is number one priority for living. If you are not safe, you cannot carry on the decent living. As simple as that. We have to offer our liberties in order to secure a good level of security." Israeli political leader Avi Primor argued that giving up liberty—and many other "comforts"—in the name of security is not only desirable but inevitable.

Those involved in social struggles in their own countries and in the international arena expressed several common themes. They accepted the questioner's premise that the security supposedly obtained by governmental intrusions into basic liberties is illusory. They expressed concern that the repressive actions of some governments, particularly the United States, would set an example to encourage tyrannical behavior elsewhere, thus undermining one claimed objective of American domestic and foreign policy.

I spent a great part of one evening talking with Sihem Bensedrine, editor of a French-Arabic online newspaper, *Kalima*, that the Tunisian government has repeatedly tried to suppress. Ms. Bensedrine has received human rights awards from Amnesty International and the European Parliament. In our talk, she described the Tunisian police and military efforts to close her publication and imprison her and her colleagues. Later, I was interested to read her answer to the question:

> What we are going through today in the occidental countries is a real regression of the civil rights and this regression is not only harmful to the occidental countries themselves, to the citizens of the occidental countries themselves. But it is also harmful to us as far as this philosophy of universal values . . . some human rights are today already disqualified in the name of this conflict of civilizations, that one tries to sell us in the name of security. It is a real cheating that those who govern the world today are leading us through, especially the American administration but also the European countries who force the citizens of the world to abandon their liberty in the name of security. The best means to continue to weaken this society is to un-secure the citizens concerning their liberty by confiscating their liberty, by removing the guaranties of human rights of which they are actually profiting. In my opinion, it is very, very important not to walk into a trap and to say that it is evident that security cannot exist without respecting the civil rights, without respecting the guarantees of the law and the guarantees of the universal values of the civil rights.

Russian participants, who are in the midst of struggles with repression in their country, sounded similar notes. The clown Antoschka said:

> To sacrifice liberty for the general safety is a legitimate, but an absurd question, because our safety does not depend on how many arms or the bombs we are going to produce, because thus we are creating the big gunpowder drum, and we collect those means which would destroy our planet, our civilization. And if it happens there would be no liberty and nothing at all what they could share.

Valentina Melnikova began by paraphrasing Benjamin Franklin's aphorism, "They that can give up essential liberty to obtain a little temporary safety deserve neither liberty nor safety," which Franklin first uttered in 1775. Melnikova went on:

> This phrase is known all over the world. We cannot immolate our freedom, we can demand from authorities to guarantee such safety that doesn't restrict our liberties nor violate our human dignity. It's

103

easy to shift the responsibility for our own safety on the state. But this is a very bad, very harmful tendency because the state that is taking away a part of our liberty loses its accountability to us.

Melnikova's last sentence echoes a concern that has animated my own career in the law. As lawyers, we seek to challenge our adversaries in free and open encounters. We have learned that behind the veil of secrecy there can too easily be deceit and trickery. When government curtails open inquiry, and retreats into repression and secrecy, it becomes by definition unaccountable, as Melnikova points out. This lack of accountability is not simply an abstract violation of rules about open government. Unaccountable leaders have this distressing tendency to rely on false information and hidden agendas, to make bad decisions, and to stifle and suppress the social and political mechanisms that lead to good decision-making.

Historian Anthony Arnove:

I think we have to reject this equation and have to understand that the policies that are being carried out in the name of security, in fact are making the world more insecure, not more secure. For example, the US invasion of Iraq [we were] told just to make the world safer, to counter the threat, the dangers of terrorism, the dangers of weapons of mass destruction. In fact, it just made the world more dangerous, more insecure, has increased instability and violence, has driven a global arms race, as countries around the world conclude that Iraq was invaded not because that it had weapons of mass destruction, but because it did not. And so, therefore, if they want a deterrent to US power, if they want a deterrent to the world's sole superpower, which has a stated doctrine of carrying out regime change in countries that aren't in its interest, which believes in the doctrine of so-called preemptive strikes, which uses terrorism as an instrument of policy, and is threatening regime change in other countries, that if they want a deterrent to that sole superpower, they had better develop a military deterrent, a nuclear deterrent if possible.

American lawyer Jonathan Granoff:

The greatest strength of the Western model of stability and security has been the capacity to limit the power of the State over the individual. And the paradigm of that has been that the individual has privacy, the individual is opaque, and the State is transparent and accountable. When that paradigm shifts, and the individual becomes transparent and the State becomes opaque, security will soon be lost. Because when there's that kind of power in the hands of the State, it will attract the kind of people, very rapidly, who want that kind of power. So the juxtaposition of security versus liberty I believe is a false juxtaposition. Our security will be obtained by wise policies that address the underlying causes of insecurity. So I think security is in limiting the power of the State over the individual, in the long term. And security will be obtained by addressing the underlying causes of violence.

The common theme of all these interjections is that an open society is best equipped to provide security for its people. Suppression of dissent, targeting suspected dissidents, and arbitrary police power create only the illusion of security. Those actions inevitably foster resentment and hostility and drive out of sight and hearing the challenging ideas that must be confronted and discussed in a complex world. One major aim of the United Nations was to provide collective security by ensuring that large-scale use of force would only be permissible with the consensus of nation-states. By listening to these voices, we can see how important that goal is. Warfare undertaken without that consensus sows resentment and injustice, with the consequences we have all observed.

Notes

1. *See, e.g.*, United States v. Railway Employees' Dep't of Am. Fed. Labor, 283 Fed. 79 (1922) (a holding that required the Norris-LaGuardia Act to undo); Lake Erie & W. Ry. v. Bailey, 61 Fed 494, 495–97 (C.C. Ind. 1893) (a judicial harangue on whether labor unions should exist); United States v. Gregg, 5 F. Supp. 848 (S.D. Tex. 1934) (unions as terrorists); see also the prosecutor's references to terrorism *quoted in* Bridges v. California, 314 U.S. 252, 275 n.19 (1941) ("union terrorism"). The criminal syndicalism statutes that were finally invalidated by Brandenburg v. Ohio, 395 U.S. 444 (1969), also contained references to terrorism. Among other perpetrators of terror recognized in Supreme Court opinions are: monopolies and trusts, United States v. South-Eastern Underwriters Ass'n, 322 U.S. 533, 553 (1944); the Ku Klux Klan, Virginia v. Black, 538 U.S. 343, 123 S. Ct. 1536 (2003); federal tax collectors, Warden v. Hayden, 387 U.S. 294 (1967); police who conduct unlawful searches, Brinegar v. United States, 338 U.S. 160 (1949) (Jackson, J., dissenting); mob action to influence a jury, Frank v. Mangum, 237 U.S. 309, 347 (1915); courts of justice who should be a "terror to evil doers," United States v. Castillero, 67 U.S. 17 (1862); patent holders, Hogg v. Emerson, 47 U.S. 437 (1848); and attacks by Native Americans, Sim's Lessee v. Irvine, 3 U.S. 425 (1799).
2. Much of the material on the French Revolution is drawn from Michael E. Tigar, Law and the Rise of Capitalism ch. 18 (new ed. 2000), hereinafter

cited as LRC2. All quoted material in this section, except where otherwise noted, originally appeared in Law and the Rise of Capitalism ch. 18. Translations are by Michael E. Tigar.

3. Mark Twain, A Connecticut Yankee in King Arthur's Court, at http://mark-twain.classic-literature.co.uk/a-connecticut-yankee-in-king-arthurs-court/ebook-page-37.asp.
4. Black's Law Dictionary (8th ed. 2004), available at http://www.westlaw.com.
5. *Quoted in* Tigar, *Whose Rights? What Danger?*, 94 Yale L.J. 970, 972 (1985).
6. The entire argument is at 1998 WL 1095. The Nichols and McVeigh trials are available at http://www.westlaw.com in the OKLA-TRANS database.
7. Morissette v. United States, 342 U.S. 246 (1952), *discussed in* Tigar, *"Willfullness" and "Ignorance" in Federal Criminal Law*, 37 Clev. St. L. Rev. 525 (1990), from which much of this discussion is drawn. All sources are cited in that article, which is available at http://www.westlaw.com.
8. The French text may be found at, e.g., http://pages.globetrotter.net/pcbcr/dr1789.html. This translation is by Michael E. Tigar. English language text is at, e.g., http://www.hightowertrail.com/Declaration.htm.
9. *See* Michael E. Tigar, *Automatic Extinction of Cross-Demands: Compensatio from Rome to California*, 53 Cal. L. Rev. 224 (1965); LRC2, ch. 2.
10. LRC2, at 295–305.
11. *Id.*
12. This is a quotation from the eminent scholar Martha Nussbaum. *See* Martha C. Nussbaum, *Skepticism about Practical Reason in Literature and the Law*, 107 Harv. L. Rev. 714 (1994). I discussed this concept in Michael E. Tigar, *Defending*, 74 Tex. L. Rev. 101 (1995). The notion here is a kind of Aristotelian rejoinder to the "no ought from an is" criticism of proposals to expand human rights.
13. From Bodin's six-volume work, De la République, *discussed and quoted in* LRC, at 301–02.
14. This discussion is drawn from LRC2, at 303–05. See also the works by Professor Janis, at 337.
15. Bentham at 371; LRC2, at 303–05.
16. See Chief Justice Marshall's musings, *quoted in* LRC2, at 306–08.
17. The cases are the Lotus case, S.S. "Lotus" (Fr. v. Turk.), 1927 PCIJ (ser. A) No. 10, at 18–19 (Sept. 7), *available at* http://www.icj-cij.org; the Barcelona Traction case, *discussed in* Buergenthal & Murphy, Public International Law 130, 161, 208 (3d ed. 2002), and Republic of Congo v. Belgium, discussed in detail below but also available on the ICJ Web site.
18. United States v. Rauscher, 119 U.S. 407 (1886).
19. *The Amistad*, 40 U.S. 518 (1841).
20. The *Paquete Habana*, 175 U.S. 677 (1900).
21. 542 U.S. 692 (2004).
22. Letelier v. Republic of Chile, 502 F. Supp. 259, 263 (D.D.C. 1980).
23. The Schooner Exchange v. M'Faddon, 11 U.S. 116 (1812).
24. The following recital is based on complaints drafted by students in the impact litigation clinic at Washington College of Law, taught by me and adjunct professor Ali Beydoun. The complaint is based on declassified documents obtained in the wake of the Hinchey report. Much valuable work

in collecting, indexing, and publicizing documentary materials was done by Peter Kornbluh of the National Security Archive at George Washington University in the District of Columbia. *See also* CHRISTOPHER HITCHENS, THE TRIAL OF HENRY KISSINGER (2000); PETER KORNBLUH, THE PINOCHET FILES (2003). There is also a film, *The Trial of Henry Kissinger,* available on DVD.

25. For an overview of the events, see John Dinges and Saul Landau's excellent book, ASSASSINATION ON EMBASSY ROW (1981).

26. Henry A. Kissinger, *The Pitfalls of Universal Jurisdiction,* FOREIGN AFFAIRS, July/August 2001, at 86.

27. *See, e.g.,* Schneider v. Kissinger, 412 F.3d 190 (D.C. Cir. 2005), *cert. denied,* 126 S. Ct. 1768 (2006). Pleadings in the case are available on Westlaw by going to the cited document.

28. Baker v. Carr, 369 U.S. 186 (1962).

29. Hamdi v. Rumsfeld, 542 U.S. 507 (2004).

30. LRC2, at 305–12.

31. This section is based on, and draws from, Michael E. Tigar, Susan C. Casey, Isabelle Giordani, Sivakumaren Mardemootoo, Paul Touvier, and *The Crime Against Humanity,* 30 TEX. INT'L L. J. 286 (1995). The material has been updated with discussion of the Papon case and its aftermath.

32. The historical material in this section is drawn from PHILIPPE BOUDREL, HISTOIRE DES JUIFS DE FRANCE (1974).

33. 8 U.N.T.S. 279; 59 Stat. 1544, 8AS No. 472, *reprinted in* 39 AM. J. INT'L L. 257 (1945) (Supp.).

34. Charter of the International Military Tribunal, art. 6, 59 Stat. 1544, 1547–48.

35. The argument that the Charter defines crimes and persons subject to its jurisdiction as separate matters was made at the Touvier trial by Arno Klarsfeld, attorney for civil parties Association of Sons and Daughters of Jewish Deportees and certain of the family members of the victims. *See* ARNO KLARSFELD, TOUVIER: UN CRIME FRANÇAIS 94–101 (1994).

36. Security Council Resolutions Establishing An International Tribunal For The Prosecution Of Persons Responsible For Serious Violations Of International Humanitarian Law Committed In The Territory Of The Former Yugoslavia, 32 I.L.M. 1159 (1993)

37. The Tribunal's Judgment is reproduced at 6 F.R.D. 69, 119, 129 (1945). *See generally* E. DAVIDSON, THE TRIAL OF THE GERMANS (1972).

38. The distinction between customary international law principles, not generally binding on a state without its consent, and peremptory norms (*jus cogens*) is *discussed in, e.g.,* Mark W. Janis, *An Introduction to International Law* 62–66 (1993) [hereinafter Janis]; Gordon A. Christenson, *The World Court and Jus Cogens,* 81 AM. J. INT'L L. 93 (1987); Ted L. Stein, *The Approach of the Different Drummer: The Principle of the Persistent Objector in International Law,* 26 HARV. INT'L L.J. 457 (1985).

39. One should interpolate the requirement of intent in order to save the prohibition from an attack on grounds of vagueness, and to ensure that one does not punish persons who were not aware of these nonstatutory norms. This principle is discussed, in the context of domestic law, in M. Tigar, *"Willfullness" and "Ignorance" in Federal Criminal Law,* 37 CLEV. ST. L. REV. 525 (1990).

40. G.I. TUNKIN, THEORY OF INTERNATIONAL LAW (Butler trans., 1974). At another point, he speaks of "the criminal responsibility of physical persons" for such crimes. *Id.* at 412.

41. *See also* 1 M. CHERIF BASSIOUNI, INTERNATIONAL CRIMINAL LAW 23 (1986).

42. *See* Article IV, Convention on the Prevention and Punishment of the Crime of Genocide, *at* http://www.preventgenocide.org/law/convention/text.htm.

43. *See* United States v. Guest, 383 U.S. 745 (1966); United States v. Price, 383 U.S. 787 (1966), *construing* 18 U.S.C. §§ 241, 242.

44. *See, e.g.,* Moose Lodge No. 107 v. Irvis, 407 U.S. 163 (1972).

45. *See* M. CHERIF BASSIOUNI, CRIMES AGAINST HUMANITY IN INTERNATIONAL CRIMINAL LAW ch. 6 (1992), *reviewed in* 88 AM. J. INT'L L. 204 (1994). Compare the views of LYAL S. SUNGA, INDIVIDUAL RESPONSIBILITY IN INTERNATIONAL LAW FOR SERIOUS HUMAN RIGHTS VIOLATIONS (1992), *reviewed in* 88 AM. J. INT'L L. 205 (1994).

46. Loi No. 64-1326 du 26 décembre 1964.

47. "Punishments pronounced for a crime become barred twenty years from the date on which the judgment of conviction becomes definitive." Penal Code, art. 133–2.

48. The history is chronicled in a superb article: Guyora Binder, *Representing Nazism: Advocacy and Identity at the Trial of Klaus Barbie*, 98 YALE L.J. 1321 (1989).

49. Judgment of Dec. 20, 1985, 1985 Bull. Crim. at 1053.

50. Arno Klarsfeld is the son of Beate and Serge Klarsfeld, who had done so much to secure passage of legislation against crimes against humanity and to bring alleged offenders to trial.

51. I am aware that this language is not really from either Hemingway or John Donne. However, my students and I, in doing the translation from the French, left it in a literal translation because Klarsfeld is doing a play on words— using in succession the different French words for carillon bell, doorbell, and death knell.

52. Much of this story is taken from Arno Klarsfeld's summation in the Touvier case, which has been published as TOUVIER: UN CRIME FRANÇAIS.

53. I use the word "mien" in the context of this trial as a kind of homage to Alexander Pope who wrote:

> Vice is a monster of so frightful mien,
> As to be hated needs but to be seen;
> Yet seen too oft, familiar with her face,
> We first endure, then pity, then embrace.

54. Military detachment of the Milice, police of the Vichy regime.

55. A local newspaper still existing in the northeast part of France.

56. Principal newspaper under the Vichy regime.

57. *See generally* THE PAPON AFFAIR (Richard J. Golsan ed., 2000), a collection of articles, essays, and interviews about the case. In analyzing the legal issues presented by the case, I have preferred to use the full text of the Cour de Cassation opinion, and have made my own translation. I have drawn on some of the information in the book.

58. THE PAPON AFFAIR at 260.

59. The formal charge was based on documents and witness statements, many of which were produced before the juge d'instruction. Thus, the defense and the reviewing court had a detailed factual context within which to discuss the legal issues.

60. The French garrison at Dienbienphu, Vietnam, engaged in battle with Vietminh forces under General Giap from March 19, 1954, to May 7, 1954. The Vietminh forces overran the French. Surviving French soldiers were taken prisoner and marched some 600 kilometers to prison camps to the North. Bernard B. Fall's book, HELL IN A VERY SMALL PLACE: THE SIEGE OF DIENBIENPHU (1966), is the classic history of the battle. The Dienbienphu defeat effectively ended the French occupation of Indochina—Vietnam, Laos, and Cambodia. The defeat there was followed in the 1950s by the French effort to hold on to Algeria, which came to an end in 1962 with the treaty recognizing Algerian independence; these events are discussed later in this book. To this day, the far right elements of French politics regard Dienbienphu and the Algerian defeat as incidents of dishonor for the French nation.

61. Moore, *Well Excuse Me!—Remorse, Apology, and Criminal Sentencing*, 38 ARIZ. ST. L.J. 371 (2006).

62. *Exile, Amnesty, and International Law*, 81 NOTRE DAME L. REV. 955 (2006). *See also* Blumenson, *The Challenge of a Global Standard of Justice*, 44 COLUM. J. TRANSNAT'L L. 801 (2006).

63. Lyrics to *Forgiving You Was Easy*, at http://www.cowboylyrics.com/lyrics/nelson-willie/forgiving-you-was-easy-2525.html.

64. Moses v. Kennedy, 219 F. Supp. 762 (D.D.C. 1963) (mandamus not available to compel prosecutors to arrest and try civil rights violators, despite mandatory language of post-Civil War statute). *See also* United States v. Armstrong, 517 U.S. 456 (1996). *See* ANGELA JORDAN DAVIS, ARBITRARY JUSTICE: THE POWER OF THE AMERICAN PROSECUTOR (2007). Lawyers for the Letelier and Moffitt families repeatedly urged the United States Department of Justice to prosecute Augusto Pinochet for the murders and cited powerful evidence of his complicity. These appeals came to nothing.

65. *See also* JEAN-CLAUDE PAYE, GLOBAL WAR ON LIBERTY (2007) (a translation from the French). *See also* Tigar, *The Twilight of Personal Liberty*, *Introduction to* Paye, *A Permanent State of Emergency*, MONTHLY REVIEW, Nov. 2006.

66. The quote is from a speech against the death penalty given at the National Assembly on June 22, 1791, and available in translated form at http://www.marxists.org/history/france/revolution/robespierre/1791/death-penalty.htm. I first encountered the quotation in 1957, when I read Arthur Koestler's book, REFLECTIONS ON HANGING (1957).

67. *See* Richard Wilson's chapter on international tribunal defense in BOHLANDER & WILSON, DEFENSE IN INTERNATIONAL CRIMINAL PROCEEDINGS (2006).

68. In addition to the Bohlander-Wilson book, *see* CALVO-GOLLER, THE TRIAL PROCEEDINGS FOR THE INTERNATIONAL CRIMINAL COURT: ICTY AND ICTR PRECEDENTS (2006). The first ICTY prosecutor, Richard Goldstone, has written a compelling history of his service, FOR HUMANITY: REFLECTIONS OF A WAR CRIMES INVESTIGATOR (2000). The court Web site is www.un.org/icty/ (click on "basic legal documents" for the statutory and regulatory basis of the tribunal's work).

69. The 2004 movie *Hotel Rwanda* dramatically depicts some of the conflict and is worth renting or buying on DVD for the quality of its production and the performances of its leading actors.

70. *See, e.g.*, DIANE JOHNSTONE, FOOLS CRUSADE: YUGOSLAVIA, NATO AND WESTERN DELUSIONS (2002). Shorter pieces taking a critical view appeared in MONTHLY REVIEW for Feb. 2003 (by Edward S. Herman) and in June 1999 (Tariq Ali).

71. As noted in the text, Ehud Olmert angrily confronted Western journalists about civilian casualties in Lebanon, citing the NATO actions, saying, "Don't speak to me of civilian casualties."

72. *See* ANGELA JORDAN DAVIS, ARBITRARY JUSTICE: THE POWER OF THE AMERICAN PROSECUTOR (2007). *See also* Tigar, *Essay, Lawyers, Jails and the Law's Fake Bargains*, MONTHLY REVIEW, July/Aug. 2001; Ellen Yaroshefsky, *Cooperation with Federal Prosecutors: Experiences of Truth Telling and Embellishment*, 68 FORDHAM L. REV. 917 (1999); Angela Davis, *Prosecution and Race: The Power and Privilege of Discretion*, 67 FORDHAM L. REV. 13 (1998); McCleskey v. Kemp, 481 U.S. 279 (1987) (nonreviewability of prosecutorial discretion in capital cases, despite evidence or racial bias).

73. *See* RICHARD J. GOLDSTONE, FOR HUMANITY: REFLECTIONS OF A WAR CRIMES INVESTIGATOR (2000), *reviewed*, Schabas, *Review*, 95 AM. J. INT'L L. 742 (2001).

74. *See* Stephen Rademaker, Op-ed, *Unwitting Party to Genocide*, WASH. POST, Jan. 11, 2007, at A25.

75. United States v. Antonelli Fireworks, 155 F.2d 631, 662 (2d Cir. 1946) (Jerome Frank, dissenting).

76. MICHAEL BOHLANDER, ROMAN BOED, & RICHARD WILSON, DEFENSE IN INTERNATIONAL CRIMINAL PROCEEDINGS 66 (2006) (footnotes omitted).

77. 242 U.S. 745, 787 (1966).

PART TWO

Group and Individual Terrorism— Non-State Actors

A. Defining Individual and Group Terrorism

When we turn from state-sponsored action to conduct of individuals or groups who do not possess state power, defining terror becomes even more problematic. A federal statute defines terrorism as "premeditated, politically motivated violence perpetrated against noncombatant targets by subnational groups or clandestine agents," and terrorists as those who engage in such activity. The federal statute that requires State Department annual human rights reports defines terrorists in the same terms.[1] These definitions are too broad to be useful. All politically motivated violence cannot usefully be labeled as terrorist, because there is a great deal of such violence in the world that most people would say is permissible. In a conflict against a repressive regime that cannot be changed by peaceful means, some governmental figures may be targeted as part of a civil war. Labeling all such conduct terrorist keeps us from thinking about the role that armed struggle has usefully and justifiably played in social change. An antiabortion crusader may kill a physician who performs abortions, and should be punished under the homicide statutes. It does nothing to help our debate about homicide or abortion to label that individual as a terrorist. I remind the reader of the many, inconsistent, and unhelpful uses of the word terrorist as an epithet in the first essay in this volume. A later essay illustrates my concern that the overbroad official standard has contributed to distressingly inconsistent and unfair results.

Those opposed to the actions of politically motivated groups or individuals will naturally use the term terrorist freely. On the other hand, as many have noted, the alleged terrorists also disdain the term, preferring to call themselves freedom fighters, guerillas, rebels, or mujaheddin. This last term is derived from the term jihad, which simply means struggle, not necessarily violent or armed fighting. As an epithet, the term short-circuits discussion of when the use of violence is defensible under generally accepted norms of domestic or international law, and when a state actor may permissibly take action against those regarded as terrorists.

Despite the difficulties, it is important to devise and apply a sensible definition that is historically sound and will be evenhandedly applied. The reader may recall my proposed definition of state-sponsored terrorism: systematic state-sponsored violence, conducted against political enemies, and in disregard of historically determined fair substantive and procedural standards. Individual and group terrorism is by definition not state-sponsored. Non-state actors may not have organized procedural and substantive rules by which they conduct their activity. Therefore, those parts of the definition are not useful.

However, terrorism involves violence against political enemies. If we accept that some violence may be justifiable against a repressive regime, there must be some limit. I suggest that the limit is historically determined in the same way that the limit on state action is so defined. For example, consider the issue of genocide. Today, the international community is united in condemning violence committed against an ethnic, national, religious, or indigenous group on account of their group membership. Several hundred years ago, intercultural violence was not so universally condemned. Similarly, a norm requiring humane treatment of political enemies during social conflict has achieved more general acceptance.

In thinking about a definition, we can look to the principles developed in ordinary criminal law. All intentional homicides are presumptively criminal. However, a homicide committed in self-defense is justified. With a justification, the situation can be judged from the point of view of the killer, whose reasonable perception of the need to use deadly force is controlling. Jurisdictions define the scope of permissible deadly force differently, and some have even abolished the historical obligation to retreat if possible from an attack before being justified in killing a perceived assailant. Standards for justifiable homicide have changed over time. In Exodus, we read that "If a thief be found breaking up, and be smitten that he die, there shall no blood be shed for him." In other words, lethal force was justified against certain kinds of thieves even if they were not invading habitation or endangering life. Justification may also prevent the conviction of someone who uses nonlethal violence because it is necessary to do so in order to avert a greater harm. People who demonstrate against illegal governmental policies may claim that they were justified in breaking the trespass laws in an effort to prevent the illegality.

On the subject of justification, American criminal law has two important characteristics. First, as suggested above, legal principles have changed over time. Second, the requirement that one judge the situation from the killer's reasonable point of view has been both controversial and elastic.

The most dramatic example of change in legal principles has been in the area of spousal abuse. Some women whose partners systematically brutalized them reacted by killing their tormentors. Because the killer is not physically able to resist abuse at the time it occurs, the killing may take place when the tormentor is sleeping or unaware of impending events. Many courts have relaxed the standards of immediacy to allow the self-defense justification to be presented to the jury. In turn, the jury will usually be told that the defendant must establish the defense by a preponderance of the evidence—it must be more likely than not that the circumstances required the use of deadly force.

Courts and legislatures have also reconsidered the reasonable point of view requirement. What and who are reasonable? When a man named Bernard Goetz shot and killed young men in a New York subway because he thought they were about to rob him, the New York Court of Appeals held that Goetz could not base his defense on his own personalized fear of people of color who behave a certain way in the subway. However, a woman who faces a battering spouse may be entitled to have the jury told that it can consider the disparity of size and physical ability between her and her tormentor. How far should courts and legislatures go in individualizing the reasonable person requirement? Most courts will not permit jurors to take the killer's racial attitudes towards potential aggressors into account. Many courts will allow fact witnesses and mental health experts to testify about the reasonable perceptions of young people and vulnerable adults. These decisions are the product of applying socially and historically determined interpretations to venerable rules.

The process of reshaping legal rules in light of new understandings is, or can and should be, rational. Deciders can and should state the reasons for change, and express their conclusions with clarity. These are characteristics of legal decision-making that is perceived as legitimate because based on defensible propositions. The process of choosing rules is not, I insist, inherently unverifiable. Some years ago, I wrote:

> When I speak of a prosaic and down-to-earth idea of justice, I mean simply that one can deduce principles of right from human needs in the present time. That is, I reject the cynical, or Stoic, or no-ought-from-an-is idea that one set of rules is just as good as another. I reject the notion, as Professor Martha Nussbaum has characterized it, "that to every argument some argument to a contradictory conclusion can be opposed; that arguments are in any case merely tools of influence, without any better sort of claim to our allegiance." Rather, again borrowing from Professor Nussbaum, my notions of justice "include a commitment, open-ended and revisable because grounded upon dialectical arguments that have their roots in experience, to a definite view of human flourishing and good human functioning." One element of such views is that "human beings have needs for things in the world: for political rights, for money and food and shelter, for respect and self-respect," and so on.[2]

Our definition must be free from hypocritical moral relativism; it must take account of the roots of terrorist conduct, and it must distinguish between terrorism and other forms of political violence. We are seeking a thoughtful definition, that reflects "thinking about terrorism."

I suggest that non-state sponsored terrorism is violence, committed in violation of historically determined norms, that is unjustifiable both in terms of its target and its extent, and done to achieve a political objective. With this definition, I mean to exclude armed struggle directed against a repressive regime, provided that the struggle is directed at appropriate targets and does not involve disproportionate use of force. The definition includes revolutionary or guerrilla activity that is designed to coerce the regime through infliction of civilian casualties, or to conscript fighters by force or putting in fear. The definition invokes historically determined standards to interdict the use of the terrorist label against movements seeking liberation from unlawful regimes. I explore this issue in more detail in a later essay.

Let us take this tentative definition and examine the ways in which it might be put to work.

B. The Colonial Roots of Terrorism and the Fallacy of Nation-Building

On August 20, 2006, the *Washington Post* carried a long article by Daniel Byman and Kenneth Pollack about Iraq's descent into civil war.[3] The authors reminded us that civil wars based on ethnic conflict had also occurred in Rwanda, the Balkans, Afghanistan, Lebanon, and elsewhere. These civil wars are characterized by actions that meet any reasonable definition of terrorism. In each of these conflicts, thousands died for political agendas and, in some, the numbers reached into the tens or hundreds of thousands. Ethnic conflict is demonstrably one of the most powerful forces contributing to terrorism.

If Byman and Pollack had more time, they might have looked back another fifty years and seen just how right they were. Basil Davidson, in his wise and trenchant book *The Black Man's Burden: Africa and the Curse of the Nation-State*, chronicled the descent into ethnic violence of sub-Saharan African countries that were one by one "liberated" from their colonial status. *Black Man's Burden* was written in 1992, when Davidson was 76. He served during World War II with resistance forces in Italy and Yugoslavia, and in the latter country developed a keen sense of what ethnic tensions can bring about. His study of Africa began in 1950 and he carefully followed the independence movements, particularly of the former British colonies.

The root questions raised by both Byman and Pollack's article and Davidson's book may be stated: What is state power? What are the principal forces that undermine the establishment and maintenance of state power along proper lines? As Davidson puts the problem, the task is "to devise and uphold a state such as citizens will accept and respect as the valid and therefore worthwhile representative of their interests and protector of their rights."[4]

When "things fall apart," and the "center [of power] cannot hold,"[5] the form that we call the nation-state ceases to fulfill its expected function. In the Western tradition, we have come to accept as normal and almost inevitable the movement towards aligning the borders of nations with the borders of sovereign states. The countries of Western Europe and the United States moved into their present borders through a historical process that is relatively familiar to us, at least in its broad outlines. In each of these countries, there remain ethnic enclaves that have maintained their own identities and, in some cases, resisted central government efforts to homogenize their cultures and overcome their different ways of being and doing. Among the Scots and Welsh are movements seeking varying

115

degrees of autonomy. In France, Brittany and Corsica harbor separatist movements. In Italy, which achieved a united government only in the nineteenth century, regional differences of culture, language, and politics are marked.

However, these differences do not in general undermine the effectiveness and perceived legitimacy of national governments. Struggle over control of state power is the struggle to direct the entire machinery of the state in the service of national policies. Because this Western world is the one closest to our own experiences and to those of our parents and grandparents, it is perhaps more difficult to see and appreciate that in much of the world our image of the nation-state simply does not reflect what is going on.

Yet, we need not look very far to see how fragile the nation-state idea can be. When the Soviet Union crumbled, it began to break apart into separate countries in which particular ethnic and cultural nationalities predominated. Fifteen years later, the process was still going on. From 1943 onwards, Josip Broz, known at Tito, was the leader of Yugoslavia, a country composed of ethnic Croatians, Serbians, Bosnians, and Montenegrins, each professing a more or less different religious faith. During World War II, each region had also been riven by controversy over support or opposition to Nazism. When Tito died in 1980, the country quickly became "the former Yugoslavia" as national groups organized around long-standing cultural and ethnic traditions demanded creation of their own separate nation-states. Within each of these entities, the violence against nonmembers of the dominant groups has been amply documented, and is one of the main reasons why the United Nations General Assembly established the International Criminal Tribunal for Yugoslavia to investigate and prosecute ethnic-based crimes against humanity.

In the former colonies of Africa, independence did not usually bring into being effective and efficient nation-states that would meet Basil Davidson's ably expressed criterion. The reasons for failure are not difficult to identify. In some instances, such as the former Belgian Congo, the economic entities that had grown up under the protection of colonial power actively opposed progressive nationalist African political leaders, and fomented secessionist and separatist sentiment. Such sentiment lurked at or just below the surface of almost every former African colony. The lines that the colonial powers drew during the nineteenth century had nothing to do with established ethnic or tribal boundaries. In governing, the colonial powers had often exploited intertribal tension by putting one group over another. Davidson chronicles conflict in the Democratic Republic of the Congo, formerly Zaire, typical of experiences throughout sub-Saharan Africa:

> When in due course the pirates who had seized power in the vast country of Zaire, in central Africa, became due for expulsion and in 1991, meanwhile, there was some let-up in dictatorial terror, it was found that the new "multiparty" state proclaimed in 1990 had fostered overnight no fewer than 230 "political parties," not a single one of which had any of the organizational and mobilizing capacity that a political party is supposed to have. This was a reversion to kinship corporations under the thinnest guise, and was going to solve precisely nothing. . . . Kinship corporations cannot produce a democratic state, whether or not they are disguised as political parties. They are bound to be enemies of the state if only because it is the state that has allowed them into the political arena through its failures in effectiveness. Being the enemies of the state, kinship corporations hasten its downfall. They point, more often than not, to a collapse of civil society and the response of *sauve qui peut*. They open the gate to fearful abuse of the common interest. They have led in Africa to terrible destructions. If the worst of these were still reserved for the 1980s, a decade that may truly be called "the decade of the AK-47," they nonetheless reached a sorry level in the 1970s.[6]

Davidson's thesis is that the colonial powers imposed their rule on African colonies in ways that doomed the prospects of democratic government in the postcolonial period. Then, when matters deteriorated in the postcolonial era, their interventions and ideas contributed nothing, or less than nothing, to solving problems. The fallacy of nation-building is that the wrong people were doing it with the wrong ideas and by wrong means.

Fast forward to Iraq, where armed conflict persists as I write this in 2007. During a press conference on August 21, 2006, George W. Bush claimed that there was progress in Iraq towards a "unified country" in which people would not be killed and maimed at the rate of more than one thousand each month in sectarian terrorist violence. He noted that "twelve million Iraqis voted" and said that this is "an indication about the desire for people to live in a free society." Fred Kaplan posted a column about the press conference on slate.com noting, "Those 12 million Iraqis had sharply divided views of what a free society meant. Shiites voted for a unified country led by Shiites, Sunnis voted for a unified country led by Sunnis, and Kurds voted for their own separate country. . . . The secular parties did very poorly."[7]

More data: The distinguished professor of history Juan Cole reported on a poll of intelligence experts in one of his 2006 internet postings. Eighty-four percent of the respondents said that the United States is not winning the war on terror and that the conflict in Iraq is the reason. Professor Cole, relying in part on Michael Scheuer's views,[8] notes that the Iraq conflict has given terrorist groups great recruiting prospects, the opportunity to fight and inflict casualties on the most sophisticated army in the world, and to establish a beachhead at the center of the world's richest petroleum reserves.

To examine this matter, we can return once again to the basics of criminal law. Terrorism, as defined above, merits a criminal sanction. The criminal law may be defined as a mechanism for imposing punishment and public condemnation on those who violate significant norms. Other mechanisms, such as civil suits and negotiation, do not lead to imposition of punishment. The decisions about which norms should be the subject of criminal sanctions, and how prosecutorial discretion should be exercised, are the subjects of earnest debate.

However, most would agree that if a system for dealing with criminal conduct does not measurably deter that conduct and, in fact, contributes to increasing it, then that system has serious flaws. Wholesale military violence in Iraq is a failure, if one considers that its objective was to deter and punish terrorist acts. If it were argued that the warfare was designed not so much to punish terrorists as to establish and support a social structure where terrorist acts would be less frequent or dealt with by civil authority, the enterprise has failed in that objective as well.

Capturing, trying, and punishing those who commit terrorist acts is a worthwhile enterprise, but only if the definition of terrorism can withstand scrutiny, the evidence adduced against accused persons is persuasive and properly obtained, and the mechanism for judging merits is termed fair. Otherwise, the sovereign apparatus of trial and punishment may itself earn the name terrorist. Moreover, when we think about criminal acts of terror, we should reflect on the limited number of tools that the criminal law can deploy—various forms of incarceration and supervised release. Some sovereigns continue to impose the death penalty. Judges can also apply traditional principles of justification and excuse to take account of reasons why people engage in harmful conduct.

I have already discussed justification defenses. Excuse defenses focus on aspects of the defendant's life and personality that make him or her less culpable. Some excuse defenses are based on the defendant's mental condition. For example, a great deal of terrorist activity has been prosecuted as genocide. Some defendants claim that by reason of their upbringing and the other influences on their behavior, they did not rationally choose to attack and kill people of a different ethnic, religious, or racial group. These defendants point to the centuries-long patterns of hatred and hostility into which they were born and in which they were raised. The criminal courts that have tried genocide cases have generally held that this sort of evidence does not provide an excuse for crime and cannot mandate an acquittal. However, the evidence may well, and in many cases does, mitigate punishment. Americans are familiar with this dichotomy. Many mental conditions will not provide an excuse for homicide but, in a capital case, must be considered by the jury as it deliberates on the life versus death decision.

Legislative bodies that make rules for criminal law can also shape rules to take account of social and historical factors. However, none of these approaches address the root causes of much terrorist behavior in any effective way.

Now we can see what we must do when we think about terror. First, we must define it in sensible way. Next, we must propose rules to punish violators. We must insist on a system that is worthy of the name "justice" within which cases will be prosecuted. We must be attentive to the proportionality between wrongdoing and punishment. Beyond all that, we must ask which forms of terrorist activity can effectively be addressed only by solving the social problems that encourage that activity.

I believe one can examine these tasks only in context. Hence, these essays follow:

C. Revolutionary Violence, Civil War, and Terrorism

We have seen that *terror* and *terrorist* are used as epithets against people who seek to gain their ends through violence, economic pressure, or even the organized use of nonviolent action. In the main, however, these words are applied to political movements that seek to destabilize or overthrow a government or to make a political point against a government or society. Crimes properly described as terrorist deserve to be prosecuted and punished not only by the states who are victims but also by the international community. Precisely because of their status as international crimes, it is important not to define terrorist offenses too broadly. Once again, we can reason through some of these issues by looking to the ordinary criminal law.

A captain of industry who calculates the risks and benefits of defrauding investors, the public, or the government deserves punishment because his or her conduct is calculated to do harm. A woman who has been battered by her spouse and finally kills him may be entitled to our understanding and to a lighter punishment than someone who commits a murder for financial gain. A young person whose criminal conduct is clearly the product of a violent and deprived childhood deserves our sympathetic understanding. Yet, each of these people has committed a serious social harm, and something clearly should be done about it.

The penal codes define offenses in terms of:

- acts (hit, take, enter, shoot, stab, set fire to);
- mental states (negligent, reckless, knowing, purposeful);
- circumstances (in the nighttime, in a dwelling, against a person); and
- results (death, bodily harm, property damage).

We expect that the criminal law will be applied sensibly and equitably. Some arguably punishable conduct may not be prosecuted for various reasons: the perpetrator is given another chance through formal or informal pretrial diversion, civil redress such as payment of damages is adequate, the perpetrator makes a bargain to testify against others, and so forth. We also know that much prosecutorial discretion is exercised more harshly against poor people and people of color. Much policing is racially biased.

We must also recognize that people are concerned about the effect of crime on themselves and on their communities. Murders and muggings may happen more frequently in some neighborhoods, but their frequency and severity affects the quality of life and the perception of personal safety of the whole community.

There are at least two ways to approach the problem of ordinary crime. One way is to devise penal laws and criminal procedures and see to their systematic and fair enforcement. The federal constitution contains many limits on how criminal conduct is to be investigated, prosecuted, and punished. Lawyers, judges, and legal scholars are deeply involved in studying how the system called "criminal justice" works.

However, almost everybody recognizes that it is futile to depend on this system to solve criminal behavior problems. The system's failures are manifest. The United States has a crime rate as high as or higher than any other advanced country. Yet, it also has an incarceration rate that is much higher than any such country, in many instances by a factor of three, four, or five. Prisons and jails are full.

Fact: 1.7 percent of white males are in prison or jail, 3.9 percent of Hispanic males, and 11.9 percent of African-American males. The United States incarcerates a far higher percentage of its people than any advanced industrial country. How are we to understand the human conditions that

these figures inadequately represent? How are we to do that while helping our students see how the rules of criminal law are used to produce
these results? Jerome Frank wisely said, in a remark paraphrased above:

> A legal system is not what it says, but what it does. Our "crimi-
> nal law," then, cannot be described accurately in terms merely of
> substantive prohibitions; the description must also include the
> methods by which those prohibitions operate in practice. . . .[9]

What does the system do? Despite the figures on incarceration, the
percentage of inmates charged with or convicted of white collar crimes
has declined. Yet, the social harm committed by these criminals is by any
measure enormous. Major public corporations have become a collection
of kleptocratic fiefdoms whose leaders enrich themselves at the share-
holder's cost, and conduct their operations at the expense of everybody
else. The corporate leaders calculate the risks and costs of their behavior
as well as its benefits. They, unlike the urban offender who will most
likely plead guilty, really do intend their harmful conduct and have a
free choice not to engage in it. The urban offender, who grows up with
progressively limited life choices, cannot be said to have acted voluntarily in the same way. That is an insight from psychology, political science,
and sociology, and an important one for me. The categories of mental
element are, in the world of what the law really does, fictions.

To make the point, suppose there was a place where crime was ram-
pant. For example, we could use a collection of outlaw corporations
where executives enrich themselves at the expense of stockholders and
the public. Perhaps our hypothetical arena of criminality would consist
of entities that make toxic products.

However, I prefer to use the example of an urban community where
poverty is the norm. I insist, however, that similar methods of analysis
are relevant regardless of where one chooses to focus. In this community example, crimes of violence and crimes against property are major
concerns. Signs of social disintegration are on corners of major streets:
drug dealing and prostitution. The housing stock is run-down. Unemployment rates are at multiples of the national average. In short, this is
an area like one we would find in many urban centers.

In this community, the ordinary methods of policing and prosecuting
yield predictable results, and the incarceration rate shows it. In addition,
the community is located in a state that has a death penalty, and mur-
derers are sentenced to death in cases permitted by that law. However,
hardly anybody believes that the system that calls itself criminal justice
can bring about a major long-term reduction in the crime rate with the

tools that the system has at its command. Some piecemeal reforms can have an impact: community policing that puts more officers walking the streets, community-based corrections systems, better lawyers in criminal courts, and serious attention to police misconduct. But these measures fall short because they do not reflect a study of the root causes of widespread criminal behavior.

Hardly anyone would suggest an unlimited increase to the amount of officially approved violence against community members until the crime rate declines appreciably. However, there will undoubtedly be proposals to approach the problem from that kind of perspective: overtly or tacitly allowing more police violence towards arrested persons; making jail conditions more onerous; increasing sentences; seeking and obtaining more death penalties—all of these are suggestions that people make under such circumstances. None of these ideas demonstrably results in long-term reduction of the crime rate. Studies that purport to show, for example, that the death penalty deters crime are fundamentally flawed. In short, simply declaring a war on crime will not bring victory. Violence must, in this sense, be distinguished from force and power. If one deployed dozens of uniformed police officers to simply walk their beats in a troubled city, that would be a show of force, and experience teaches that such an approach often curbs crime. Negotiation with community leaders, and even with those associated with gang activity, with the promise that force will follow if peace does not, is a use of power.

In the international sphere, use of force to produce a cease-fire in times of hostility is sometimes essential in order to forestall a humanitarian crisis. For example, in 2006, the Lebanese Shiite Muslim group Hezbollah took hostile action within the state of Israel. Israel responded with a hugely disproportionate use of military violence that displaced nearly one million people, killed hundreds of civilians, and destroyed much of the fragile Lebanese social, political, and economic infrastructure. The United States had the power and credibility to force a cease-fire pending negotiations on a longer-term solution, but it decided not to use that power. The point remains the same, regardless of context. Protecting life and seeking longer-term solutions are twin goals.

The fact that, in suppressing urban crime, unrestrained application of official violence does not prevent political officials from seeking and obtaining support for ever more official violence against alleged wrongdoers.[10] On mature reflection, however, it is clear that simply sharpening the limited set of tools that the ordinary system possesses, whether in a punitive or palliative way, will not bring one closer to a solution. Those tools address symptoms and not causes.

In a war on crime, one casualty is inevitably fundamental values rooted in the Constitution. It is beyond debate that when police and prosecutorial discretion are unregulated, they are exercised against poor people and people of color. The justified perception that the system is loaded against certain people increases resentment and helps perpetuate the cycle of resistance to social norms.

The causes of urban crime have been debated, but they surely include poverty, past and present racial and ethnic discrimination, unemployment, poor housing, lack of equal access to public services, and lack of education. Children in communities, like those of which we are speaking, become socialized at an early age to patterns of behavior that limit their life choices and predispose them to antisocial behavior. These problems and concerns did not arise overnight. They have been woven into the tapestry of American history from the outset. Therefore, a sensible and long-term approach to a perceived crime problem requires one to take a long historical view.

In taking that view, it is not necessary to abandon a continuing commitment to preventing crimes, and to isolating and punishing those who commit them. The longer-term analytical approach goes hand-in-hand with the need for enforcement. As one works on the underlying causes, the insights gained may foster reforms in the existing system that calls itself criminal justice—for example, by increasing the transparency and perceived legitimacy of police, prosecutorial, and judicial systems. In turn, such changes can produce lasting benefits in terms of community attitudes. After all, the system in which we live always depends to some great extent on the willingness of people to obey the law, and their perception that the society is, at least to some extent, being operated in a fair way.

If you agree with at least some of this analysis of how one can approach a problem of widespread urban crime that threatens the peace and stability of a community, the next question might be: Why not apply the analysis to the problem of terrorism? Why should one declare a "war on terror" and leave matters there? Of course, terrorist crimes are punishable assaults on people and property. However, we ought to reflect on how in the long term we can understand and address the root causes of such behaviors. We ought to reflect that abandoning constitutionally based limits on police and prosecutorial action is a questionable strategy for many demonstrable reasons.

The ordinary system of criminal law has not ever drawn a straight and inevitable line between deviant behavior on the one hand and prosecution and punishment on the other. A great deal of behavior that the penal laws define as criminal of course goes undetected, or when it becomes apparent, unsolved in terms of identifying perpetrators. Penal laws are often relics of a former time or overbroad responses to events that get the legislature excited. The police, prosecutorial, and court systems would be swamped if there was a direct and complete correlation between observed criminality and punishment. Indeed, these systems, and the incarceration structures built to serve them, are already overloaded in the United States today.

The point here is that police, prosecutorial, judicial, and ultimately jury discretion have always mediated the relationship between crime and punishment. As I have said, discretion is often exercised in provably discriminatory ways, but the discretion exists. Therefore, when we think about crime, including terrorist crime, there is a serious question beyond whether it can logically or properly be defined as criminal. That question is real and important, as the legislative tendency to overcriminalize as a solution to problems that ought to be handled in some other way is often in evidence. Additionally, one should ask whether particular conduct that is arguably prosecutable should in fact be prosecuted, or whether the community's long-term interests would be served by doing something else.

What is needed, more than anything else, is a sense of history.

Having outlined some of these issues in the context of ordinary crime, let us consider some of the activity that has been labeled terrorist, at one time or another, in various places. If we survey alleged terrorism from, say, 1790 onwards, a consistent and interesting picture appears. One can identify three distinct types of activity that have been labeled terrorist within some reasonable sense of the term.

1. Terrorism in Anticolonial Struggles

Many groups using terrorist tactics are involved in anticolonial struggles against an occupying power. To refer back to an earlier discussion, the occupying powers are, in almost every case, guilty of state-sponsored terrorism in their efforts to combat the anticolonial uprising. If this hypothesis is true, then one might well argue that in addition to measures that directly confront terrorism and terrorists, one needs to understand the roots of such conflicts and to break the cycle of violence that they engender.

2. Terrorism During a Civil War

Closely related is terrorist activity used by revolutionary groups seeking to overthrow a noncolonial government. We see this in the struggles for

124

power in many former colonies and dependencies, such as Nicaragua, Colombia, and Peru.

3. Ethnic and Religious Hostility Terror

We see this form of terrorism in Ireland and the former Yugoslavia. In some instances, the killing and other violent activity is also part of an effort to overthrow or eject a governmental presence. However, this form of violence deserves separate consideration because its causes and potential cures differ from those we see when the activity is motivated solely or mostly by political considerations.

4. Transnational Terror

The attacks of September 11, 2001, were conducted across an international frontier. Their target was a nation-state that does not hold explicit governmental power over any country in which the attackers and their supporters reside. However, their target country does exercise considerable influence in the region from which the attackers come. Sometimes, an even more direct link appears in transnational terror episodes, as when a revolutionary group in a colony commits attacks on the mother country.

The categories are not airtight or mutually exclusive. A given act or campaign of terror can have aspects that fall within more than one category. However, each category is worthy of separate consideration because the solutions to different acts of terror will differ. One might add other categories, and in an earlier essay we have seen the tendency to label many kinds of force or violence as terrorist. However, I have decried that tendency. Overuse of the term terror both trivializes the subject and helps to justify extreme reactions to problems that can best be solved without hyperbolic characterizations.

With this introduction, let us consider some historical events that might logically fit into one or more of these categories.

a. Ireland

In Ireland, throughout the nineteenth century, the British used their power as occupier to impose a series of restrictions on religious and political freedom and to put down resistance to their rule by a variety of devices that resembled those the French used during the reign of terror. For its part, the Irish anticolonialist movement used assassination and other forms of terrorist activity as political weapons. When the British conceded Ireland's demand for independence in 1921, the struggle continued over the fate of Ireland's six Northern counties, which remained part of the United Kingdom. For several years, the Irish "anti-treaty forces" continued a military struggle to make the six counties part of a unified Irish state.

Thereafter, the Protestant majority in the six counties, supported by British political and military power, and Irish nationalists made for a three-way military and political battle in which thousands died. This violence was in some respects a continuation by guerrilla-type warfare of the anticolonial struggle. However, on the streets of major Northern Irish cities such as Belfast, there were killings with no conceivable military purpose: Catholic against Protestant. The religious divide mirrored to some extent an economic gap between Protestant communities and the poorer Catholic communities. The violence therefore became ethnic cleansing terror.

Additionally, into the 1990s and 2000s, Irish nationalists committed periodic bombings in England, which were transnational terrorist activities.

b. Kenya

In sub-Saharan Africa, the leaders and active followers of every movement for colonial liberation were subjected to harsh treatment at the hands of the colonial powers. Kenya provides an example. The Kenyan movement for independence from Great Britain traces its roots at least to the late 1920s. In 1928, Jomo Kenyatta, who was to become Prime Minister of independent Kenya in 1963, published a newspaper that dealt with tribal issues and claims relating to land farmed by Africans. He was a leader of a movement to improve conditions for Africans and for eventual independence. After World War II, the demand for independence became focused and strident. The independence movement consisted of different groups, but one of the most influential—in terms of forcing the British government's hand—was the so-called Mau Mau uprising. The Mau Mau, called Muingi by the Kikuyu tribal leadership, was paramilitary in nature. Its members were armed mostly with spears, whips, and machetes. It conducted deadly raids on white settlements. In the international press, these killings were portrayed as the central element of the African uprising, but this was not so. By 1960, when Britain began to yield to independence demands, the death toll from some twelve years of fighting stood as follows:

- 68 white settlers killed, probably by Mau Mau forces;
- tens of thousands of African rebels killed by British troops, with the British government claiming 11,503 and scholars saying it was at least twice that;

- more than 1,000 alleged rebel sympathizers hanged after trials that did not comport with recognized standards of fairness;
- 63 British soldiers and police killed; and
- slightly more than 2,000 African and Asian British sympathizers killed.

Most of the combat deaths occurred in military sweeps conducted not only against alleged Mau Mau rebels but also against other Kenyan rebel groups that were also fighting for independence.

Jomo Kenyatta was never a member of the Mau Mau. He was a leader of the Kenya African Union, an influential proindependence group. However, in 1953 he was tried for allegedly organizing the Mau Mau uprising and sentenced to seven years hard labor. His trial is generally considered to have been manifestly unfair and the evidence against him to have been manufactured by the British. At sentencing, the judge said that Kenyatta had "successfully plunged many Africans back into a state which shows little humanity."

c. South Africa

Beginning with the National Party's electoral victory in 1948, in an election in which most blacks did not have the vote, that party imposed the apartheid system of racial separation on the country. By 1953, all people of color had been purged from the voter rolls. The government's repressive policies and practices would qualify as state-sponsored terrorism by any means, as well as violating international law norms in other respects. The African response was to organize along two lines. There were relatively peaceful aboveground movements, of which the African National Congress was the most well-known. However, the government banned the ANC: it was a crime to mention its name, be a member of it, or to possess or read its literature. ANC leaders were also banned, which then made it a criminal offense to mention their names in public. However, there were nonbanned organizations that continued to carry an antiapartheid message. South African newspapers were forbidden to report on operations of the security forces in a critical way. I can recall being in Johannesburg in 1988 when South African police seized all copies of a liberal newspaper because it carried photographs of security forces rounding up activists.

Along a parallel track, there was armed struggle. The South African government portrayed this struggle and its leaders as terrorist. In 1963, the government arrested Nelson Mandela and others based on evidence of their leadership roles in Umkhoto Ne Sizwe, or Spear of the Nation, an armed resistance movement. There is no question that Umkhoto Ne Sizwe was responsible for violent acts that might merit the name terrorism. As the South African government justified its own actions and sought international support for them, it often invoked the picture of Umkhoto Ne Sizwe violence.

d. Algeria

Although the struggle for Algerian independence is often, and rightly, termed anticolonial, the official French position was that Algeria was not a colony. It was, in French parlance, a "département d'outre mer," or DOM; that is, administratively a part of metropolitan France. By now, there are only a few of such outposts, including the French Caribbean islands of Guadeloupe and Martinique, French Guiana, and the Indian Ocean Reunion Islands. The idea that Algeria was "part of France" was a powerful rhetorical device as the struggle for Algerian independence got under way, as well as a legal fiction that lent support to France's treatment of Algerian fighters for independence.

Algeria was valuable to France for many reasons, not least its large reserves of natural gas. French and American engineers worked after World War II to build vast gas pipelines, mainly to supply Western Europe. After the war, France shared the fate of other European powers and witnessed its imperial outposts erupt into revolutions—1954 was a bad year for French colonialism. Between March and May, the Dienbienphu fortress in French Indochina fell to North Vietnamese forces under the command of General Giap. For a time, it appeared that the United States might take an immediate and direct role to bail out the French, and there was talk of using nuclear weapons. In the end, however, the issue of Indochina's future was on the table for discussion in Geneva. Those talks yielded nothing of value, and the United States gradually invaded Indochina with ever-larger contingents of troops.

In Algeria, as elsewhere in North Africa and the Middle East, opposition to the colonial powers grew. On November 1, 1954, a number of pro-independence groups formed the Front de Libération Nationale. Ahmed Ben Bella was a principal FLN leader. His political outlook was socialist, nationalist, and secular. He served in the Free French army during World War II and was decorated for extraordinary bravery. After the war, he became involved in the armed struggle for Algerian independence. The French government arrested him in 1956 through the tactic of diverting a Moroccan aircraft, on which he was traveling, into French territory.

He was tried and remained in prison until Algerian independence. His crimes consisted of participating in armed resistance.

After Algerian independence in 1962, Ben Bella became the country's first president. He lost an internal power struggle, and was ousted in 1965 and placed in custody until 1980, when he went into exile. The Algerian independence battle was marked by violence on both sides, in the pattern of a colonial power resisting the forces of independence.

Following Algerian independence, there was extraordinary violence that logically can be classified as terrorist. French people who had exercised financial and political influence in Algeria, including many whose families had been there for several generations, were opposed to independence. This group had various names, such as colons, pieds-noirs (literally, black feet). Many of them immigrated to metropolitan France. Some of these formed the Organisation de l'Armée Secrète (OAS). The OAS began in late 1962 to conduct bombings and killings of public officials who had either supported Algerian independence or who had acquiesced in it. These bombings were organized under the name Project Delta. Among the targets were socialist and communist political figures and, as chronicled in the book *Day of the Jackal*, President de Gaulle himself.

In Algeria, political and religious strife mirrored that in other North African and Middle Eastern countries. The lines of argument were virtually the same as those in Iran, whose situation is the subject of another essay in this collection. The dominant religion of this region is Islam, although there are several contradictory and antagonistic strands within that faith. Islamic fundamentalism, somewhat like Christian fundamentalism, has flourished among the poor and dispossessed. In addition to a messianic message, its advocates and practitioners have often been a center of community organization and mutual assistance. Indeed, because Islamist political organizations were often banned by colonial powers, the social service and religious side of fundamentalism developed as an organizational device that the authorities would allow. In the battle for independence from colonial rule, the tensions between religiously motivated and nationalist-secular fighters were suppressed or glossed over in the interest of having a united movement for freedom from colonial rule. However, once indigenous leaders were installed, they became jealous of the power and influence that religious Muslim organizations continued to exercise. These religious groups, of which the Muslim Brotherhood of Egypt and Syria is an example, have great support among the poor due to the clarity of their political-religious ideology[11] and to their network of social service and charitable activities.

President Nasser achieved power in Egypt in a 1952 military coup with the backing of the Muslim Brotherhood, but came to see it as antithetical to his more secular and nationalist ideology. Today, Islamic political-religious organizations are indissolubly involved in charitable activities. This close linkage becomes significant in the first amendment and due process litigation discussed later in this section.[12]

e. Peru

Since at least the 1990s, and in the face of growing economic problems and repressive government, a guerrilla movement known as Shining Path or Sendero Luminoso has grown up. Sendero, and government forces fighting it, have both been responsible for mass killings and disappearances. It is legitimate to ask whether the Peruvian government has committed state-sponsored terrorism. Sendero's tactics have provably included conduct that meets the proposed definition of individual and group terror: violence, committed in violation of historically determined norms, that is unjustifiable both in terms of its target and its extent, and done to achieve a political objective. I include this brief mention of Peru because the armed struggle there evokes some of the thoughts of Che Guevara that I discuss later in this essay.

f. Afghanistan

In the wake of the September 11, 2001, attacks, the United States invaded and occupied Afghanistan, displacing the fundamentalist Islamic group known as the Taliban. Afghan politics are actually somewhat more complicated than Taliban versus anti-Taliban. Because the Afghan conflict promises to endure, it is useful to recall some recent history. In 1973, the Afghanistan monarch Zahir Shah was overthrown in a coup d'etat led by his brother in law Sardar Mohammed Daoud. In 1978, another coup followed, led by the Communist Democratic Party of Afghanistan. The ensuing years saw divisions within the communist movement and Muslim groups who opposed the political and religious policies of the new government. Beginning in 1979, the United States armed, trained, and supported Islamist mujahadeen fighters who battled the Communist government. The Soviet Union sent troops to occupy Afghanistan and to support the government; troop losses were enormous. Many Afghanis also emigrated to live in refugee camps in Pakistan and Iran. In his 1982 State of the Union address, President Ronald Reagan said, "We support the mujahadeen" of Afghanistan. The Islamist forces that today operate along the Afghani-Pakistani border, including those loyal to Osama bin Laden, were in fact financed and armed by the United States.

This series of short summaries will not command agreement from everyone. Responsible historians debate the evidence and the conclusions to be drawn from it. However, for me, these vignettes provide a basis for commenting upon the different types of non-state-sponsored terrorism and evaluating responses and solutions.

In colonial and postcolonial settings, an interesting pattern emerges. First, of course, the colonial power conquers and occupies the subject territory. Its occupation is almost invariably supported by methods that would qualify as state-sponsored terrorism. At some point, resistance breaks out. The colonial power tries to isolate the leaders and put down the uprising, again by means that are usually disproportionate to the social harm that the rebels are causing.

In this process, and as part of its governing strategy, the colonial power pits one social group against another in ways that create lasting difficulty. For example, in sub-Saharan Africa, colonial powers played one tribal group against another. In Iraq, the British occupiers put Sunni Muslims into positions of power over Shiite Muslims. In Iran, the British and Americans supported the Shah's despotic rule and sponsored the overthrow of parliamentary institutions that were nationalist and progressive. In Ireland, the British consolidated economic and political power by overt discrimination against Catholics. As former colonies achieved independence, the resentments that had been reinforced by colonial policies continued and spawned instability and violence. Thus, when the anticolonial terror was over, ethnic and religious hostility took over as a source of violence. The likelihood of this turn of events was heightened when colonial independence was coupled with the installation of a regime that the former colonizer supported, in contradiction to the popular will. In the former Yugoslavia, the major powers supported creation of a strong central regime in the wake of World War II. That regime would be built by the anti-Nazi partisans and would unite the different ethnic groups. Once that regime began to fracture, the old hatreds and enmities became the basis of ethnic violence.

When we consider anticolonial and revolutionary terror, our sense of history can help to distinguish legitimate from illegitimate uses of violence in the context of social struggles. Terminology is difficult in these situations. A colonial power claims to exercise legitimate control over a territory and to simply be enforcing the laws of that place. Yet, international law may be clear that the colony should be freed from control. During an internal revolutionary struggle, several overlapping and contradictory sets of norms may be invoked by partisans of each side. For example, in South Africa, the apartheid government and the resistance were each responsible for violent acts. Apartheid and all its corollary doctrines violated fundamental human rights norms generally accepted and enforced by the international community. Lacking means of redress within the existing government, disaffected people were entitled under those same norms to engage in resistance that would in turn be conducted within certain defined limits.

Even without resorting to an international law analysis, we all have opinions about what kinds of violence are or are not legitimate in the context of social struggle. That is, we may wish that a sovereign state will put down a rebellion, but argue that its tactics should be as humane as possible, both because of our wish to spare innocent life and our feeling that choices of tactics now will have a long-term impact on the society's well-being. We may believe that rebels have a just cause, yet express concern about their tactics, hoping that they will not target civilians and use violence in a disproportionate way. Indeed, killing noncombatant civilians and inflicting disproportionate social harm characterize a rebel movement as comparatively weak. That is, if the movement feels compelled to blow things up and kill people simply to gain notice and to exert pressure, this is a sign that the movement lacks the popular support that would be necessary to topple the regime by mass organization.

Interestingly, these topics were discussed in a 1961 book by Ernesto "Che" Guevara, the Argentine-born physician who became a central figure in the Cuban Revolution. Guevara was part of the Cuban government after the triumph of the Cuban revolution in 1959. In the 1967, he went to Bolivia to assist a rebel movement in that country. He was captured and killed by the Bolivian military in October 1967.

Guevara was a prolific author. His book, *Guerilla Warfare*, deals with issues of proportionality in the context of a revolutionary struggle. His writings seek to draw a line between legitimate and illegitimate uses of violence in the context of a social struggle. He wrote:

- Be sure that a center of work is not destroyed unless the moment is decisive, since this brings with it as a consequence massive unemployment of workers and hunger.
- When a revolutionary movement has acquired support in suburban areas, it should operate selectively and carefully, in order to achieve "a savings of lives and of the precious time of the nation."
- Acts of sabotage are very important. It is necessary to distinguish clearly between sabotage, a revolutionary and highly effective method of warfare, and terrorism, a measure that is generally

ineffective and indiscriminate in its results, since it often makes victims of innocent people and destroys a large number of lives that would be valuable to the revolution. Terrorism should be considered a valuable tactic when it is used to put to death some noted leader of the oppressing forces well known for his cruelty, his efficiency in repression, or other quality that makes his elimination useful. But the killing of persons of small importance is never advisable, since it brings on an increase of reprisals, including deaths.

- There is one point very much in controversy in opinions about terrorism. Many consider that its use, by provoking police oppression, hinders all more or less legal or semi-clandestine contact with the masses and makes impossible unification for actions that will be necessary at a critical moment. This is correct, but it also happens that in a civil war the repression by the government in certain towns is already so great that, in fact, every type of legal action is suppressed already, and any action of the masses that is not supported by arms is impossible. It is therefore necessary to be circumspect in adopting methods of this type and to consider the consequences that they may bring for the revolution.

- Sabotage has nothing to do with terrorism; terrorism and personal assaults are entirely different tactics. We sincerely believe that terrorism is of negative value, that it by no means produces the desired effects, that it can turn a people against a revolutionary movement, and that it can bring a loss of lives to its agents out of proportion to what it produces.

Guevara drew upon his experience in armed struggles aimed at seizing state power from repressive regimes, principally the Cuban revolution that brought down the Batista government that the United States had supported. In the Cuban struggle, racial, nationalist, ethnic, and tribal divisions did not play a dominant role.[13] However, when we survey the places where terrorist violence is most horrific and intractable, these divisions appear as dominant themes. They overlay the colonial experience and the perception of foreign domination, and potentiate the incidence and intensity of conflict.

Historians and political figures underestimate the power of religious ideology. Even after fundamental social change, old attitudes and ideas live on and become the focal point of organization against the new order. The French revolution promised to make a new world and a new legal order. Yet, when it came time to draft the Civil Code, the Code Napoleon, which was to enshrine the new order in its legal structure, the drafters were powerless to overturn religion-based ideas about family life and so the Code simply reflected those rather than fundamentally altering them.

Events validate Ruskin's adjuration: "No more dangerous snare is set by the fiends for human frailty than the belief that our own enemies are also the enemies of God."[14]

In the history of criminal law, we can find instances where criminal sanctions, more or less draconian in character and application, were deployed in order to crush a popular movement regarded as dangerous. For more than a century, from about 1720 onwards, English authorities formulated and enforced offense definitions that essentially outlawed a way of life practiced by peasants in Wiltshire. More than one hundred offenses, even so minor as going disguised in a wood, were punishable by hanging. The sanctions contributed to breaking the back of peasant resistance, but only by exercising state power in a gratuitously violent way. In some societies and situations, military and paramilitary forces exist alongside more formal and regularized instruments of punishment.

The formal criminal law has limited power to achieve fundamental social goals, and overuse of that power leads to failure or induces the state to become a terrorist. Employing military violence to punish without trial breeds resentment and opposition, and ultimately fails because the root causes of social unrest remain.

Criminal law is also and inevitably backward looking. Its mechanisms evaluate past conduct in order to inflict a present punishment. Yet, by the time the trial takes place, it becomes clear that the criminal law process is unhelpful or even irrelevant. For example, in 1968, the Lyndon Johnson administration brought conspiracy charges against Dr. Benjamin Spock, Rev. William Sloan Coffin, and three other activists who had been encouraging young men to resist conscription into the Vietnam War. Spock and three others were convicted of conspiracy. By the time the court of appeals reversed their convictions in 1969, popular and judicial attitudes towards the war and the draft had shifted in Spock's direction. That shift continued and, in 1977, President Jimmy Carter issued a large-scale amnesty that covered most draft resisters. In retrospect, the Spock prosecution was a historical artifact even before the legal proceedings had run their course. This suggests that using the criminal law to address draft resistance failed to address any of the social issues of that time in a helpful way. The Carter amnesty was a gesture of reconciliation made necessary by the thoughtless use of the criminal process.

This is not to say that criminal law is worthless in confronting large-scale resistance to established order. In the 1960s, throughout the American South, church-burnings, murders of civil right leaders, and a host of related crimes were pandemic. There existed criminal laws against such behavior, and federal government resources to use them. To the extent those laws and resources were used, the federal interest in civil rights was visibly reinforced. To the extent that federal officials were hesitant or resistant, they created the appearance of tolerance for law-breaking. Invocation of the criminal law could not directly affect attitudes towards racial justice for the future. However, the criminal law can and does enforce standards of behavior, and it is easier to act yourself into right thinking than to think yourself into right acting.

The conduct of those who commit wholesale violence designed to coerce and frighten is criminal, but it important to define and use criminal sanctions in ways that focus on unlawful conduct while leaving open discussion about legitimate goals. The erosion of this distinction is the most obvious failure of the policies followed by colonial powers in the instances discussed above.

Historical myopia dominates much discussion about terrorism in and originating from the Muslim world. What are the elements of this Islamic radicalism that infuses the terrorist rhetoric? I believe the most important historical strand is the Islamist view of the Western and therefore largely Christian powers as colonial occupiers. The key word of Islamic radical anti-Western discourse is "crusader," recalling the Western assaults on the Arab World of a thousand years ago. The Crusades are sometimes described in simplistic terms as an effort by Christian monarchs to liberate the holy places from Islamists. "Crusade" in French is "croisade," a battle for the cross. As an organizing principle, religion is a handy device that has plenty of emotional power.

Yet, underneath the religious symbols, the Crusades were in fact a contest about economic power in the Mediterranean. At the root of today's violence is a contest about self-determination which is in turn about control of resources. The poorest and most victimized of the world's people sit atop the world's largest petroleum reserves. From the Crusades onwards, Western powers have sought to impose their will on this territory and its people. The successive histories of costly failure should give us pause. Can we expect that punishment—in the context of trials or of military encounters—will make for a different result?

Criminal law is not concerned only with efficient punishment of those perceived as wrongdoers, which is a view one might entertain from reading the popular media. Justice Felix Frankfurter, quoting Daniel Webster and the Lord Chief Justice of England, reminded us that " 'In a government like ours, entirely popular, care should be taken in every part of the system, not only to do right, but to satisfy the community that right is done' and that 'justice must not only be done but must manifestly be seen to be done.' "[15] Prosecution and punishment in high profile cases commands domestic and transnational support only if conducted openly, evenhandedly, and fairly. The following essays continue this theme, first with an example and then with some proposed prescriptions.

D. The People's Mojahedin of Iran—Case Study of a Flawed Policy

The ideas I have expressed above can best be evaluated in the light of concrete situations. What follows is a case study of antiterrorism legislation and prohibitions in actions.

The official United States response to alleged terrorism includes designation of groups as foreign terrorist organizations (FTOs). Once an organization has been designated, it becomes a crime to provide material to support it, its alleged members are subject to exclusion or removal from the United States, and financial institutions are required to report any of its financial activities of which they become aware. Essentially, the foreign terrorist organization's access to funds is blocked.

Under the Anti-Terrorism and Effective Death Penalty Act of 1996, the legal criteria for designating a foreign terrorist organization are:

- the organization is a foreign organization;
- the organization engages in terrorist activity, or terrorism, or retains the capability and intent to engage in terrorist activity or terrorism; and
- the terrorist activity or terrorism threatens the security of U.S. nationals or the national security of the United States.[16]

Terrorism, as noted above, is defined as "premeditated, politically motivated violence perpetrated against noncombatant targets by subnational groups or clandestine agents."[17] Terrorist activity is defined broadly to include almost any use of unlawful force or violence to influence governmental conduct.

In the past, the designation as an FTO automatically expired after two years, but in the wake of the September 11, 2001, events, the law was changed to make any designation effective until explicitly revoked by Congress, the Secretary of State, or overturned by a court order.

In order to evaluate this method of combating terrorism, let us review the case of the People's Mojahedin Organization of Iran (MEK), which the Secretary of State designated as a foreign terrorist organization in 1997. According to some commentators, the designation was part of a Clinton administration effort to encourage better relations with the government of Iran. MEK challenged the designation in court. In its opinion, the court of appeals set out the problem facing any FTO that wants judicial review:

> The statute before us is unique, procedurally and substantively. On the basis of an "administrative record," the Secretary of State is to make "findings" that an entity is a foreign organization engaging in terrorist activities that threaten the national security of the United States. This language—"findings" on an "administrative record"—is commonplace. We encounter it day in and day out in cases coming from federal agencies. But unlike the run-of-the-mill administrative proceeding, here there is no adversary hearing, no presentation of what courts and agencies think of as evidence, no advance notice to the entity affected by the Secretary's internal deliberations. When the Secretary announces the designation, through publication in the Federal Register, the organization's bank accounts in the United States become subject to seizure and anyone who knowingly contributes financial support to the named entity becomes subject to criminal prosecution. Any classified information on which the Secretary relied in bringing about these consequences may continue to remain secret, except from certain members of Congress and this court. There is a provision for "judicial review" confined to the material the Secretary assembled before publishing the designation. Because nothing in the legislation restricts the Secretary from acting on the basis of third hand accounts, press stories, material on the Internet or other hearsay regarding the organization's activities, the "administrative record" may consist of little else. . . .
>
> At this point in a judicial opinion, appellate courts often lay out the "facts." We will not, cannot, do so in these cases. What follows in the next two subsections may or may not be facts. The information recited is certainly not evidence of the sort that would normally be received in court. It is instead material the Secretary of State compiled as a record, from sources named and unnamed, the accuracy of which we have no way of evaluating.

The court began its consideration of the MEK by quoting a CIA report of 1993, which concluded that the organization:

> is the largest and most active Iranian dissident group. Its primary goal is the overthrow of the Iranian Government, after which it would seek to establish a non-theocratic republic. . . . The MEK's history, marked by violence and terrorism, belies its claim to uphold democratic ideals. Formed in the early 1960s, its origins reflect both Marxist and Islamic influences, and its history is studded with anti-Western activity.[18]

Much of this CIA conclusion is doubtless true, but the statement as a whole is seriously misleading. MEK has existed for several decades. It is secular, leftist, and nationalist. It has advocated armed struggle. It is not, and has never been, an Islamic fundamentalist group by any definition. Its leadership is dominated by women, and it rejects the idea of a theocratic state or of a government based on Islamic law.

MEK was one of many groups that opposed the Shah of Iran. Until the Iranian people overthrew the Shah in 1979, official United States policy was to support his government. The Shah's constitutional monarchy, although it oversaw intellectual and social progress, was in fact quite repressive of its adversaries. The Shah had been head of state in Iran since 1941. However, in 1951, the Iranian Parliament under the leadership of Mohammed Mossadegh decided to nationalize Iran's oil. British and American intelligence operatives, led by the CIA, engineered a military coup that eventually resulted in Mossadegh being deposed and the Shah's designate becoming prime minister. Iran's oil resource exploitation was dominated at that time by British and American interests.

Throughout the 1960s and early 1970s, a number of anti-Shah groups operated in several countries, including the United States. In this country, American intelligence operatives cooperated with the Shah's secret police, the SAVAK, to hunt down, keep track of, and persecute members of these groups. This covert cooperation was revealed in hearings conducted under the leadership of Senator Frank Church; the Church Committee's secret report was leaked to the press in 1975.

If one takes the view that nationalization of oil resources, as Mohammed Mossadegh had planned, was anti-Western and Marxist in some reasonable sense of the term, then that part of the CIA description is literally true. However, propping up the Shah with an unpopular coup, and supporting his repressive policies, was contrary to American values and probably to American long-term interests. Sooner or later, the Shah's regime was bound to fall, and the longer and stronger the

American support for it, the more virulently anti-American would be the regime that replaced it.

During the 1970s, I represented a few Iranian students in the United States who were allied with the Shah's secular opponents. They were the sort of progressive, intelligent people that one might welcome as new leaders of an Iranian government. However, when the Shah's regime fell, it was replaced by one based on Islamic religious law and principles. So, MEK and its allies maintained their opposition status. There was no doubt that some part of MEK's activity was focused on preparing for armed conflict, and that people allied with MEK committed acts of violence against the Iranian government. There is also some evidence that people associated with MEK participated in the 1979 embassy takeover in Tehran.

Because the new Iranian government had taken American embassy workers hostage, the United States severed diplomatic relations. In 1997, the Clinton administration wanted to take a step that the Iranian government would welcome. Iraq not Iran, its neighbor, had become the United States' designated antagonist. There seems little question that the FTO designation of MEK was motivated by diplomatic considerations. The factual basis, which was and remains mostly secret, could easily be constructed because, after all, there was armed struggle in Iran, and MEK was participating in it. Given the broad definition of national security that the United States is accustomed to using, that prong of the FTO test was easy to satisfy. After all, American foreign and military policy towards Vietnam was based for years—at least in part—on the fiction that the United States was part of the Southeast Asia region.

MEK protested the FTO designation, leading initially to the judicial opinion quoted above. For a half-dozen years, the case wobbled back and forth between the State Department and the court of appeals. The court granted MEK some limited judicial review, giving it the right to inspect the nonclassified portions of the State Department record on designation. Based on this limited disclosure and with ample judicial deference to the Executive Branch, the court upheld the designation. In that litigation, the government was permitted to file classified information with the court, which neither MEK nor its lawyers were permitted to see, and on which the court could base its decision.

Government agencies—executive, legislative and judicial—make many important decisions based on secret information. Grand juries indict people, Congress committees receive classified information, commanders order military action, and all of these things may be done based on secrets. However, when government wishes to take action against an individual or organization, there is a presumption in favor of disclosing the evidentiary basis for that action to the target and for providing some sort of adversary hearing to test the evidence. One powerful reason for this is that the due process clause seems to require it. Learned Hand put the matter in this way:

> We agree that there may be evidence—"state secrets"—to divulge which will imperil "national security"; and which the Government cannot, and should not, be required to divulge. Salus rei publi-cae suprema lex. The immunity from disclosure of the names or statements of informers is an instance of the same doctrine. This privilege will often impose a grievous hardship, for it may deprive parties to civil actions, or even to criminal prosecutions of power to assert their rights or to defend themselves. That is a consequence of any evidentiary privilege. It is, however, one thing to allow the privileged person to suppress the evidence, and, toto coelo, another thing to allow him to fill a gap in his own evidence by recourse to what he suppresses.[19]

Also, there is the practical reason that underlies our concepts of due process and the adversary system. Unchallenged evidence may well be wrong. Investigators who know their conclusions will not be tested in the crucible of inquiry are likely to exaggerate or even falsify. This lesson has been learned in far too many cases to doubt its cogency.

However, the saga of MEK did not end with the designation. There were two at least two more chapters to the story.

One chapter began in 2001, when the Justice Department indicted seven Iranians in Los Angeles for aiding MEK by, among other things, raising and sending money. The defendants denied the charges, but defended their right to support MEK and to raise money for its chari-table activities, of which there are concededly many. The case is *United States v. Afshari*.[20]

By way of background to this indictment, one should note that in the year 2000, 228 members of the House of Representatives and thirty United States Senators called on the Clinton administration to revoke MEK's FTO designation. In August 2001, Senator Mary Landrieu of Lou-isiana wrote to Secretary of State Colin Powell that the FTO label had been attached "almost mindlessly."[21]

The defendants moved to dismiss the indictment against them. United States District Judge Robert Takasugi held the material support statute unconstitutional. He focused on the difficulty in moving from a largely unreviewable designation based on secret evidence to a blanket prohibition on meaningful association with the designated group.

The problem Judge Takasugi identified is not new, but the entire FTO process revives a way of governmental thinking and acting about national security that harks back to the 1940s and 1950s and has largely been discredited since that time. As the Cold War became chillier, and the issues of loyalty and security were being debated, President Truman issued an executive order whereby the Attorney General would designate organizations as communist."[22] Membership in or "sympathetic association with" any such organization would then be a basis for restricting access to federal employment. In addition, private groups used the list as a basis for adverse employment actions in the private sector and for campaigns against public figures who associated with the listed organizations. The Attorney General used whatever information he might be able to gather in making the list.

Although the Attorney General's list procedure was never directly overturned by an authoritative judicial decision, the idea of blanket legal sanctions against an entire group was bit by bit undermined and discredited in a series of Supreme Court decisions.[23] In addition, there is widespread agreement that the loyalty-security programs and policies of the 1950s and 1960s accomplished little if any useful purpose and in fact harmed a good number of people, not to mention their chilling effect on public discourse about important issues. Labels such as "communist," "fellow traveler," and "pinko" were attached to all manner of groups and individuals working for disarmament, peace, civil rights, civil liberties, and economic reform.

FTO designations, like the Attorney General's list and all other blanket condemnations, suffer from two constitutional infirmities. The first infirmity is procedural: the designations are done without an adversary hearing and may not be given effective judicial review. Of course, establishing bureaucratic categories is a normal function of government in the modern age. All agencies do it. However, the normal run of agency action does not immediately affect the rights of political action and association. In addition, the usual targets of agency listing are in the United States, and will have notice of the adverse action and a real opportunity to seek whatever judicial review may be available. This is not true of most FTO designees.

Moreover, most FTOs are indeed foreign, and the U.S. Court of Appeals for the District of Columbia Circuit has held that for that reason they are not entitled to the same due process protections as people and entities within the United States. That principle, though supported by precedent, is questionable in a time when foreign entities have an increasingly important role in the American economy. It makes good political sense to treat those entities with the same fairness extended to domestic entities, in anticipation that equivalent ideas of comity will rule in foreign courts where U.S. entities appear.

The second infirmity of FTO designations is that they threaten first amendment rights. A person can be affiliated with an organization in many ways. An individual can provide financial support. The Supreme Court has held that, in effect, money is speech and that limitations on giving financial support to political organizations must be narrowly tailored so as not to interfere with the right of political expression and association. However, as many courts have noted, money is fungible. I may send one-hundred dollars to an organization that engages in peaceful political action as well as allegedly unlawful violence. I may earmark the money for the constitutionally protected activities, but I have no real control over whether the organization's leaders actually use it for that purpose. Therefore, the reviewing courts have held, the federal government can block bank accounts and close funding channels to such groups.

In a famous judicial opinion about Vietnam War protests,[24] the court used the term "bifarious" to describe activities that involve both lawful and unlawful elements. When the lawful activity is constitutionally protected speech and association, the line between it and unlawful activity is also the line between what the Bill of Rights protects and what it does not. Therefore, judging a bifarious undertaking involves first amendment line drawing. When government draws those sorts of lines, it must ensure that it does not restrict protected speech and that the rules it establishes are clear and unambiguous.

To return to our funding discussion, blocking all funding channels does inflict harm on the lawful and protected organizational activities. After all, the governmental decision is based at least to some extent on the content of speech. At a minimum, therefore, the organization is entitled to due process judicial review of governmental action. However, as we have seen, that judicial review is truncated. A person whose car was repossessed by the finance company would have more right to review and challenge the evidence against him or her than these organizations have.

Now we turn to the case of someone who gives the organization financial or other support. Federal law makes it a crime to do that if the organization is an FTO. At least one court of appeals has held that the indicted individual has no right to judicial review of the FTO designation in her criminal case. That is, she cannot demand that the government produce the evidence on which the designation was based, and then challenge the evidence as inadequate to support the designation. She cannot even litigate a claim that the FTO designation was politically motivated rather than based on evidence. We have seen with respect to MEK how political motivations, and wildly inconsistent ones at that, are involved in that FTO designation.

Since 2002, the executive branch has used the FTO designation power predominantly to designate Islamist organizations. The wisdom of these political choices is no doubt a matter for executive decision in the first instance. However, because the pattern of designations has an effect on so many people, and because the entire campaign against alleged terrorists is a legitimate subject of public controversy, it is important that the reasons for designating any particular organization be subject to review and debate. In the period from 2001 through 2006 and beyond, so many executive branch pronouncements involving Islamist countries, organizations, and individuals turned out to be based on faulty reasoning, incorrect information, and at times outright mendacity.

The labeling process is governmental action that harms those designated because they are then the objects of public scorn and obloquy. A historical review of the American experience with McCarthyism yields evidence in support of this assertion.[25]

Even if one accepts, as I do not, the idea that an executive branch designation may permissibly be based on secret and unreviewable evidence, the situation of people and entities who are subject to adverse governmental action based on such a designation is quite different. Denying judicial review under those circumstances violates the fundamental principle of which Learned Hand spoke in the quotation above. When government turns from broad-based regulation to individual punishment, an entirely different set of due process protections come into play under the fifth and fourteenth amendments. When the potential punishment is a criminal conviction, the sixth amendment provides even more stringent guarantees, including the right to confront the evidence against one.

Prosecuting someone based on an unreviewed and unreviewable executive order has never been countenanced in United States judicial history. During World War II, there were prosecutions for violating price controls. The Supreme Court held that the defendant could not challenge the price control regulation he was accused of violating. However, the Court noted that the regulations were subject to judicial review at the time they were issued, and the accused might have sought review at that time.[26] The review would have been on a public record, not based on secret evidence. Also, the issue of price controls did not involve any curtailment of protected political speech.

The price control cases represented the outer limits of nonreview. The Supreme Court held that someone who had refused induction into military service might obtain judicial review of his classification as eligible to serve. That is, even though we were at war, and raising an army through the military draft was of prime importance, nobody could be convicted of refusing service without being able to challenge his classification. That is, people who claimed exemption due to religious training and belief, hardship, or service as a minister, could refuse to obey an order to join the military and defend a criminal prosecution based on a claim that their draft board acted without a basis in fact, committed a procedural error, or misapplied the law.[27]

The FTO cases present a stronger case for review. Unlike the usual price control or draft board case, the initial designation is fraught with the possibility of political motivation untethered to an evidentiary record. The judicial review of the FTO designation is meaningless to the individual defendant in at least two ways. First, the organization itself and not the individual must seek review, and if the organization does not, the right is waived. Second, as we have seen, the review itself is hardly worthy of the name. These considerations make reliance on the price control cases improper.

There is another crucial distinction between the FTO designation and an individual prosecution. We can accept the idea that a restriction on funding may curtail some protected speech because, as noted, money is fungible, but political affiliation is not fungible in that way. That is, one can—arguably—classify an entire organization in a particular way, even though the classification may be overbroad. However, an individual cannot be punished for affiliation with such an organization without proof that he or she intentionally associated with it, specifically intending to further its known unlawful aims. In turn, conduct such as speech, publication, and petition cannot be proscribed or made the basis for liability, unless the conduct is intentionally done under circumstances that create a clear and present danger of imminent lawless action.

This principle was clearly expressed in a 1961 Supreme Court case, *Noto v. United States*.[28] Noto was prosecuted for being a member of an organization that sought to overthrow the United States government by force and violence. The organization was the Communist Party USA.

144

In retrospect, it is fairly clear that neither the Communist Party as a whole nor Noto in particular presented any danger that the government would be overthrown. The overreaction to the alleged threat a revolutionary group within our borders is now well-understood, as are the dangers to free expression created by official pursuit of the Party and its members.

However that may be, the Supreme Court reversed Noto's conviction. Justice Harlan wrote the opinion for the Court, and made several points that are relevant here. He noted that in our system of government, "guilt is personal." It is impermissible to measure the culpability of a defendant by the intent and actions of others. The *Noto* principles have been applied in later cases, including that of Dr. Benjamin Spock, Reverend William Sloane Coffin, and others for an alleged conspiracy to induce young men to resist the military draft during the Vietnam War. In a lengthy and scholarly opinion, the court of appeals reversed the convictions. It held that because this line between lawful and unlawful is also the line between protected and unprotected, the line drawing must be done *strictissimi juris*. This term, borrowed from the *Noto* opinion, simply means with extraordinary care to respect the rules against vagueness and overbreadth.

The Spock court also cautioned against another manifestation of "guilt by association": seeking to establish the guilt of one person by showing the use of acts and declarations of others. No, said the court, when an alleged agreement clearly includes constitutionally protected elements, proof of adherence to the unlawful bargain must come if at all from the accused's own words and deeds.

In the process by which organizations are classified as terrorist and their members and sympathizers targeted for punishment, there are three principal evils. I have spoken of overbreadth—sweeping together protected and unprotected conduct. I have noted the constitutionally suspect substitution of collective guilt for individual liability.

For me, however, the most dangerous aspect of this process is the executive branch's claim of unreviewable discretion. As the MEK story tells us, the power to classify can be used in perverse and illogical ways. The executive's claim to unchecked power is expressed most stridently in times of danger.

No doubt the three issues of overbreadth, guilt by association, and reviewability will be litigated in the dozens of cases spawned by the executive branch's insistence on using a certain version of the criminal law as an antiterror instrument. In the MEK case, the U.S. Court of Appeals for the Ninth Circuit reversed Judge Takasugi's order dismissing the indictments and rejected claims touching on all three of the issues I have mentioned.

The court of appeals denied a rehearing en banc and the Supreme Court denied certiorari, leaving the government free to put the defendants on trial. However, several court of appeals judges dissented from the denial of rehearing, joining in a forceful opinion by Judge Alex Kozinski, a principled conservative jurist.

Judge Kozinski's opinion began with the incontestable proposition that the first amendment protects a person's right to contribute money for political or religious purposes. One may disagree with the Supreme Court's easy assumption that money is speech for constitutional purposes, but that is the law. Judge Kozinski acknowledges that the court of appeals has also held that there is no first amendment right to contribute money to a terrorist organization. As I have noted above, there is some difficulty with such a categorical statement, because some people will give money to an organization that conducts illegal activities intending only to support its lawful work. Criminalizing all contributions done with any purpose in mind is an instance of overbroad regulation of speech.

Nonetheless, accepting Judge Kozinski's proposition for the sake of discussion, he then focuses on the key issue of reviewability. Who says that MEK is terrorist? The executive branch, to be sure. However, as I have noted above, the U.S. Court of Appeals for the District of Columbia Circuit sent the case back to the State Department on initial review, apparently finding the designation inadequately supported. The *Afshari* defendants made the contributions for which they were indicted during the time when the FTO designation review process was still ongoing and thus during a time when the designation had not been held proper. Judge Kozinski argued that criminalizing conduct done before an authoritative and final administrative decision violates due process and free speech.

Judge Kozinski also argued that the designation and review process itself violates the Supreme Court's holdings requiring full, prompt, and fair judicial review of any administrative determination that interferes with otherwise protected speech. He cited the cases invalidating state laws that declared books and motion pictures to be obscene.[29]

Finally, Judge Kozinski addressed the conclusion that the designation could not be reviewed in a criminal prosecution. He cited another obscenity case, *McKinney v. Alabama*.[30] In *McKinney*, the defendant was prosecuted for having a magazine that had already been declared obscene. The Supreme Court held that he was entitled at his own trial to litigate the issue of obscenity—that is, of first amendment protection.

Four other judges joined Judge Kozinski in urging review by the full court of appeals. The Supreme Court's denial of certiorari may simply have reflected the Court's general, though not invariable, practice of waiting until a course of litigation is finally over before hearing a case. Neither I nor Judge Kozinski argue that MEK is a benign organization, or that all of its members are blameless. The capabilities, intentions, and actions of MEK are legitimate subjects of debate. However, when the purpose of that debate is to punish MEK or its members, or to deprive them of a protected interest, the constitution requires that certain rules be followed. Following those rules, collectively known as due process, is indispensable to achieving results that are reliable and that will command the community's respect.

The MEK story is one of very many, notable cases because its fairly long history permits us to see the substantive, procedural, and political problems with the FTO designation process.

Shortly after September 11, 2001, the Bush administration classified a number of organizations as terrorist. As in the case of MEK, it did so without clear standards and without a demonstrable factual basis. There have been successful judicial challenges to some of these classifications, and many cases are pending as I write. But, the consequences of these designations bear notice.[31]

Anna Husarska works with the International Refugee Center in New York and writes frequently for the *New York Times.* Her December 4, 2006, op-ed piece for the *International Herald Tribune* noted that in the wake of September 11, Congress conceded power to the Executive Branch to classify as "terrorist" virtually any organization that uses arms or other dangerous devices to accomplish political ends.[32] The Bush administration's new list included those who have taken up arms against repressive regimes in many parts of the world. Ms. Husarska noted, for example, that refugees from repressive regimes in Burma and Myanmar were classified as terrorists. With the classification comes ineligibility to enter the United States as a refugee. For those in the United States who lend support to members of these groups, even for humanitarian purposes unrelated to armed struggle, criminal liability awaits, as the MEK case shows.

A related issue is raised because a person who provides material assistance to a designated terrorist organization is ineligible for asylum in the United States. Thus, someone who was forced to provide food or household services to a terrorist group, and who would therefore be a candidate for asylum because he or she would face persecution on return to the native country, is denied relief on account of that unwilling service.

147

Overbreadth, guilt by (even unwilling) association, and lack of review all merit the name thoughtlessness. A thoughtful response to an urgent problem requires precision, discernment, and mechanisms that ensure reliable fact-finding. Otherwise, beneficial and constitutionally protected social and personal conduct is chilled or even punished, and wrong-headed policies persist.

However, there is a chorus of opinion that somehow a strict adherence to traditional ideas of due process and free expression must now yield to an alleged unprecedented emergency. I next examine such assertions from several perspectives.

E. The Fourth Amendment, Privacy, and Social Danger

A claimed social danger is the key element of arguments to narrow or abolish guaranties of democratic rights. Personal privacy, and autonomy, particularly the freedom to develop and hold political opinions, has historically been one casualty of such claims. The invasions have taken different forms at different periods. During and after World War I, alleged German sympathizers were hounded. H. L. Mencken chronicled some of the ways in which even people with German-sounding names, or who spoke German, were targeted. That time also saw a worldwide upsurge of socialist sentiment, which was reflected in American electoral politics of that time. The socialist candidate, union leader Eugene V. Debs, got almost a million votes in the 1920 presidential election, and he was in Atlanta federal prison at that time for having seditiously opposed the war. Socialist candidates won elective office in several American states.

Woodrow Wilson's Attorney General, A. Mitchell Palmer, who served from 1919 to 1921, claimed that communists were about to overthrow the American government. The "red scare" sentiment had actually begun somewhat earlier than Palmer taking office, and was fueled by a number of apparently coordinated bombing attacks in eight American cities, on June 2, 1919.

Palmer, however, seized political advantage from these events and directed what came to be known as the "Palmer Raids." About 10,000 people were rounded up—radical unionists, leftists, immigrants. Palmer's assistant, J. Edgar Hoover, went on to head the Federal Bureau of Investigation, which was founded in 1924 but was simply a renaming of the Justice Department bureau of investigation that Hoover also headed. Many of those arrested were prosecuted under the Espionage Act of 1917 and the Sedition Act of 1918 for speeches and organizing against the war. A number of immigrant leftists were rounded up and deported.[33]

Public support for the Palmer Raid tactics, initially widespread, faded over time as people reacted to revelations of official lawlessness. Professor Zechariah Chaffee of Harvard Law School wrote tellingly of the chilling effect these official actions had on movements for social change.[34] Nobody who reviews the history of that time with a discerning eye believes for a moment that the surveillance, raids, roundups, prosecutions, and deportations did anything to make America safer.

In the 1930s, fear of socialism led to passage of laws interdicting speech and association, and creation of the House Committee on Un-American Activities to investigate alleged subversion. After World War II, the activities of the legislative and executive branches in the name of security and loyalty littered the legal landscape with the shards of shattered lives. The excesses of that time have been documented in books, articles, and movies.[35] Of course, during World War II, Japanese-Americans were rounded up regardless of their actual opinions and actions, and sent to concentration camps. In the American South, state and local officials in the 1950s and 1960s borrowed from the techniques of federal officials and began their own investigations and prosecutions of civil rights leaders for alleged plots to do violence.

The courts interceded to try and turn back the tide, but were not wholly successful.[36] When even partial redress came for those harassed, fired, or prosecuted, it was usually late and after the victim had spent a lot of time and money seeking vindication. I sketch this history briefly only to note the overzealous nature of official judgments about the nature and extent of danger, and how officials in such times commonly overstep constitutionally permissible limits.

Other essays in this book deal with the substantive constitutional issues raised by these events, principally those arising under the first amendment. The first amendment provides an independent basis for holding that a person's political and religious views are shielded from governmental intrusion. This essay is concerned with the principles enshrined in the fourth amendment guaranty against unlawful search and seizure and the fifth amendment protection of due process. Another essay will address the international law issues involved in such things as sending suspects to foreign countries where they will be tortured.

From the 1920s and through the rest of the twentieth century, the technology of surveillance became more sophisticated. If there were telephones, the lines could be tapped. Conversations could be recorded with hidden microphones. Ever smaller and more sophisticated cameras could record people's movements. With the advent of global positioning systems that are now a part of almost every cellular telephone, tracking people and their conveyances is ever easier. A series of book-length studies appeared in the 1960s lamenting the demise of privacy and wondering what might be done about it.

Of course, it is not only government that collects information about people: private companies mine data as a marketing device, and in ways that threaten privacy. However, this essay is concerned with governmental conduct, generally for the announced purpose of detecting and prosecuting crime, but specifically in the context of combating alleged terrorist threats. Therefore, it is well to review some basic ideas about search and seizure. The fourth amendment reads:

> The right of the people to be secure in their persons, houses, papers, and effects, against unreasonable searches and seizures, shall not be violated, and no warrants shall issue, but upon probable cause, supported by oath or affirmation, and particularly describing the place to be searched, and the persons or things to be seized.

The fifth amendment says that "no person shall . . . be deprived of life, liberty, or property, without due process of law." For those who drafted the Constitution, this language had a specific historically determined meaning. They wrote it based on their own experience and that of dissidents in England.

During the colonial period, tax evasion was a popular pastime. The Boston Tea Party was only one dramatic example. In order to enforce taxes, the British authorities employed writs of assistance, which were orders obtained from complaisant judges authorizing customs and revenue officers to enter premises where goods were stored and search at large and at will. Colonial resistance to the writs of assistance was widespread. The most famous challenges were those mounted by Massachusetts lawyers led by John Adams and James Otis. On the Boston Common in 1761, James Otis delivered a famous denunciation of the writs. Of that speech, John Adams later wrote, "[T]hen and there the child Independence was born."[37]

In England, at about the same time, arose two cases involving the English radical John Wilkes. Lord Halifax, then Secretary of State, issued a paper authorizing royal officers to search Wilkes's premises and papers for evidence of crime, including sedition—which was simply speech criticizing the Crown. Wilkes was arrested and thrown into the Tower of London—and expelled from Parliament. He sued and won. Two cases, *Wilkes v. Wood* in 1763, and *Entick v. Carrington* in 1765, decided that the executive branch of government had no authority to issue warrants and that Halifax should pay damages. Every lawyer who participated in writing the Constitution and its Bill of Rights was familiar with the writs of assistance struggle and with *Entick* and *Wilkes*. They wrote the fourth amendment with those cases in mind.[38]

One may wonder why it is important to restate this rather elementary history. The reason is that the executive branch of government has, within the past three decades, repeatedly denied that the fourth amendment's plain language means what it says, and that somehow a vague requirement of "reasonableness" can trump the amendment's specific commands.

Most recently, the executive branch has engaged in widespread interception of telephone conversations, and even more widespread intrusion in e-mails and other electronic communications, without a judicial warrant and without particularized suspicion as to particular persons and events.

There are three distinct aspects to fourth amendment protection, reinforced by the fifth amendment guaranty of fair judicial proceedings. The three aspects are: the meaning of "persons, houses, papers and effects," the Warrant Clause, and the particularity requirement.

1. Persons, Houses, Papers, Effects

As government use of electronic surveillance became widespread, an interesting constitutional question arose: What, exactly, was meant by "persons, houses, papers, and effects?" One could define "houses" with reference to ideas about property, although with an expansive view that would also protect people in their rented rooms. "Papers" was clear enough to drafters who had in mind searches against political dissidents based on allegedly subversive writings. "Effects" and "persons" might be given a narrow interpretation, but the Supreme Court began in the 1960s to see that the fourth amendment worked together with other constitutional provisions to protect a certain idea of personal security rooted firmly in the Framers' avowed intentions.

Into the dispute about electronic surveillance wandered Sidney Silverman. He was a notorious gambler in the Washington, D.C., area. One of his gambling operations was set up in a row house. In the house next door, the FBI set up their own installation. This was in 1958, well before any legislative authorization for this sort of thing. FBI agents drove a spike through the party wall separating the two houses, and installed what was known as a spike mike. By this means, they overheard incriminating conversations, and on that basis obtained a warrant to arrest Silverman. The government claimed that their surveillance was no more intrusive than, say, listening under the windows of an apartment building. The Supreme Court disagreed, holding that the ¼" penetration of the spike mike into Silverman's proprietary premises was enough to violate the fourth amendment.[39]

The debate over that ¼" legitimately raised a concern about what the fourth amendment truly protects as technology increases the government's ability to intrude. Along came Charles Katz, whose conversations the government overheard by attaching a microphone to the outside wall of a telephone booth that Katz habitually used to conduct gambling operations. If one took a narrow view of the Silverman case, the analysis would end when the evidence showed that the microphone stuck like a limpet to the phone booth wall and did not penetrate by so much as a millimeter. However, the Supreme Court held that the fourth amendment protects "people, not places," or as it might more accurately have said, people in addition to places.[40] We are all entitled, as a matter of the fourth amendment and of the Framers' theory of the human condition, to a zone of privacy within which to conduct our lives. Intrusions into that zone must be justified by probable cause and, subject to limited exceptions, approved beforehand by a neutral and detached judge. That protected zone is no longer defined entirely by property law and old ideas of trespass.

Of course, there are some intrusions that cannot be justified even with that procedural protection: the first amendment says that as to matters of faith and belief, "Congress shall make no law. . . ." The scope of permissible search is defined in the first instance by the scope of criminal law. There must be probable cause with respect to an offense, and if the constitution forbids criminalizing certain conduct, it by the same reasoning limits searches to discover evidence of that conduct.

2. The Warrant Clause

The fourth amendment Warrant Clause embodies three fundamental ideas, of which two are expressed in its text. First, it reflects the Framers' concern with separation of powers into distinct branches, each with limited power. This idea is expressed in the requirement of a judicial warrant. The role of judges was thought indispensable to this design. Chief Justice Marshall's opinion in *Marbury v. Madison*, which upheld this judicial role, put the issue beyond significant debate. Second, the magistrate must have probable cause, which is beyond mere suspicion and surmise.[41] Third, and implicit in the amendment, the Framers understood from *Entick* and *Wilkes* how unchecked executive power could be used to threaten other fundamental rights, such as freedom of expression. Given that Wilkes was not only pursued but barred for a time from

Parliament, executive power could also be used to undermine the legislature's legitimate powers.

Curbing executive power was important to those who had overthrown a king. Madison wrote in Federalist No. 45, "We have heard of the impious doctrine of the Old World, that the people were made for kings, not kings for the people."[42]

Madison's idea is expressed in article three of the Constitution, which defines the judicial power. However, when it comes to searches and seizures, the Warrant Clause adds an additional, mandatory, and specific command that limits executive action. In the battles against political dissidents, whether labeled terrorist or not, the executive branch has claimed that the President or his designee can authorize searches and seizures without a warrant, despite the Constitution's plain language. This power is said to derive from the President's control over foreign affairs and his role as commander-in-chief of the military.

The issue of presidential power to order searches has been litigated many times, and the controversy continues. The Supreme Court has rejected the idea that the President's power with respect to foreign affairs, or his position as commander-in-chief of the armed forces, confers an implied power to authorize electronic surveillance, mail tampering, and other searches. Of course, the national power to control borders may authorize searches of varying degrees of goods, persons, and even mail coming into the country. However, the generalized powers of the President do not trump the specific words of the fourth amendment.

As a matter of constitutional logic, the matter could not be otherwise. Power with respect to foreign affairs does not reside exclusively with the President. The Senate ratifies treaties and confirms ambassadors. Congress appropriates funds for foreign missions, foreign aid, and military activity. Article three of the Constitution gives the judicial branch express authority over cases "arising under . . . treaties," and over cases involving foreign diplomats and aliens. Under the general grant of power over cases arising under federal law, the Court finds, interprets, and applies customary international law. It has done so in a series of cases, even when the executive branch would have wanted a different result, as in the case of *Banco Nacional de Cuba v. Sabbatino*, in which the Court upheld a Cuban decree that nationalized the sugar industry. Another example is the Court's decision in *Hamdan v. Rumsfeld*, holding that the executive branch must obey and apply the provisions of treaties that confer rights on detainees. The Court has held that international law is federal law and that states are not free to make and apply international law principles on their own.

As I have stressed in many of these essays, long experience teaches that nominally independent review of executive action helps to prevent errors. All of us can recall cases where the police, FBI, or other law enforcement agency got matters very wrong. Death row inmates, convicted after trials, are found to have been innocent victims of police negligence or even outright fraud. People suspected of being disloyal, or revolutionary, or terrorist—or whatever is the current term of opprobrium for social outcast dissenters—are found to have been wrongly accused. Given the fears of Islamic fundamentalist violence, the risk of wrongful classification is heightened by the documented tendency of law enforcement to engage in ethnic profiling.

Of course, a warrant requirement before a search or seizure, or a prompt judicial hearing afterwards, is no guarantee that every invasion of liberty will turn out to have been justified. Judges are as susceptible as other humans to a climate of fear. And, judges who stand against executive power in troubled times find themselves subjected to a barrage of criticism from the executive, but some independent review is better than none.

If it be said that secrecy is essential for some kinds of cases, that is no reason to depart from the warrant requirement. There is even a special court—the Foreign Intelligence Surveillance Court—established by Congress to rule on electronic surveillance requests in cases involving noncitizen subjects. That court operates under special procedures and largely in secret. Indeed, there is a great deal of evidence suggesting that this special court is not independent enough, and that it ought to scrutinize applications more critically. Regardless of that criticism, it is captious to say that laws that were on the books before September 11, 2001, did not contain mechanisms to accommodate so-called anti-terrorism searches and still comply with the warrant clause. I return to this theme a little later, after discussing a third central concept of the fourth amendment.

3. Particularly Describing

Beyond the Warrant Clause, the fourth amendment also responded to the colonial period writs of assistance by requiring that the warrant "particularly describ[e]" the "place to be searched, and the persons or things to be seized." Officers were not to be given permission to rummage and ransack. Executive officers complain that complying with this requirement would hinder intelligence operations, which they say require compiling huge quantities of data and then sifting it to determine what is relevant and what is not. They are saying, for example, that they need to intercept tens of thousands of personal e-mail or telephone messages that they have no particular reason to believe are being sent in furtherance of crime, based on the possibility that something will turn up. Coupled to this assertion is an effort to redefine the level of legitimate concern that someone's conduct must raise in order to justify searching that person's premises or property, and even arresting that person.

To see this issue in context, we should review the history of the most broadly intrusive form of search known to the law—electronic surveillance, or the wiretap and bug. A wiretap is an interception of a telephone conversation by monitoring the actual landline connection. A bug is a hidden microphone. In these days of cell phones with digital signals, there should perhaps be a third word, and maybe there is, but I do not know it. Electronic surveillance is the inclusive term.

In the Communications Act of 1934, Congress prohibited wiretaps. The Supreme Court developed the idea that government agents could lawfully record a conversation if one party consented. But, the idea that there could be a warrant for electronic surveillance ran into heavy resistance. After all, a microphone in somebody's home, or a tap on a telephone, is an undiscerning piece of hardware. It picks up everything that is said within range, including intimate conversations, legally privileged discussions, and all of the vocalization of everyday life. If a live human is monitoring the microphone, he or she can turn it off at certain times or when a discussion that seems privileged begins—or even when matters irrelevant to the investigation are being discussed. This possible option disappears when the number of taps and bugs is so great that there are not enough human agents to listen to all of them in real time. And even if there were enough agents, the listener would still be aware of intimate and privileged conversations in the process of deciding not to record them.

In short, a wiretap or bug is inherently the sort of "general search" that those who wrote the constitution expressly discountenanced by requiring particular description. Their dislike of the general search was rooted in their experience with the ransack roving searches permitted by the writs of assistance during the colonial period.

The Supreme Court addressed this issue in *New York v. Burger*,[43] and it held that New York's statutory provisions for electronic surveillance warrants violated the fourth amendment. Burger was decided in 1967. However, federal law enforcement agencies very much wanted the lawful authority to use electronic surveillance; they had, as we shall see, been doing it without lawful authority for decades.

Congress responded to this demand and to the Burger holding in Title III of the Crime Control Act of 1968, which also contained many other provisions that investigative agencies and prosecutors had sought. Warrants would be available for electronic surveillance:

- based on a higher degree of probable cause than for an ordinary search warrant;
- only for certain very serious crimes; including espionage and other national security offenses;
- for limited but renewable periods;
- when authorized by a senior Justice Department official;
- with detailed requirements for preserving the evidence gathered; and
- subject to requirements to minimize the intrusiveness of the surveillance.[44]

This new power was extensively used in organized crime investigations, and to a lesser extent in other cases.

4. Executive Branch Seeks More Power

As of 1968, therefore, the Congress had accepted the three central ideas of the fourth amendment: scope of protection, warrant requirement, and prohibition on general searches. The legislative response in the 1968 Act did not sufficiently guard against general searches, but at least the concept had been recognized there. When Richard Nixon became President in 1969, he authorized use of the expansive 1968 Act powers, including electronic surveillance, against political dissidents. However, for the Nixon administration, those powers were not enough. Some of the excesses committed were part of the chain of events that led to Nixon's impeachment and resignation. However, the litigation over presidential power and searches continued.

To see this litigation in perspective, we can return our gaze to the early 1960s. When Robert Kennedy was Attorney General, the FBI and IRS installed a number of wiretaps and bugs, mostly directed at alleged organized crime figures. Kennedy always claimed that he did not know these things were going on, but there are reasons to doubt that assertion.

The bugs and taps in Las Vegas, for example, were set up with the connivance of the telephone company, and the FBI set up a dummy corporation—the Henderson Novelty Company—to handle the billing for the company's services. When the bugging operation was discovered, some of those who were overheard filed civil suits against the FBI agents and the telephone company. When some of those same people were prosecuted for various crimes, the bugs and taps became an issue in their cases. In another case, the IRS and FBI rented a room at the Sheraton Carlton hotel in Washington, D.C., and put a spike mike through the baseboard so they could record and overhear conversations in the adjacent suite, which had been leased by a prominent lobbyist named Fred Black.

In 1966, then Solicitor-General Thurgood Marshall learned of the widespread illegal electronic surveillance, and began disclosing it to the defense and to the courts in criminal cases where the fruits of tapping or bugging had been used. The Supreme Court finally held, in *Alderman v. United States*,[45] that the government was obliged to disclose illegal surveillance to the defense and to the court, so that there could be a hearing as to whether unlawfully obtained evidence had tainted the government's evidence.

The Alderman case involved alleged organized crime figures who had been active in Las Vegas. However, the Supreme Court consolidated that case with *Ivanov v. United States*. Ivanov was a Soviet national who worked as a chauffeur for a Soviet trading company. He was arrested as his cohorts—who were Soviet diplomats—were receiving classified information from an American engineer involved in armaments work.[46]

The Court did not decide in *Alderman/Ivanov* whether the electronic surveillance of Soviet premises in the United States was lawful. However, the decision led to countless motions in criminal cases to compel the government to disclose surveillance. I wrote one such motion in *United States v. Dellinger*, the Chicago 8 conspiracy case that arose from demonstrations at the 1968 Democratic National Convention in Chicago. If the government had used statutorily authorized methods, the 1968 statute required disclosure. If it had used unlawful methods, *Alderman* required disclosure.

In response to the motion, the government did make a disclosure, but not the one we expected. It said that there had indeed been electronic surveillance, but did not provide details. Instead, it made the claim that the surveillance concerned matters of national security, as to which the President had the authority to act without a judicial warrant and without having to account for the nature and extent of the search.

In their court filing before Judge Julius Hoffman, the Justice Department produced letters to FBI Director J. Edgar Hoover from Presidents Roosevelt, Truman, and Eisenhower, each authorizing electronic surveillance without a judicial warrant. The Department claimed that these letters somehow established a precedent for such activity. They did not and could not. That an unlawful practice has been done does not legalize it. Presidential letters do not form a system of rules on which reliance may be placed. The executive branch does indeed have some powers to make binding rules, but it does so lawfully only in accordance with rules about notice, comment, and publication, and within boundaries set by Congress.

Judge Hoffman declared the warrantless surveillance lawful. Several other federal judges followed his lead. Then, on January 9, 1971, U.S. district judge Warren Ferguson held that national security wiretapping without a judicial warrant violates the fourth amendment, at least in cases involving domestic activity. The case, *United States v. Melvin Carl Smith*,[47] involved an alleged member of the Black Panther Party. I was Smith's lawyer on this issue. On January 25, 1971, Judge Damon Keith in Michigan followed Judge Ferguson's lead and reached a similar result. Judge Keith's decision reached the Supreme Court, and the Court agreed with Judges Keith and Ferguson.[48] That decision led the government to dismiss the charges against Mr. Smith rather than disclose the details of surveillance.

All of this deciding and legislating left one major issue open for debate as of the mid-1970s: electronic surveillance of foreign targets and foreign diplomatic missions. Fictional accounts of secret agents and diplomatic intrigue have told us of hidden microphones and secret wiretaps. Secret agents operate from embassies and consulates under cover of diplomatic status that confers a certain immunity from search and arrest. The fictional stories are based on fact. That sort of thing happens, and it is outside the realm of detailed legislative and judicial oversight. This is an inevitable consequence of the tensions of the world in which we live. The activity sometimes goes by the name intelligence gathering, although history records so much incompetence that intelligence might be the wrong word.

While recognizing this reality, it is important for the sake of responsible government to insist that these intelligence activities be limited to their narrow and historically defined purpose, that they be subjected to review by the legislature, and that if individual rights are infringed in the process, there be some redress. Without vigilance, the intelligence agencies become a law unto themselves. The Rockefeller Commission in 1975 revealed that the CIA had greatly overstepped its role and was conducting domestic surveillance activities that clearly violated legal and constitutional standards. The committee headed by Senator Frank Church reported in 1975 and 1976 that foreign secret police agencies were being allowed to operate in the United States. More recently, torture has been carried out under the mantle of secrecy, and in violation of the constitution, laws, and treaties of the United States. The executive branch under the leadership of every President since World War II has used secret agents and secret deals to destabilize foreign governments with whom the United States was at peace. The history of American intervention in foreign political activity has been documented over and over.

The main point here is not necessarily that all the secret actions were wrong or unlawful, though most of them no doubt were. Rather, the permissible secrecy with which intelligence agencies surrounded themselves to carry out their accepted functions became a cover for activity that ought to have been reviewed by legislative officials as part of the process of open government. The debates over these issues are well-documented.

So we may confront the range of devices that the executive branch insists are necessary to fulfilling its duties, or at least tolerable as within its lawful powers. Unjustified or punitive detention, rendition to foreign countries and torture are the subject of other essays. As to each of these, judicial review should be available, and conduct that violates laws, treaties, and customary international law is unacceptable.

The more limited issue here is that of electronic surveillance. After the *Alderman/Ivanov* decision, the prosecution in several cases had to confront the issue of foreign national security. It seems some defendants had visited or telephoned foreign embassies for various reasons—usually unrelated to the matters being tried in their cases—and been overheard on wiretaps or bugs. It was certainly embarrassing for the government to acknowledge that these devices existed, particularly when some of them had been installed by burglarizing the embassy premises or getting entry on false pretenses such as repairs and renovations. The solution in most of these cases was simply to reveal the existence of surveillance under a protective order that bound all parties and their lawyers to secrecy, and to acknowledge with a shrug of shoulders that indeed this sort of surveillance did happen in the world. The disclosures, when they occurred, did not excite much comment because at the same time the world was learning of similar activity done by most countries with respect to embassies on their territory.

However, the problem was more acute when the overheard material actually did relate to conduct that the government wanted to prosecute. The Carter administration brought matters to a head when Attorney General Griffin Bell authorized a months-long tap and bug at the home of a South Vietnamese national as part of an espionage investigation. This took place five years after the Supreme Court had held that warrantless searches were unlawful. The target of this surveillance was not like an embassy visitor or employee; the surveillance was aimed at him and avowedly designed to gather evidence to be used in a criminal prosecution. Attorney General Bell claimed that the surveillance was within his power to authorize because it was about foreign national security and not aimed at a domestic organization.

We will never know what the Supreme Court would have done with this case, even though the Court's members were aware that it was happening and that it was on the way. Fearful of such a confrontation, the Justice Department proposed and Congress passed the Foreign Intelligence Surveillance Act (FISA) to provide for a special court, composed of article three judges but operating largely in secret, to handle warrants for national security electronic surveillance where the target was not a U.S. person. This latter limitation has not meant a great deal because the "non-United States persons" targeted generally spend a lot of time talking to United States persons in which the government is also interested.

Getting a warrant under FISA has not proved difficult. The FISA court has never turned down an application. The FISA appeals court, another specially created and staffed entity, has upheld prosecutors sharing FISA-authorized surveillance with intelligence agencies. Not surprisingly, prosecutors in cases having foreign connections greatly prefer FISA surveillance warrants to the ones obtainable under the 1970 law.[49]

FISA makes it much harder for a defendant to challenge the legality and extent of electronic surveillance through provisions that impose secrecy, minimize disclosure to the defense, and give considerable deference to the initial decision that surveillance should take place. When challenging surveillance under the 1970 Act, the defendant will almost always have access to the surveillance application, to test it for adequacy and truth. When a FISA surveillance is involved, the application remains secret, to be examined only by the judge without input and argument from defense counsel. A FISA surveillance may obtain thousands of conversations that include privileged and irrelevant material, but the statute mandates that any "minimization"—or privacy protection—is to take place after the fact by sequestering or ignoring the private or privileged matter.[50] In one recent case, the FISA surveillance lasted several years and yielded nearly 90,000 intercepted telephone conversations. Just storing and evaluating this mass of material was a formidable challenge—and that was just one case of hundreds.

After the events of September 11, 2001, Congress hastily passed the Patriot Act, which expanded the permissible scope of foreign intelligence electronic searches. Investigators could obtain a warrant to search a group of telephones that a suspect might be using, rather than identifying a single one. This provision further eroded the particularity and general search limitations that the Supreme Court recognized in *New York v. Burger* as essential. Such searches inevitably sweep irrelevant conversations of uninvolved people into the surveillance net.

One could make a case that FISA does not quite comply with the fourth amendment requirements of probable cause and particularity. After all, the FISA judges hear government applications that may never see the light of day; therefore, there is reduced incentive for governmental candor in seeking warrants. The judges may tend over time to regard themselves as cogs in the government's prosecutorial machinery rather than independent arbiters.

Regardless of such possible criticisms, the courts have generally upheld FISA and warrants obtained under it. The point for present purposes is that FISA gives the executive branch surveillance powers that, by congressional design, go right up to the edge of what the constitution permits, if not beyond. FISA represents a deliberate legislative judgment and an implicit recognition that the executive branch does not enjoy a freewheeling generalized power to search and seize.

Because electronic surveillance is inherently rather general, and of late has become more so, there is an erosion of this relationship between probable cause to believe that a particular person is committing a particular crime, and the scope of overhearing that will be permitted. To put the matter differently, the probable cause requirement provides a necessary nexus between objective proof and a particular description of what is to be seized. The data mining approach of electronic surveillance satisfies neither end of the nexus link.

Beginning in 2001, however, the administration of George W. Bush decided that the expansive surveillance power already in existence was not enough. Secretly, and often without even lawfully required notice to selected members of Congress, executive officers began intercepting electronic communications, including e-mail and telephone. They put in place other programs of surveillance. When these programs were revealed, the executive branch criticized the media for reporting on them and there were even rumblings that newspaper editors might be prosecuted. Administration officials declined to provide details of surveillance programs, but justified them with general assertions that public danger, foreign conflict, and the general words of congressional responses to the September 11, 2001, events justified them.

I think that all of this executive action is contrary to the Constitution. The executive branch response to revelations of it is at best unconvincing and at worst dangerous nonsense. Those who wrote the Constitution regarded separation of powers into three branches of government as the most important principle of democratic government. No more kings, they said. Drawing on English tradition, they provided a strong legislature, and enumerated its powers in the constitution's first article. They provided for a judicial branch possessing all the characteristics that they hoped would ensure its independence of function and temperament. Although some, such as Patrick Henry, doubted that the judiciary would be equal to the task of restraining excesses of executive power—particularly when the executive appeared in command of the military—even those doubters believed that the specific provisions in the Bill of Rights were the minimum necessary to empower the judiciary's restraining hand.

A claim of executive power to conduct searches and seizures without judicial authorization presumptively flunks the constitutional test. Such a claim is fundamentally inconsistent with the constitutionally mandated separation of powers. In practice, the surveillance techniques fall afoul of every fourth amendment requirement. It is, in this context, fruitless to argue that these are new times and that new measures are needed. Those who wrote the constitution knew of the danger of subversion, having themselves been subversive revolutionaries. They were aware of the power struggles between the English Crown and Parliament, and yet they wrote of legislative independence.[51] They had protested the way in which subservient judges were appointed and kept under control. They wrote into the constitution a definition of treason and yet, did not, in the Bill of Rights, legislate a treason or subversion exception.

Seen in historic context, the constitutional limits on searches are born of the same idea that gives us the first amendment guaranty of free speech and press. In the realm of assertedly dangerous speech, the answer is "more speech," unless and until the circumstances are so dire that governmental intervention may be justified. That stopping point is well beyond the place where people are getting together and talking about the wisdom, propriety, and necessity of committing violent acts. By a parity of reasoning, the probable cause and warrant requirements bar the government from seizing private information until a judicial officer rules that there is a precise and detailed reason to believe that a crime is being committed. And, to complete the thought, so long as people are engaged in the robust and often fractious debate that the first amendment protects, the Constitution forbids defining their conduct as a crime.

F. Judge Richard Posner, Terrorism, and the Constitution[52]

A distinguished federal judge, Richard A. Posner, has argued in a slim book, entitled *Not A Suicide Pact*, for recognizing extraordinary executive powers.[53] I believe that his assertions that new dangers to national security require relaxing constitutional safeguards are mistaken: historically, factually, and as a matter of sound constitutional interpretation. Ironically, the cover of his book is some proof that he is wrong. The book's cover reproduces the camera image of a September 11 terrorist getting through airport security on that day. Yet, almost everyone would agree that if the airport security requirements that now exist had been in place that day, he would probably have been stopped. The airline industry had been vocal in lobbying against the imposition of such requirements because it did not want to inconvenience passengers. The industry had resisted installing reinforced cockpit doors, which airlines such as El Al had been using for years, and so on.

Judge Posner's views are worth exploring for several reasons. First, he is an intelligent and eloquent observer. Second, his views command attention. Third, he says publicly what many judges privately believe—that the constitutionally based rules about human rights must now give way in the face of allegedly new and different dangers. Indeed, he even advocates what he terms civil disobedience, by which he means that public officials should at times ignore or refuse to follow authoritative human rights rules designed to restrain official conduct. Even though police, prosecutors, and lower court judges are forbidden to engage in such disobedience, Posner's view is the sort of thing that encourages them to find ways to manifest their desire not to follow the rules, an issue I deal with in more detail below.[54]

Judge Posner's chosen title is curious, because the phrase "not a suicide pact" evokes the three Supreme Court decisions in which the term appears. Taken together, these decisions are a rebuke to Judge Posner's central thesis.

The first decision is *Kennedy v. Mendoza-Martinez*,[55] in which the Court invalidated a statute that divested Americans of citizenship as a punishment for leaving or remaining outside the United States to avoid military service. The imposition of such punishment without constitutionally required safeguards was impermissible, the Court held.

The second decision is *Aptheker v. Secretary of State*.[56] Herbert Aptheker was a Marxist scholar and a member of the Communist Party. The Subversive Activities Control Act made it a crime for him to have or use a passport. The Supreme Court held that this statute violated Aptheker's

163

constitutionally protected right to travel, even though the Communist Party had been held to be a subversive organization, in an order upheld by the Supreme Court in 1961,[57] and the Cold War was fully under way.

Finally, in *Haig v. Agee*,[58] the Court upheld Secretary of State Haig's action in revoking the passport of Philip Agee. Agee, a former CIA agent, embarked on a campaign to reveal the identities of CIA agents in countries where they were operating and drive them out of business. The Supreme Court upheld the State Department action, taken after appropriate procedures.

In sum, these three cases address allegedly serious national security threats. Organized resistance to military service poses dangers. The Communist Party was thought to pose significant danger, although there were those who persuasively argued at the time that the danger was greatly overstated in ways designed to undermine fundamental constitutional values. That argument looks quite convincing with the retrospect of forty or more years. The *Agee* case is controversial but the situation it addressed was at the time regarded as serious, and the government argued that Mr. Agee's conduct could compromise very important U.S. interests. Mr. Agee was entitled to a due process hearing on the passport revocation and, in fact, obtained full judicial review of the statutory, regulatory, and factual basis for the Secretary's actions.

Not one of these cases supports any part of the Posner proposals, which include truncated judicial review—or no review at all—of detention, relaxation of interpretive standards governing first amendment rights, and almost complete deference to executive decisions that may result in torture and death.

In each of these cases, the adversary system brought out the reasons for and against a particular decision that would affect personal liberty. The cases are in that sense monuments to procedural fairness, including judicial review, and the right to counsel who will challenge the government's assertions about what may or must be done to protect national security.

There is also a question of perspective here, raised not only by Judge Posner's book but also by much writing and speaking on this subject. More than 3,000 people died in the September 11 attacks. Since that date, 150,000 Americans have died as a result of gun violence, and more than 4,000 from hit-and-run vehicle accidents. Deaths from preventable illness number in the hundreds of thousands. Deaths of soldiers in Iraq reached nearly 3,000 by the end of 2006, and the death toll of Iraqi civilians is variously estimated from several hundred thousand to about 600,000—and Iraq did not possess weapons of mass destruction nor was it culpably involved in the events of September 11. This book is titled "Thinking About Terrorism" because I perceive an overreaction to dramatic events. I candidly acknowledge thinking Judge Posner's book is based on an overreaction.

Judge Posner seeks to turn the history of constitutional adjudication on its head. He correctly notes that because our Constitution is short, written, and difficult to amend, development of constitutional doctrine takes place principally by judicial interpretation, with contributions by executive and legislative interpretations and actions. From there, he leaps to the conclusion that in times of danger, such as he believes the present to be, the Supreme Court should adjust the constitutionally based rules to allow executive, and to some extent legislative, acts that had been held to violate the Constitution. Amending the Constitution, he says, is too cumbersome and there is the risk of overreaction in the amendment process

I begin by addressing the fundamental premises of the Posner book. Judge Posner's principal line of argument is that at this historical moment, the courts and Congress, and presumably everyone else, must accord almost limitless deference to the decisions made by the executive branch. Not only should one refrain from challenging decisions to conduct a war with hundreds of thousands of human casualties, but one should also tolerate incursion into traditionally protected areas of free expression and personal privacy.

This argument rests upon two myths. The first is a myth of executive supremacy.[59] The second is a myth about what Posner terms "the present emergency."

As to the first myth, Judge Posner writes: "In United States v. Curtiss-Wright Export Corp.,[60] the Supreme Court held that the United States acquired the powers of a sovereign nation by its successful revolution against Great Britain rather than by a grant in the Constitution: the nation is prior to the Constitution."[61] In a related remark, Judge Posner claims that "National defense, not limited to defense against human enemies, is a core sovereign power and moreover one that is traditionally exercised by the executive."[62] Neither of these statements is true, and neither one supports an argument for unreviewable executive power.

In these times, those who seek to uphold executive power against challenge usually cite *Curtiss-Wright*. That case arose during the military conflict in South America known as the Chaco War. Between 1932 and 1935, Bolivia and Paraguay battled over the Gran Chaco region, mistakenly thought to contain mineral deposits. On May 28, 1934, Congress by joint resolution authorized the President to interdict sale of arms to belligerents in that conflict, and made it a crime to violate any

165

presidential proclamation made under the joint resolution. That same day, President Franklin Roosevelt issued a proclamation carrying the resolution into effect and forbidding arms sales. He revoked the proclamation on November 14, 1935. Curtiss-Wright and some of its officers were indicted for violating the terms of the proclamation.

The defendants challenged the President's exercise of power to issue the proclamation. The Supreme Court, over Justice McReynolds's dissent, held that the President had properly exercised his power. Justice Sutherland's majority opinion contains a great deal of language unnecessary to the Court's holding. The Court might have simply recited the long list of Congressional enactments authorizing the President to impose and maintain embargoes for various purposes. That list begins in the earliest days of the republic. However, Justice Sutherland speaks more broadly and in terms that Judge Posner is not alone in misconstruing.[63]

First, Justice Sutherland says that the power over foreign affairs never resided in the thirteen original states. As Louis Fisher has pointed out, this is not quite true. Fisher writes, "Sovereign powers in 1776 came initially to the Continental Congress and the separate states, not to the President, a position that did not exist at that time."[64]

Beyond the issue of historical analysis, the ultimate source of power over foreign affairs is irrelevant to the question of where those powers reside under the Constitution. The Supreme Court has squarely held that the national government has exclusive power over relations with foreign states. States cannot make foreign policy.[65] Wherever any given power of government can be said in some metaphysical sense to come from, the exercise of all powers is defined by the Constitution itself.

Justice Sutherland does not deny this fundamental truth. He notes that even if there were no written constitutional provisions about foreign affairs, such powers would have resided in the national government. That may be a stretch, as the Constitution was drafted in large measure because the Articles of Confederation had created doubts about the lines of authority between the general government and the states. Sutherland takes his argument beyond the text and intent of the Constitution, and cites cases upholding national governmental power "not in the provisions of the Constitution, but in the law of nations."[66]

It is important not to overlook Sutherland's use of the phrase "law of nations." It puts the entire discussion into context. The United States, in the transnational community, lives under a regime of rules that are implicit in the transnational order. These rules embrace obligations of states towards one another, and in their dealings with individuals. They embody principles that existed before the United States was formed. However, these norms do not confer unlimited power on the United States to act in transnational relations; rather, the United States is obliged to limit its unilateral exercise of sovereign power in the transnational arena by rules derived from treaties, customary international law, and peremptory norms of international law. By this time, some seventy years after Justice Sutherland wrote, it is clear that these norms include prohibitions on aggressive war, genocide, and torture, among other crimes. Thus, the national governmental power of which Sutherland speaks is a limited one. We can understand that the United States government violates these norms at times, but that does not deny their existence any more than the fact that murders occur is an argument that the norm against murder does not exist.

The Supreme Court has repeatedly looked to the law of nations as a source of norms that govern and regulate the conduct of all three branches of government. For example, in *The Paquete Habana*,[67] in 1900, the Supreme Court held that the Navy had violated the law of nations by seizing fishing vessels during the Spanish-American War—that is, during active hostilities. The case teaches two important lessons: the judicial branch judges the executive, and the executive is bound by the law of nations. In *Banco Nacional de Cuba v. Sabbatino*, which I mentioned above, the Supreme Court applied a principle of the law of nations to validate a Cuban executive order nationalizing sugar; this decision was displeasing to the executive branch, and reaffirmed the judicial role in interpreting and applying the sovereign power and in placing limits on its exercise.

Moreover, this somewhat limited sovereign power to act in the transnational arena has never been understood to reside solely in the executive branch of government. Rather, it is shared among the three branches, as a moment's reflection on the two Supreme Court decisions mentioned above will reveal. Justice Sutherland's long list of embargo provisions and actions underscores the way in which executive power, even in the conduct of foreign relations, is limited by the powers that the other branches possess. Typically, the Congress recognizes a threat and authorizes the executive branch to deal with it by restraining certain kinds of commerce. The President does not act alone. When the President exercises power in a controversial way, what happens? During Thomas Jefferson's presidency, an instructive case arose.[68]

In 1807, Congress authorized an embargo on foreign seaborne commerce, as a measure of retaliation against British and French interests.

The embargo was controversial, and it caused great hardship to commercial interests on the Eastern seaboard. It did not have the desired political effect, and on the domestic scene caused Thomas Jefferson's party to lose a great deal of political support. However, having been authorized by the Congress, it was held constitutional.[69] Seafarers resorted to evasion and smuggling. One congressional response was a statute of 1808 that permitted the federal customs collector of each port to detain any ship ostensibly bound for a domestic port whenever, in his opinion, the ship was actually headed to a foreign destination. The statute seemed to repose unfettered discretion in the executive branch.

Enter Justice William Johnson, Jefferson's first Supreme Court nominee. Johnson, a well-respected South Carolina lawyer and judge, took his seat on the Court in 1804. As was the custom at that time, he sat as a trial judge on circuit and, in that capacity, heard a challenge lodged by a ship owner who had been refused clearance to leave the port of Charleston. The owner, Adam Gilchrist, claimed that his ship was bound for Baltimore, and was laden with rice and cotton. The collector of customs apparently suspected that the ship was really headed overseas.

Justice Johnson heard evidence and, with a written opinion, issued a writ of mandamus on May 28, 1808, directing the collector to clear the ship. Justice Johnson held that the courts had the power to construe the Congressional grant of power and to keep executive actions within lawful bounds. His language was polite, but his message was clear.

Jefferson, hearing of the decision, was angry. He asked Attorney General Caesar Rodney to draft a letter evaluating Justice Johnson's decision. Rodney complied, and among other arguments, said that the court lacked jurisdiction because the Congress had given the President unreviewable power over the issue of port clearances, and that the President had exercised that power in telling collectors not to clear any vessels carrying certain kinds of cargo even though there was evidence the cargo was bound for a domestic port. Jefferson had in effect ordered that ships carrying certain foodstuffs and other articles that logically would be shipped abroad should be kept in port, regardless of their stated destination.

Upon receiving Rodney's letter, Jefferson authorized it to be published, and it appeared in a Charleston newspaper in the summer of 1808. Justice Johnson was appalled at Rodney's misstatements of fact and law, and at Jefferson's having had the letter published. He knew both men well, and professed his respect for them. However, he wrote a reply and then waited a few weeks before releasing it for publication. The reply stands as an important document in the history of judicial review, and as a cogent assertion of the role of judges in the constitutional system. Johnson began by saying that he would not have replied to a newspaper editor's criticism of his opinion. Editors have an unlimited right to comment. He went on:

> The official acts of men in office are proper subjects for newspaper remarks. The opinion that cannot withstand a free and candid investigation must be erroneous. It is true that a judge may, without vanity, entertain a doubt of the competency of some of the editors of newspapers to discuss a difficult legal question; yet no editorial or anonymous animadversions, however they may have been characterized by illiberality or ignorance, should ever have induced me to intrude these observations upon the public. But when a bias is attempted to be given to public opinion by the overbearing influence of high office, and the reputation of ability and information, the ground is changed; and to be silent could only result from being borne down by weight of reasoning or awed by power.[70]

So here is a judge not awed by power, asserting judicial independence. Johnson noted that participating in seaborne commerce is a fundamental right, unless there be a law to restrain it. Congress had passed such a law, limited to vessels bound for foreign ports. The President had interpreted his power under the law very broadly, interdicting vessels based on their cargos rather than on evidence of destination. Johnson reiterated his conclusion that the President had acted outside the bounds of his lawful authority.

He declined to rest his decision upon inherent judicial power:

> The jurisdiction of the court, as is properly observed by the attorney general, must depend upon the constitution and laws of the United States. We disclaim all pretensions to any other origin of our jurisdiction, especially the unpopular grounds of prerogative and analogy to the king's bench. That judicial power, which the constitution vests in the United States, and the United States in its courts, is all that its courts pretend to exercise. In the constitution it is laid down, that "the judicial power of the United States shall extend to all cases in law or equity, arising under this constitution and laws of the United States, and treaties made, or which shall be made," &c. The term "judicial power" conveys the idea, both of exercising the faculty of judging and of applying physical force to give effect to a decision. The term "power" could with no propriety be applied, nor could the judiciary be denominated a department of

government, without the means of enforcing its decrees. In a country where laws govern, courts of justice necessarily are the medium of action and reaction between the government and the governed. The basis of individual security and the bond of union between the ruler and the citizen must ever be found in a judiciary sufficiently independent to disregard the will of power, and sufficiently energetic to secure to the citizen the full enjoyment of his rights. To establish such a one was evidently the object of the constitution. But to what purpose establish a judiciary, with power to take cognizance of certain questions of right, but not power to afford such redress as the case evidently requires?[71]

The Gilchrist case does not stand alone. It is simply a dramatic example of the way that judges have and exercise the power to control presidential action even in the field of foreign affairs. The *Curtiss-Wright* holding is in that line of authority, for it upholds presidential exercise of a power granted by Congress within the limits of that Congress had set.

If we are to look into the theory of American government, and to look as Judge Posner claims to do into the time before the Constitution was adopted, we can find clues in the Declaration of Independence. One principal charge against King George was that "He has affected to render the military independent of, and superior to the civil power." The Declaration contains a number of other specific allegations directed at the impermissible—to the colonists—idea of unbridled executive power. The colonists knew a great deal about English legal history, and particularly the seventeenth century events that restricted royal power. The Declaration's denunciation of King George echoed a well-understood principle of English law. In the early part of the seventeenth century, the king claimed to Parliament that he was using his executive power in deploying the military, and that this was a matter of executive discretion. Lord Coke replied, "God send me never to live under the law of conveniency or discretion. Should the soldier and the Justice sit on one bench, the trumpet will not let the cryer speak in Westminster Hall."[72]

As I have noted elsewhere in this book, the Supreme Court has repeatedly examined and rejected executive branch claims of complete immunity from judicial review when national security is at stake. From the Supreme Court's holding that President Jefferson could not hold Aaron Burr's alleged confederates in military custody,[73] to the scrupulously fair treason trial of Burr himself, through the holding that the President had no authority to impose martial law on Hawaii during World War II, and in dozens of other cases, the principle of separation of powers and judicial responsibility has been upheld.

One can also look to another episode in American constitutional history, not usually mentioned in the modern debate. When Franklin Roosevelt became President in 1933, his administration faced an unprecedented economic crisis. In his inaugural address,[74] he promised decisive action in the name of national security. For the next several years, the Supreme Court, the Congress, and the executive branch wrestled with the means to address economic crisis within constitutional limits. The Supreme Court struck down the initial efforts to address the crisis and in a series of later decisions gave its assent.

Another aspect of Judge Sutherland's discussion requires comment. He quoted a statement made by John Marshall during a Congressional debate in 1800, before Marshall was named to the Supreme Court: "The President is the sole organ of the nation in its external relations, and its sole representative with foreign nations,"[75] and went on to cite other authorities upholding presidential power to conduct negotiations with foreign nations. Along the way, Justice Sutherland noted that often the details of presidential reasoning and action may legitimately be held secret. None of this reasoning undercuts the amenability of presidential conduct to judicial review and, therefore, it does not lend credence to the Posner myth of executive supremacy.

John Marshall's statement was made before he was a judge and in the context of a discussion of presidential power concerning extradition. The Supreme Court has held that executive branch decisions concerning extradition are subject to judicial review to ensure compliance with international law.[76] More broadly, if one wants to know what John Marshall thought about judicial review of executive action, there is a rich store of his judicial writings, which have the virtue of placing the matter in context and also of being authoritative declarations of the law of the land.

In *Marbury v. Madison*,[77] Chief Justice Marshall made clear that Marbury was entitled to his commission as a judge, and that only the unfortunate fact of his having filed his request for mandamus in the wrong court stood in the way of issuing mandamus to the Secretary of State. Marshall recognized only a narrow area within which presidential action might escape judicial scrutiny.

Then, when he sat as judge in the treason trial of Aaron Burr, Marshall held that even the President of the United States was subject to judicial process, and must obey a subpoena for relevant documents.[78] The *Burr* opinion on that subject has since been recognized as authoritative, in the litigation surrounding a criminal investigation of President Richard

171

Nixon.[79] The executive branch possesses an executive, or state secrets, evidentiary privilege, and Justice Sutherland is correct in referring to it. However, judges decide whether the privilege is properly invoked; it is not a blanket authorization to withhold evidence. The Supreme Court has noted that "Judicial control over the evidence in a case cannot be abdicated to the caprice of executive officers."[80] Dean Wigmore has written that "A court which abdicates its inherent function of determining the facts upon which the admissibility of evidence depends will furnish bureaucratic officials too ample opportunities for abusing the privilege."[81] In sum, the judicial role faced with challenged executive action is based on deference and not surrender. Executive supremacy, in the sense that Judge Posner imagines it, is a myth.

The second myth that Judge Posner invokes is captured in his phrase "the present emergency," as though the dangers to national security in the present moment are so much different and greater than at other times to justify prescriptions to enlarge unaccountable power and shrink personal liberty. Perhaps, one might say, there is a present emergency of that kind. If there is, and if it is to be invoked in the way Judge Posner advocates, then the burden of proof lies on him. As a judge, he knows that the factual basis for restricting constitutional guaranties is a matter of evidence and not of speculation.

As I have noted in earlier essays, many books have been written about the failed policies and false premises of the executive branch since September 11, 2001. Many responsible historians point out that the American invasion of Iraq has polarized opinion in the Muslim world and drawn young men and women into the armed struggle. If these views make sense, then one answer to the threat of terrorism is to change foreign and domestic policy and not to erode constitutional guaranties.

A look backward at American history would also be instructive. To be sure, there have been many crises during which the executive branch invaded civil liberties and the judicial branch proved compliant. But, as we look back at every such episode, we see that the executive branch usually overstated the danger and made false claims about the suitability of its chosen means to deal with it. Jefferson's response to Burr's threat,[82] the political response to Native American claims,[83] the nineteenth and early twentieth century furor over aliens, the Palmer Raids after World War I,[84] the Japanese relocation,[85] imposition of martial law in Hawaii,[86] the excesses of the McCarthy period, urban uprisings in the 1960s,[87] organized crime—all of these chapters teach us that easy statements about a present emergency must be taken with skepticism, not to say cynicism. In each of these crises, hyperbolic rhetoric obstructed rational thought

172

and political decisions were made that in retrospect seem unwise and even dangerous.

When thinking in the same space about executive power and emergency, it is well to recall Justice Robert Jackson's concurring opinion in the *Steel Seizure Case, Youngstown Sheet & Tube v. Sawyer.*[88] In 1951, during the Korean conflict, there was a strike at the nation's steel mills. President Truman reacted by ordering the mills seized and operated by the federal government, invoking his powers and President and commander in chief. There was no doubt that the nation was embroiled in a conflict, which was eventually to cost nearly 55,000 American lives, and the lives of 600,000 Korean soldiers and more than two million Korean civilians. The Supreme Court held, 6-3, that the President overstepped the constitutional bounds on his authority.

Justice Jackson's concurring opinion drew on his experience as Solicitor General and Attorney General as well as his judicial and lawyering experience.[89] His analysis of the issues is a persuasive response to Judge Posner's thesis. Justice Jackson began with a cautionary word about judicial and executive decision-making in a time of crisis:

> That comprehensive and undefined presidential powers hold both practical advantages and grave dangers for the country will impress anyone who has served as legal adviser to a President in time of transition and public anxiety. While an interval of detached reflection may temper teachings of that experience, they probably are a more realistic influence on my views than the conventional materials of judicial decision which seem unduly to accentuate doctrine and legal fiction. But as we approach the question of presidential power, we half overcome mental hazards by recognizing them. The opinions of judges, no less than executives and publicists, often suffer the infirmity of confusing the issue of a power's validity with the cause it is invoked to promote, of confounding the permanent executive office with its temporary occupant. The tendency is strong to emphasize transient results upon policies—such as wages or stabilization—and lose sight of enduring consequences upon the balanced power structure of our Republic.

While Justice Jackson had supported the Japanese relocation, based on what he then knew, he warned that with respect to matters over which coordinate branches have some responsibility, "Presidential claim to a power at once so conclusive and preclusive must be scrutinized with caution, for what is at stake is the equilibrium established by our constitutional system."[90]

173

So long as a President is directing military activity in a foreign theater of war, it will be difficult for courts to intervene directly in the day-to-day business of fighting. We are left to debate the fraudulent pretexts for war that were presented to Congress and the people, and to trust that eventually the rules of transnational law relating to aggressive war will prevail. We are forced to recognize the limits on American power as deployed by the executive branch, as demonstrated by military setbacks that can be seen as showing that the entire enterprise was ill-considered and wrong. The freedom to hold that kind of debate, and the government's obligation not to lie to the people about the issues, remain the most fundamental guarantors of democratic rights. There is judicial power and duty to see that the debates are not chilled.

Judge Posner's book does not speak much about foreign adventure, however. He is talking about domestic institutions that have historically been under the control of Congress and the courts. He deploys rhetoric about foreign conflict and domestic threat to argue that courts should defer to the executive branch. To those matters, the Steel Seizure case is one reminder that executive power is reviewable and accountable.

I turn now to an analysis of Judge Posner's specific proposals. He first advocates a weighing test for determining the social good and social harm from curtailing a given right, such as the right to judicial review. Judges must somehow calculate and weigh the interests of national security against the harm done to individuals by torturing them, detaining them without judicial review, or otherwise invading liberties that have long been recognized as fundamental. He acknowledges that judges are not experts in national security, perhaps overlooking the irony that he—a judge—is writing this book.

The Posner analysis is in modern dress but revives an old debate. Judge Posner is fond of equations. As an appellate judge, he has given district judges a formula to calculate the elements of decision on a motion for preliminary injunction, including likelihood of success on the merits, social harm, and relative equities. Of course, a wise reader will note that most of these elements cannot be quantified in any but the most subjective way, and that the equation is therefore a misleading effort to make objective something that is not.

In the 1950s, the Supreme Court advanced various formulas to balance away free speech rights in the face of alleged dangers to national security.[91] Freedom of expression was the loser. Many, and I was among them, were heartened when the Court seemed to return to the far more protective test of "clear and present danger."[92] National security— meaning, the security of the entire nation—or its way of life, is a hugely important though ill-defined interest. Weighed against this would be the rights of relatively small numbers of people, at least compared to the entire national population. The characterization of interests involved in this sort of balancing puts individual and group rights at a great disadvantage.

Turning then to the actual balancing process, the government will always assert the national security interest robustly and generally. Its lawyers will resist specific and detailed factual inquiry into the nature and source of threats. It will argue that the individual's rights to discover falsehood, to challenge the legality of evidence, and even to have effective counsel all pose dangers to national security. In times of perceived danger, judges often heed these arguments. Therefore, the result is that, in the judging process, the balance is being struck not only by judges who are not experts in national security but by judges who, like Justice herself, are proceeding with blindfolds on.

The full-dress use of the adversary system to probe government wrongdoing is not simply an ideological preference. It is a proven way to get the truth. When the journalist Quentin Reynolds died in the crash of an Air Force plane, his widow could not sue for damages because the causes of the crash were said to be secrets of national security.[93] The Supreme Court, even while proclaiming that the judiciary must control the evidence even when national security is at stake, accepted the government's assertion of the need for secrecy. Sixty years later, the airplane records were unsealed; the crash was due to a maintenance error having nothing to do with secrecy.[94] The government had played the national security card without any factual basis. I have cited other examples of government doublespeak and outright mendacity throughout this book. The litany continues in the present moment, with revelations of governmental misconduct in high profile national security cases.[95]

These examples should warn us. Abstract agreement that governmental power is greater during times of danger proves nothing. The lesson of history is clear that dispensing with procedural and substantive safeguards leads to bad decisions that do not lessen, and may actually increase, danger. The lesson is also that we do not need an elaborate theoretical justification for judicial timidity in the face of executive power. Judges, including those on the Supreme Court, have often demonstrated that sort of timidity without having to read a learned treatise about it. The list of mistaken decisions based on abdicating a vigorous and independent judicial role is long.

Finally, one cannot responsibly treat this sort of balancing as a series of isolated judicial decisions. Judicial control of executive action is at best a hit-and-miss process. Not all cases of alleged abuse get to court even if the courts have not been shuttered by legislative action. The due process clause does not generally provide a right to counsel in civil and habeas corpus actions, and the quality of counsel in criminal cases is uneven. Torturers and jailers know that the risks of their actions being reviewed and, if reviewed, criticized are fairly low. We can understand this idea in our daily lives. We all deal with bureaucracies. We have become accustomed to the way that lower level decision makers operate in seeming independence from the rules that are supposed to govern their conduct. Secure in their jobs, they act out their imperial fantasies to our unending frustration. This is not a universal scenario, but it happens often enough and particularly when the lower level decision makers have an agenda of their own. Having seen this scenario at work in our daily lives, we have little reason to tolerate it when those in high office act it out.

Every approved weakness in the review process of high-level action further encourages lawlessness at the lower levels, which is one reason people truthfully say the government becomes a recidivist when it does wrong and gets away with it.

Turning to the broader issue of constitutional interpretation, Judge Posner takes up a theme that he has developed in his writings:[96] Constitutional rights are those created by justices of the Supreme Court who loosely interpret the Constitution to keep the document flexible and adaptive. Posner traces the evolution of different constitutional rights over time to demonstrate that there are practical reasons for not allowing those liberties to remain static.

Posner reasons that as long as one agrees that constitutional rights need to be adaptive to remain relevant as times change, one should accept that Justices and judges should feel free to alter the scope of rights in times of national emergency because, at those times, the Constitution could not be amended quickly enough to be responsive. He finds support in the way the Supreme Court has reinterpreted the scope of constitutional rights over time. He also endorses the idea of judges experimenting with boundaries and making adjustments to assure optimal levels of security and freedom. Posner recognizes a tension between this idea and that of basic inalterable principles such as free expression and procedural fairness. For example, he doubts that there could be any justification for allowing citizens to be tried before military tribunals.

Posner suggests that, in some circumstances, the exercise of unauthorized power in conflict with civil liberties is necessary and desirable, as when one must torture a terrorist to obtain vital information. Without much explanation, he denies the validity of concerns that the government will abuse this overreaching privilege by exaggerating public fears to create more power, or by maintaining the power after threats have passed. He also suggests that curtailing civil liberties to prevent a terrorist catastrophe would actually protect civil liberties in the long run, because terrorism hurts civil liberties by intimidating people into forgoing their civil liberties. For example, he suggests that terrorism prevents people from exercising their right to speak freely in criticizing Islam for fear of retaliation and this method of stifling of liberty is as effective as a direct constraint on civil liberties by the government.

On the subject of torture, Judge Posner seems to accept that at times it will occur and will be justified. He does not base his view that torture is sometimes useful and permissible on any of the usual anecdotal justifications. The "torture the terrorist" hypothetical has been the subject of much learned debate. I have expressed my own view in this way:

> I am prejudiced against torture. I am also prejudiced against the posturing and tergiversation that has lately gone on about torture. The media, even including respectable academic publications, use phrases like "the debate about torture" without a hint of irony. We are seeing memo after memo leaked from the Bush administration, showing that torture of detainees is a standard policy, and that those high-ranking officials who approve of it fall over themselves thinking up defenses to criminal prosecutions for torture and ways to make sure there will never be any judicial review. The norm against torture has become peremptory, jus cogens, and non-derogable. Given my prejudice about universal jurisdiction and its corollaries, you can guess what I think about the prosecutability of many American officials.

> I have heard people pose hypotheticals about torture. What if you knew that somebody had planted a bomb, and torture might make them reveal where it was? These days, when we think about "somebody," we usually picture a somebody who is a somewhat different color and a rather different religion that ourselves. My answer is, first, is our "knowing" on the same level as knowing that Saddam Hussein had weapons of mass destruction? Second, let us assume that sometimes the norm against torture will be violated, and after the fact somebody might want to say that the torturing is excused or justified.

> Change the hypothetical slightly. Talk about murder instead of torture. The criminal law has rules about excuse and justification. It is administered with discretion. The trier of fact sometimes makes

177

unauthorized exceptions. Punishment may be mitigated under certain circumstances. Yet all of these considerations could not possibly lead us to say that the norm against murder should not exist or not be enforced. The hypotheticals conjured by apologists for torture tell us absolutely nothing of value.[97]

Judge Posner takes a different approach. Posner asserts torture is an effective way of gaining information and could prevent the deaths of thousands or millions of people. He argues that torture is not constitutionally prohibited as cruel and unusual punishment if it is performed prior to conviction and solely to obtain information. It should be governed by a shocks-the-conscience notion, which will vary in permissibility depending on the stakes involved. He concedes that the authority to torture should not be codified, because it would be impossible to specify the situations in which it should be used, individuals might erode the boundaries of such authorization, and officials would take the decision to torture with less gravity if it were expressly authorized. Instead, he believes it would be safer to force officials to assume the political and legal risks of disobeying the law in order to torture someone when they must do so.

The differences between our positions are great. Torture has never been proven to avert harm to thousands or millions of people. Intelligence operatives tell us that torture in secret prisons has prevented attacks, but when asked to prove their point they draw the curtain of secrecy across the matter. If one balances an individual's right to be free from torture against the hypothetical prospect of saving many lives, the individual is likely to come out on the short side of the equation. However a judge— or anybody else—who wants us to quantify harms and benefits should insist that the counting be done in the open by verifiable means.

One of Judge Posner's most endearing qualities, in his scholarship and judicial activity, is his dedication to reliable and verifiable empirical research. In his discussion of torture, he seems to have taken leave of his most cherished academic values. His view is not visibly rooted in the long history of coerced interrogation, nor in present-day analysis of psychological and physical science. And, of course, his conclusions cannot be based on rigorous analysis of the data about current and recent infliction of torture, because the torturers refuse to give out that sort of information: They just say, "trust us."

In any event, the "individual versus the many" equation is false. When it is revealed that the United States openly and unapologetically engages in torture, and that even when its leaders condemn torture the perpetrators of it go unpunished, there is measurable harm. When the most powerful nation excuses torture, its use obtains a certain cachet that ensures it will be used in many other places. All of us remember the adverse impact on United States short-run and long-run interests from the Abu Ghraib revelations. These, too, are harms. Judge Posner is trying to count and weigh things that can only be assigned values in a subjective way. Then, he loads the scale by always making the individual who is about to suffer from governmental conduct overcome the huge burden of comparing his or her poor lot to the massive interests of government and society. This form of counting reminds one of the nineteenth and early twentieth century prosecutions of workers for trying to organize unions. The workers were guilty of conspiracy in restraint of trade for withholding their labor because everybody *knew* that the individual worker must bargain with the individual corporation.

I think we should begin from the premise enshrined in transnational law—written and customary. The norm against torture is non-derogable. Torture cannot be justified by reasons of state or the defense of superior orders. A torturer, like a killer, may have a defense of justification or excuse, as those concepts appear in the general criminal law. The defense of justification requires proof by the accused, generally by a preponderance of the evidence, that the otherwise prohibited conduct was the lesser of evils, as would be the case if the accused pleaded self-defense. The conduct may be excused if the accused suffers from a mental disability or was unable to form the intent to break the law.

Judge Posner's shock the conscience test revives Justice Frankfurter's now discredited method for judging outrageous police conduct.[98] The test has been discredited in the context of constitutional adjudication because it relies entirely on subjective impressions. When, as Judge Posner seems to argue, the "shock" is to be "weighed" against some potential harm from not doing torture, the alleged test is too vague to be applied in any consistent way, and provides a broad avenue for escaping liability.

In any case, any proposed test for permitting torturers to escape criminal liability must survive the "void for vagueness" test. The Supreme Court has held that a jury instruction permitting jurors to assess liability based on such ideas as conduct being "reprehensible" is unconstitutionally vague because it provides no guidance to potential defendants, prosecutors, judges and jurors.[99] Such a standard is not a norm at all, but simply an excuse for decision makers to act as they wish.

Another of Judge Posner's themes is the authority to detain and punish. In his discussion, he moves seamlessly from descriptive to prescriptive statements, thus concealing fundamental issues about fairness and reliable outcomes. He notes that aliens outside the United States have historically been held not entitled to habeas corpus relief in U.S. courts. The Supreme Court has even held that an alien who is physically present but who has not been legally admitted may not be entitled to habeas relief. Posner also notes that under current law, an alien who is a suspected terrorist can probably be "detained indefinitely without violation of the Constitution."[100] He goes on to say that unlawful combatants can be denied most constitutional rights granted to criminal defendants and, if they are foreigners, can be denied habeas corpus as well. If caught in another land and detained outside of the United States, suspected terrorists have no prisoner of war rights and could even be tortured without violating the Constitution, because the Constitution only applies to foreigners within the United States when it applies to foreigners at all.

Posner's entire argument on this score seems uninformed by the Hague and Geneva Conventions, which have long defined and protected the rights and duties of combatants and noncombatants during transnational armed conflict. During conflicts not covered by these conventions, for example uprisings within a nation-state, detailed rules of transnational law—many of them discussed in earlier essays in this book—lay out the obligations of sovereigns to act in ways that protect individuals and help to ensure reliable outcomes.

In discussing the rights of U.S. citizens, Judge Posner believes that habeas corpus should be available. He justifies this view based on his own weighing of the risks and benefits of unreviewable detention. However, given what he sees as the entirely new conditions of today, he says that any detained citizen should have the burden of proving that he or she is not a terrorist. In this context, he also argues that conditions may warrant holding suspects incommunicado and permitting the government to rely on secret evidence.

To address Posner's broadest contentions, one should look back at events since September 11, 2001. The Bush administration has attempted to create a legal no man's land, in which people who are imprisoned and interrogated are held incommunicado, even away from visits by such agencies as the Red Cross. They do not have counsel. They have no access to any evidence that might prove they are being wrongly held. If they are mistreated—and all agree that many of them have been—they have no recourse to any judicial forum.

Forget, for the moment, humanitarian-based rules. In the legal landscape envisioned by the administration, all the rules that are designed to produce reliable outcomes have been suspended in favor of unreviewable executive discretion, the exercise of which is justified by generalized statements that these efforts are necessary.

It is true that habeas corpus, as a common law writ, requires jurisdiction over the persons of the detainee and the custodian, and that detentions outside U.S. territory are problematic under these conditions. The Supreme Court has rebuffed the effort to declare the American military base at Guantanamo entirely off-limits to judicial review. One might greatly expand the scope of review by recognizing that in analogous contexts the territory of the United States is a broad concept. For example, in *United States v. Corey*,[101] the defendant's sexual abuse of his stepdaughter in any apartment that had been rented by the U.S. Embassy in the Philippine was within the "special . . . territorial jurisdiction of the United States."[102]

However, if one is concerned, as Judge Posner claims to be, with reliable outcomes, then in a world riven by conflict with U.S. military and intelligence agents acting all over the world, one should address the issue from a different direction altogether. The root question is how one can secure obedience to peremptory norms of international law in the current context. Since World War II, and in light of its lessons, the arc of history tends towards vindicating claims for justice, and punishing those who engage in torture and crimes against humanity, even as they invoke technical defenses to liability.

Those who plan illegal renditions and torture are in the jurisdiction of U.S. courts. The intelligence product of this illegality flows back to them. Judge Posner has no suggestions on how courts might play their constitutional role in reviewing that sort of behavior. By describing the apparent paucity of existing legal tools, and mixing in his own prescriptions, he avoids the question entirely.

When he discusses the fourth amendment protection against unlawful searches and seizures, Judge Posner is similarly shy about judges doing what the Framers envisioned and the Constitution seems to command. He suggests that any search and seizure (with or without a warrant) is acceptable if reasonable. Reasonableness depends on the nature of the threat and the nature of the search or seizure. Posner argues that the less intrusive the search and seizure, the more reasonable, and that electronic surveillance and data mining are minimally intrusive. In determining the level of intrusion, Posner considers time, space, convenience, fear, and embarrassment. He suggests that, where machines are performing the search and seizure, and the information cannot be used for purposes beyond information gathering, there is no need for fear or embarrassment. However, this assumes that the information is secure and would never be abused. He insists that abuse would not occur, given the transparency of the government today. He reasons from the premise that electronic surveillance and data mining are minimally intrusive that, given the "present emergency," the government could constitutionally "intercept *all* electronic communications inside or outside the United States," as well as conduct warrantless electronic surveillance within the United States, and perform data mining on all databases containing voluntarily surrendered personal information.[103]

To accept the first premise of this astounding argument, one would need to overrule a dozen or so Supreme Court decisions that have construed the fourth amendment's text. One would also have to reject—without any evidence other than Judge Posner's conclusory assertions—the findings of studies that have documented the malign effects on political and religious liberty of unharnessed governmental surveillance.[104] There are two parts to that amendment—the warrant clause and the reasonableness clause. I have addressed this issue in another essay in this book.

What I have said contains answers to Judge Posner's claims about the "present emergency." He invokes the term as a claim that the world has changed in some fundamental way and the danger he sees is paramount. Certainly, terrorism has had center stage in public discourse. Although by late 2006, voters' concern with a mounting death toll in Iraq and economic issues began to eclipse it. If we are speaking of death risks, ordinary crime, unsafe products, and environmental depredation kill many times more people than terrorism, yet few propose remaking the constitutional compact in order to deal with them.

I earlier listed emergencies of various kinds that the American nation has faced and survived. Judge Posner does not delve into history to prove to us that the "present emergency" is more dire than any of those, nor why we should adjust our constitutional compass in response to it.

A part of the problem with Judge Posner's argument is his continued reliance on a skewed system for evaluating risks and benefits. One consequence of wholesale data collection has been that people have been kicked off airplanes due to no fly lists. People have been detained for no reason except that their names wound up on watch lists maintained by the FBI. In one recent case, a civil rights lawyer in Colorado was repeatedly stopped by police, handcuffed, and held while the local and state officers contacted the FBI, learned first that he was on a watch list, and were then authorized to let him go on his way. With the wholesale surveillance has come the spate of public warnings to report suspicious activity. To whom? Well, to relatively untrained police officers for a start. Recently, five Muslim clerics were fulfilling their religious duties by praying in an airport waiting lounge. They were arrested and detained. They missed their flight. After a number of hours, the police let them go. They posed no harm to anyone. One might argue that in each of these incidents, the inconvenience to specific people was relatively minor compared to some ill-defined risk of a major terrorist event and, therefore, every single instance of invasion of personal liberty, taken one by one, would be permissible. Such an argument misses the point of constitutional governance.

It is also difficult to see a justification for claiming that government is transparent. I have litigated national security issues for forty years, and have found that the executive branch is as opaque as it can possibly be. The history of national security litigation, discussed at many places in this book, bears out this observation. The FBI has many law enforcement tools. Its recent history of putting those tools to use has been an embarrassment. The FBI spent millions to create a computer system for organizing data and the entire project has been a failure. FBI agents continues to interview witnesses, take notes, and create written reports in the same way that they did fifty years ago. In 2004, I tried a case involving tens of thousands of telephone intercepts. The FBI's recording methods were mostly classified, but the information that we did obtain showed that recordings were lost and damaged, equipment routinely failed, and that millions of dollars were wasted on equipment that quickly became obsolete. The FBI agent in charge of the technology during ten crucial years had almost no formal education or equivalent experience in computer technology. The technology of unregulated surveillance creates a sea of raw data in which the collectors are drowning. My thought: Why give additional and unregulated power to people who cannot effectively use the tools they already have?

Judge Posner's recipe for regulating religious exercise, speech, and publication is a curious brew. He contends that advocacy of certain ideas, such as "radical [Islam]," should be sufficient to allow the government to monitor people who attend services and speeches where such views are espoused.[105] Again, he believes the benefit of investigation—presumably, identifying potential terrorists—outweighs the potential harm of intimidating people who might wish to practice their religion by attending Islamic services or sharing Islamic views.

Judge Posner believes that advocacy of certain aspects of "radical Islam" has no redeeming social value. He claims that Islam is more likely to produce violence than Christianity, as "Jesus Christ was the opposite of a warrior priest; Muhammad, in contrast, was a general."[106] He concludes that investigating Islamic advocacy, as well as profiling Muslims, is practical and therefore acceptable.

One theme of this book is that thinking about terror requires a sense of history. Judge Posner's characterizations of religious views and origins lacks that sense. Judge Posner was raised Jewish; his bar mitzvah was on January 11, 1952.[107] Presumably, he is familiar with the Jewish reverence for fighters. If he attended any Passover Seders, he would have dipped a finger in wine and counted out—with some satisfaction—the plagues that G*d visited on the Egyptians. As for Christianity, it perplexes many people that so kindly a fellow as Jesus seems to have been advertised as justifying killings in Ireland, Bosnia, and Iraq, not to mention the religious wars from the medieval period onwards. Posner does not discuss King David, the Inquisition, puritanical witch hunts, or the like. He similarly does not address who would be determining which aspects of religious speech have value, if the government were allowed to infiltrate and monitor assemblies involving any advocacy of beliefs that he or some other official determined to be without value.

Perhaps Judge Posner has not read Mark Twain's *War Prayer*, which captures the spirit of much killing done in the name of this or that deity:

> O Lord our Father, our young patriots, idols of our hearts, go forth to battle—be Thou near them! With them—in spirit—we also go forth from the sweet peace of our beloved firesides to smite the foe. O Lord our God, help us to tear their soldiers to bloody shreds with our shells; help us to cover their smiling fields with the pale forms of their patriot dead; help us to drown the thunder of the guns with the shrieks of their wounded, writhing in pain; help us to lay waste their humble homes with a hurricane of fire; help us to wring the hearts of their unoffending widows with unavailing grief; help us to turn them out roofless with little children to wander unfriended the wastes of their desolated land in rags and hunger and thirst, sports of the sun flames of summer and the icy winds of winter, broken in spirit, worn with travail, imploring Thee for the refuge of the grave and denied it—for our sakes who adore Thee, Lord, blast their hopes, blight their lives, protract their bitter pilgrimage, make heavy their steps, water their way with their tears, stain the white snow with the blood of their wounded feet! We ask it, in the spirit of love, of Him Who is the Source of Love, and Who is the ever-faithful refuge and friend of all that are sore beset and seek His aid with humble and contrite hearts. Amen.[108]

Islamic scripture contains many martial passages. However, as historian Juan Cole points out, it also speaks of harmony and peaceful coexistence. Indeed, as Professor Cole has noted, in the Middle Ages, Jews in Islamic communities were regarded as "people of the book,"[109] and not persecuted as they were in Christian Europe. Almost any religious ideology can be and has been invoked as the basis for violence and, in almost every collection of scripture, words will be found to cover the situation.

Judge Posner's move from an inaccurate perception of religious history to an endorsement of ethnic profiling is similarly unsupportable. The prospect of terrorism is daunting, but no more potentially dangerous than a dozen other potential social ills. Even before the events of September 11, 2001, ethnic prejudice was not only at work but operated in a misleading way. Immediately after the April 19, 1995, bombing of the Murrah Building in Oklahoma City, authorities rounded up Arabs as suspects, without probable cause and based solely on preconception.

Judge Posner also considers whether advocacy of violent acts can or should be banned. He concludes that such speech can cause harm, both imminently and in the long run, and deploys the analogy of someone who published the recipe for a hydrogen bomb. He does not examine the difference between aiding citizens and nations in building a weapon that could kill millions and stating dislike for those same millions. Posner concludes that there need be no imminent threat to prevent certain types of advocacy and, while it would currently be unwise to prevent such speech, it would not be unconstitutional.

I have spent decades defending those who advocate dissident views. I recognize that hateful speech that endorses violence poses a genuine problem in an open society. Posner's hydrogen bomb analogy is inapt and unhelpful. The international community has methods for dealing with nations who want to make a hydrogen bomb. Those methods may be of limited utility in practice, but devising and using them has nothing to do with making constitutional doctrine about speech.

In an earlier discussion, I saluted the Supreme Court's emphatic declaration the state can punish only advocacy done with the intent to cause imminent lawless violence, and that in fact creates a clear and present danger of such violence. I noted that the test Judge Posner proposes—a kind of formless balancing—had in fact resulted in manifest injustice during times of past alleged emergencies.

While Posner does not believe that advocacy speech needs to be prevented at the present time, he does advocate the prevention of certain types of publication. He proposes that the government should be able to enjoin, in advance, any publication that deliberately leaks any national security information that has been classified according to proper statutory criteria. Such criteria do not now exist but could and should be developed. Courts should then review the government's proposed reasons for preventing publication in camera. By "in camera," he may also mean ex parte. If so, then the lamentable history of government lying to judges about the basis for its action must be considered. If "in camera" simply means shielded from public view by a protective order, then the procedure may be adequate.

The substance of Posner's proposal is not adequate. He seems to want more statutory definitions of what government may keep secret, more injunctions against publishing, and more punishment of publishers. Executive branch officers have often expressed the urge to censor and punish those who publish inconvenient truths. Under present law, they hesitate to do so. Instead, they attack the reporters and publishers as unpatriotic. Reporters, editors, and publishers are chilled by these assaults.

Thus, there is an uneasy truce that in fact results in less information about governmental wrongdoing than seems optimal. In 2002, as the George W. Bush administration conducted its fervent campaign to go to war in Iraq, many media outlets hesitated to examine and criticize the factual, legal, and geopolitical basis for warmaking. When media sources reported on warrantless national security wiretapping, they were accused of disloyalty.

Judge Posner's proposal to add formal sanctions to the evidently effective informal ones is unnecessary and unwise. In the present emergency, an emboldened and not a frightened free press seems a better solution, and one that the Constitution's authors would approve.

Judge Posner also considers the right to conceal from the government personal information voluntarily given to others. In order to function in today's society—get a driver's license, open a bank account, take out a loan, have a medical exam, compute and pay taxes—people are compelled to reveal an enormous amount of personal information. Posner considers whether the government should be allowed to data mine such information. Among the objections to data mining are that people may be inhibited to speak or act freely or that personal information will be used for purposes other than that for which it was ostensibly gathered.

Posner emphasizes that, in data mining personal information, a machine reviews the raw batches of data. Humans are involved only when some information has been flagged. He analogizes this process to the use of a drug-sniffing dog at an airport. He asserts that electronic data mining thus mitigates the fear of embarrassment and the censorship of candor. He moves from this assumption to say that the only objection to such electronic practices stems from a concern that the information will be abused for non-national security purposes. As to this, he presumes that the information will not be so abused.[110] He discounts other objections beyond misuse and minimizes to the point of asserted irrelevance the history of governmental abuse of personal information.

He asserts that people operate these days with a lower expectation of privacy in a society where personal information is required on a regular basis. He reasons that, just as people do not mind doctors looking at their bodies because they are only medically interested, people will not mind government workers looking at their private information because they are only interested in protecting national security. He concludes that the invasion of privacy will be repaid with increased security, again assuming that value added in one aspect of a person's life can replace value lost in another.

These assertions and arguments are castles in the air. All of us share details, even intimate ones, about ourselves for a number of purposes. In those encounters, we are often given and often expect assurances that the data will not be used for any other purpose. Indeed, there are elaborate structures to guarantee compartmentalization, and Judge Posner takes little if any account of them. For example, governmental dissemination of tax return information is limited by statute. Our doctor, lawyer, and religious advisor visits are governed by evidentiary privileges, professional obligation, and (in many instances) by detailed statutes and case law principles. We submit to a search at the airport in order to board a particular flight.

"Data mining" is another name for taking all of this kind of information and combining it to form a picture of someone's beliefs and associations in order to assess supposed national security risk. Someone who proposes to breach all these historic barriers should be required to explain why, and in some detail, but Judge Posner does not do this. The idea that disclosure of private facts is presumptively wrongful is not a new invention. It dates, in modern garb, to an 1890 *Harvard Law Review* article by Charles Warren and Louis Brandeis.

Beyond the many academic studies of how personal privacy has been eroded in the past several decades,[111] we can each delve into our own experiences to see how radical a departure Judge Posner proposes. I suspect that every reader of these words has some private data about his or her activities and thoughts that he or she very much wishes would remain private and not shared with strangers—let alone with government investigators. In a time when identity theft is front-page news, I think people are more concerned with how data is shared in the computer age than Judge Posner assumes.

Another problem is data mining is the incorrect assumption that two plus two equals four in the world of computer algorithms. A piece of private data from one source, coupled with a piece of private data from another source, can produce an insight or suspicion about a broader picture than either item of data suggests by itself. Lawyers put together puzzle pieces in almost every trial to yield a coherent picture that no one puzzle piece would reveal. That is what data miners do. Trial lawyers also know that given the same puzzle pieces, two observers can and often do come to different conclusions.

A person who tells his regular physician that he engages in extramarital sex, and his psychiatrist that his sexual dalliances are with other men, willingly gives that information, plus his Social Security number, to those providers so that the visits are covered by insurance. That same person may disclose a history of road accidents and traffic tickets to an insurance company, again along with a Social Security number. He may then go online to a chat group that focuses on religious or political issues and discuss political ideas. If he holds a professional license, say as a doctor, he may have disclosed many personal details to licensing agencies. And so it goes. Posner is saying that it matters little to the individual or the society as a whole that government can mine and cross-reference this data and use it for investigative purposes. Perhaps in an age where there are few secrets because of the Internet, this sort of thing is very easy to do. But, when our hypothetical person sits down for a tax audit, or is being looked at by airline security personnel, government possession of a complete picture of one's private life will legitimately make one uncomfortable.

Judge Posner's reliance on the nonhuman character of computer data mining contradicts elementary principles of judicial reasoning. Let us begin with an airport sniffer dog. There is a lot of controversy about such dogs, because canines do not have a natural love for cocaine odor or bomb residue odor. They have to be trained by humans. They learn a system of rewards for making good guesses. After training the dog, humans bring the dog to the airport at a chosen time to inspect chosen baggage. Dog searches are not indisputably reliable.[112] Therefore, the analogy is not apt.

Computer searches are designed by humans to operate on data chosen by humans and to evaluate that data under criteria chosen by humans. The humans in charge from September 11, 2001, onwards have demonstrably used impermissible ethnic criteria, behaved unlawfully with respect to important personal freedoms, relied on bad intelligence, lied about important issues, and sought to impose a veil of secrecy on governmental operations. Regardless of what one thinks about the wisdom or propriety of the human activity, the results of data mining are worth no more than the credibility of the people who plan it, do it, and use it. This is a fundamental idea of the law of evidence: A document or tangible object is worth no more in evidence than the credibility of a sponsoring witness. Trial judges and trial lawyers apply this lesson every day, and appellate judges do so every so often. If the police officer testifies about a gun he took from the defendant, the gun is irrelevant unless we believe the officer about where he got it.

The Supreme Court has developed a well-articulated vision of privacy, as essential to personal security, freedom of thought, the inviolability of personal intimate relations, and other elements of "individual right."[113] Judge Posner fails as well to take account of this course of decision.

In sum, Judge Posner's prescription for dealing with individual terrorism has many and dangerous side effects. To say that more intelligence officers and other government agents should operate under even less demanding controls, when the present system is so obviously flawed, makes no sense at all. The fundamental principles of separation of powers and judicial review are not born of the Founding Fathers' baseless dreams. They rest in some part upon a historically and socially determined view that people are rational and that institutions can be. They rest upon an argument that review, debate—checks and balances, if you will—are a good idea because they lead to more reliable results in the real world. If an executive officer wants to search, detain, or punish someone, requiring him or her to present evidence that will be evaluated fairly by a neutral judge increases the chance that the decision will be made reliably as well as fairly. For those who wrote the Constitution, this was common sense, and it remains so today. Just as the constitutional answer to "dangerous speech" is "more speech" and not suppression, the rational procedural response to danger is "more due process."

There may be arguments for deference to the duties, powers and expertise of executive officers, but deference is not surrender. Deference cannot properly be accorded when, in addition to claiming limitless power, the executive argues that even the nature and potential uses of such power must remain secret.

In *Marbury v. Madison*, Chief Justice Marshall wrote of the heavy presumption that executive action is subject to judicial scrutiny. However, he also acknowledged that under the Constitution, there are certain acts that the President might take or authorize for which he is "accountable only to his country in his political character and to his own conscience."[114] Marshall chose his words carefully. He did not say that the President may act like a king, free of all constraint. Rather he said that within narrow limits the President is subject only to the constraints imposed by the political branches of government; that is, by the legal duties that the Congress might impose, by impeachment if necessary and, ultimately, by the electoral process. Secrecy traduces all constitutional mechanisms of accountability; for it prevents them from taking place.[115]

I would say to Judge Posner: Yes, the Constitution is not a suicide pact. To me, that means we should not blow it and ourselves up in the vain hope of quashing terrorism by unconstitutional means. More prosaically, I invite him to read John Henry Faulk's story of the chicken snake, in the Foreword to this book.

G. Military Commissions, Fairness, and America's Image

The points I have made above are, it seems to me, underscored by the United States' efforts to deal with alleged foreign terrorists held in Guantanamo or in secret prisons in theaters of armed conflict. In October 2006, the Congress passed the Military Commissions Act (MCA), a response to the Supreme Court's decision in *Hamdan v. Rumsfeld*. The Act sets up a complex system for trying people detained in Guantanamo and other facilities. Under the Act, people designated as unlawful enemy combatants will be tried by military commissions. The commissions need not follow rules of evidence, and can accept and consider evidence obtained by coercion under certain circumstances. The trial procedures to be followed will be worked out in litigation over the coming months and years, as civilian and military lawyers represent clients caught up in the system.

It is already apparent that prosecutors intend to use hearsay evidence derived from "interviews" of people captured and held. The interrogators, the translators, and the persons interviewed will be unavailable for cross-examination. As all trial lawyers know, the hearsay rule is designed to ensure reliable outcomes by excluding evidence that poses a high degree of danger of unreliability. The out-of-court declarant may not have accurately seen, remembered, or related the event. These difficulties are magnified when the hearsay report involves translation. The declarant may not have personal knowledge of the event: there is a big difference between "I know A took up arms" and "I saw A take up arms." One must keep in mind that most of those detained at Guantanamo—nine out of ten—were turned in to authorities by their countrymen in order to receive a bounty from the American authorities. The going rate in Afghanistan was $5,000.

The offenses for which these detainees may be tried include violations of the treaty-based laws of war and of provisions that echo federal criminal law prohibitions on giving material support to terrorism. One difficulty is that the offense definitions criminalize the conduct of people who took up arms against the American invasions of Afghanistan and Iraq, although under international law a person who shoots at an invader is, under most circumstances, immune from punishment for doing so. As one military lawyer put it during a seminar on the legal rules formulated by the Bush administration on enemy combatants, "We can shoot at them, but it is a crime for them to shoot back."

In the MCA, Congress has created a class of persons to be tried for crimes committed against American interests. It has ignored the constitutional language that provides that "the trial of all crimes shall be by jury," and that "in all criminal prosecutions" the accused shall enjoy certain rights. To be sure, Congress has authority to prescribe rules for trial of cases arising in the "land and naval forces," but that language means that some people can be tried for some offenses under military justice procedures. Those procedures guarantee substantial procedural fairness and judicial review.

The MCA begins with the assertion that a military commissions is "a regularly constituted court, affording all the necessary 'judicial guarantees which are recognized as indispensable by civilized peoples'" for purposes of the Geneva Convention.[116] The tension between that statement of intent and the detailed procedures in the Act and regulations issued under it raise challenging issues. The Supreme Court has held that a congressional statute will not be construed to deny basic rights unless the Congress has unequivocally said so.[117] At that point, of course, constitutional inquiry becomes necessary.

There are cases arising in World War II in which the Supreme Court approved the use of military commissions under certain circumstances. The litigation over the MCA will determine how far Congress and the President can take those exceptional cases and create a system of trials that fall below elemental standards of fairness. The leading case is *Ex parte Quirin*,[118] in which the Court upheld use of a military commission to try German saboteurs. Interestingly, as the Supreme Court pointed out in *Hamdan v. Rumsfeld*,[119] the Supreme Court exercised its review power in *Quirin* while the trial proceedings were pending in order to determine the legality of what was going on. *Quirin* holds that Congress had authorized the President to create and invoke military commissions to try offenses under circumstances permitted by the laws of war. Thus, congressional authorization is the first step. *Hamdan* held that absent such authorizations, the President has no power to create military commissions whenever he pleases; his power is limited by the Constitution and by principles of international law. The MCA purports to authorize military commissions. It does not, and could not constitutionally, authorize procedures that deny due process and violate fundamental norms of international law.

In thinking about these points, consider the results of a British Broadcasting Corporation poll conducted between November 3, 2006, and January 9, 2007. Pollsters interviewed more than 26,000 people in Argentina, Australia, Brazil, Britain, Chile, China, Egypt, France, Germany, Hungary, India, Indonesia, Italy, Kenya, Lebanon, Mexico, Nigeria, the Philippines, Poland, Portugal, Russia, South Korea, Turkey, the United Arab Emirates, and the United States. Pollsters reported that most respondents, including those in the United States, disagreed with U.S. foreign and military policy. Respondents thought that U.S. conduct in the Middle East "provokes more conflict than it prevents." Two-thirds of respondents disapproved of the way that Guantanamo detainees are being treated.[120]

The poll is no doubt subject to caveats about sample size and polling technique, but its essential findings reflect the attitudes being displayed in many forums around the world. The view that U.S. proceedings against alleged terrorists are tinged with impropriety can harm the international struggle for human rights in several concrete ways. As we have seen, a sometimes well-founded criticism of proceedings against alleged terrorists—state-sponsored or otherwise—is that the political motivation of the pursuer reveals that the claim of human rights violations is hypocritical or cynical.

After all, to repeat the observation of Judge Jerome Frank, "The legal system is not what it says, but what it does." The discretionary application of criminal law is perhaps the most cogent illustration of this point. One reason to support the creation and operation of truly transnational tribunals is that they are more likely to reflect, in their substantive rules and in the cases brought to them, the values of the broader transnational community. Such broad-based influence tends to flatten out unbecoming disparities. A transnational court has a chance to escape domination by the great powers whose malign influence stunted the growth of human rights law until the early twentieth century.

Such a court could have procedures that permit access by victims of state-sponsored and other terrorism without an unreviewable veto power by prosecutors. This is, to be sure, a difficult issue. In the United States, we have a system in which public prosecutors are almost always the final arbiters about whether a given case will or will not be brought. Other countries allow some degree of participation by private lawyers representing victims' interests. The system of private prosecution for felony once dominated English criminal procedure, and was replaced by public policing and prosecutorial systems beginning in earnest in the 1700s.

In Spain, a private individual can commence a prosecution under certain circumstances. As discussed in an earlier essay in this book, the courageous human rights lawyer Juan Garcés filed criminal charges against Augusto Pinochet. The examining magistrate was Baltasar Garzón, who permitted the case to go forward. For several years, the Spanish state apparatus failed to support the case and took steps to derail it, but those efforts were not successful. The precise legal mechanisms of these events is not so important as the lesson. All systems of public prosecution run the dual risks of improvidently proceeding and unwisely refusing to proceed. The former risk can be controlled by the judges who hear the case, if they are armed with legal rules to constrain unlawful discretion. The latter risk can be met only by rules that permit victims and the broader community to present cases and to require that the allegations be taken seriously.

The United States' objection to the International Criminal Court has focused on the issue of prosecutorial discretion, but for the wrong reasons. The U.S. officials have not wanted to take the risk that Americans will be prosecuted. They are worried about "too much justice" rather than "not enough."[121]

H. Conclusion

"Not what it says, but what it does" is an aphorism with many instructive meanings. The way a legal system is operated says a great deal about the sovereign who runs it. To say "we are against terrorism" and then to prosecute selectively or unfairly weakens or contradicts the message.

This book is born of an idea: The surest and best defense of democratic institutions is to respect them. Some years ago, Kevin McCarthy and I wrote a play about Irish lawyers, and we put these words into the mouth of Ireland's "liberator," Dan O'Connell:

You, sir, in the front row. You look well-fed enough to be a lawyer. You certainly know this simple, beautiful and inflammatory notion. Every time you stand before a jury in a criminal case, you are drawing all over again the most important line the law can draw—between the idea of reasonable doubt and the reality of some poor soul on trial for his life or his liberty. And you take on the sacred duty to persuade that jury to set aside intuition and prejudice and walk that line.

John Mage, reviewing the autobiography of the great progressive lawyer Victor Rabinowitz, wrote, "In the U.S. system, all significant legal and political questions are given legal form. This has proved effective for its rulers, not least by limiting in advance the types of permissible answers." Mage is right and therefore one must understand both the possibilities in and the limits on struggle over principles of legal ideology.

The "legal form" is most significant in criminal cases. The way a society fashions and applies the rules of criminal law provides the most basic possible information about how its leaders view the human condition.

As for Mage's other comment, about limits: For the two halves of this book—the two basic kinds of terrorism—the lesson to learn is about immanence and transcendence. In defining and combating terrorism, the task is first to understand and even-handedly apply the principles we already know and understand. We devise definitions with a sense of history. We respect boundaries about procedural fairness and democratic rights. This is the inward-looking process of seeing what is immanent, inherent, indwelling. We must also recognize that any decision made in the name of any sovereign is a moment in history, and that the present is also history. We are led to receive properly the lessons of the past by recognizing that those lessons will themselves be tested by events, now and in time to be. Judgments about the historic events now going on will be reviewed, and actions done based on that review. We should try to see those future, transcendent, effects in order to protect our children's future.

I end this book where it, and I, began. I spoke these words in the immediate aftermath of September 11, 2001:

Both state-sponsored terrorism and insurgent group terrorism are criminal. I have no doubt that there must exist the duty and the right and the power to investigate and to judge the killings of innocent people. But the legitimate right to conduct those investigations, and to inflict that punishment, lies only with those who accept the following obligations:

194

- To struggle against all forms of terrorism, by whomever committed
- To use means that honor and do not trample upon the tradition of human rights
- To understand the reasons people will follow the lead of those who sponsor terrorism, and
- To support the legitimate struggle of those people to live in dignity in accordance with those norms of human rights that have become norms of international law in the past three score years.

To put the matter another way, the only kind of justice worthy of the name is social justice. Social justice includes both process and legitimacy. It includes process because that has been the lesson of history for three millennia. It includes process because we have seen the cost of doing otherwise. We have seen how the arrogance of power has detained people without probable cause, refused or subverted impartial judicial review of detention, and drowned out calls for reason and proof with strident cries for vengeance. Hundreds of people, perhaps more, are being held right now while our government disregards these guaranties. The department that calls itself Justice is using this excuse to repeal dozens of guaranties of procedural fairness, not only in so-called terrorism investigations, but across the board.

Social justice includes legitimacy because the proper exercise of force can only be in the context of redressing the social ills that have led people to follow false echoes.

Notes

1. 22 U.S.C. § 2656f(d) (2000). *See, e.g.*, United States v. Afshari, 426 F.3d 1150, 1154 n.4 (9th Cir. 2005), *reh'g denied*, 446 F.3d 915 (2006), *cert. denied*, 127 S. Ct. 930 (2007).
2. *Quoted in* Tigar, *Defending*, 74 U. Tex. L. Rev. 101 (1995).
3. *The Mideast Domino Theory*, Wash. Post, Aug. 20, 2006, at B1. Byman and Pollack are at the Brookings Institution; they released a report on Iraq in Feb. 2007. *See* Karen DeYoung & Thomas Ricks, *No U.S. Backup Strategy for Iraq*, Wash. Post, Mar. 5, 2007, at A1.
4. Basil Davidson, The Black Man's Burden 227 (1992). This book, which draws on Davidson's long experience in Africa and the Balkans, is an indispensable guide to understanding the divisions and difficulties now being faced in Middle Eastern societies.
5. The quoted lines are from William Butler Yeats's poem, *The Second Coming* (1920), and were written about the social turbulence of that time. The poem continues, "Mere anarchy is loosed upon the world, The blood-dimmed tide is loosed, and everywhere, The ceremony of innocence is drowned." The text is

available in SELECTED POEMS AND TWO PLAYS OF WILLIAM BUTLER YEATS (M.L. Rosenthal ed., 1962), and online with a Google search.

6. BASIL DAVIDSON, THE BLACK MAN'S BURDEN 227–28 (1992).
7. The column and reportage on the press conference is at http://www.slate.com/id/2148197/ under the title *What a Moronic President*.
8. MICHAEL SCHEUER, IMPERIAL HUBRIS: WHY THE WEST IS LOSING THE WAR ON TERROR (2004).
9. United States v. Antonelli Fireworks, 155 F.2d 631, 662 (2d Cir. 1946) (dissenting opinion).
10. Sara Sun Beale, *The New Media's Influence on Criminal Justice Policy: How Market-Driven News Promotes Punitiveness*, 48 WM. & MARY L. REV. 397 (2006).
11. *See generally* OLIVIER CARRÉ & GÉRARD MICHAUD. 1983. LES FRÈRES MUSULMANS: EGYPTE ET SYRIE, 1928–1982 (1983); RICHARD P. MITCHELL, THE SOCIETY OF THE MUSLIM BROTHERS (1969).
12. *See generally* Nicole Nice-Petersen, *Justice for the "Designated": The Process That Is Due to Alleged U.S. Financiers of Terrorism*, 93 GEO. L.J. 1387 (2005).
13. In pre-revolutionary Cuba, racial discrimination was a major social issue.
14. JOHN RUSKIN, THE JOYS OF FESOLE 291 (1891) (published together with the essay from which this quotation is drawn, entitled *Our Fathers Have Told Us: The Bible of Amiens*. There are other versions of this utterance. I first heard it in 1962 during a Parliamentary debate, quoted by Konni Zilliacus, M.P.
15. Jt. Anti-Fascist Refugee Comm. v. McGrath, 341 U.S. 123, 172 n.19 (1951) (concurring opinion).
16. 8 U.S.C. § 1189 (2000).
17. 22 U.S.C. § 2656f(d) (2000).
18. People's Mojahedin Org. of Iran v. U.S. Dep't of State, 182 F.3d 17, 20 (D.C. Cir. 1999).
19. United States v. Coplon, 185 F.2d 629, 637 (2d Cir. 1950).
20. The reported decisions in the case are United States v. Afshari, 209 F. Supp.2d 1045 (C.D. Calif. 2002), *reversed*, 426 F.3d 1150 (9th Cir. 2005), *on denial of reh'g*, 446 F.3d 915 (9th Cir. 2006), *cert. denied*, 127 S. Ct. 930 (2007).Humanitarian Law Project v. Deaprtment of Justice, 393 F.3d 902 (9th Cir. 2004).
21. Greg Winter, *Aiding Friend or Foe Is Issue in Case*, N.Y. TIMES, Mar. 22, 2002, at A13, col. 6.
22. Jt. Anti-Fascist Refugee Comm. v. McGrath, 341 U.S. 123, 172 n.19 (1951) (concurring opinion).
23. Decisions that undermined the use of "investigation" and "publicity" to target alleged subversion included Watkins v. United States, 354 U.S. 178 (1957). The legal landscape is well-described in THOMAS I. EMERSON, THE SYSTEM OF FREEDOM OF EXPRESSION, at chs. VIII, XV, XIX (1970).
24. United States v. Spock, 416 F.2d 165 (1st Cir. 1969).
25. *See, e.g.*, VICTOR NAVASKY, NAMING NAMES: THE SOCIAL COSTS OF MC-CARTHYISM (2003) (excellent study). On the use of unreliable evidence during this period, *see* Greene v. McElroy, 360 U.S. 474 (1959).
26. Yakus v. United States, 321 U.S. 414 (1944).
27. *See* Yakus v. United States, 321 U.S. 414 (1944) (in prosecution for violating price controls, defendant cannot claim controls invalid or improper in his criminal case; that claim must be made in an administrative hearing

challenging the controls when they are first issued; dissent by three Justices); Falbo v. United States, 320 U.S. 549 (1944) (refusal to submit to induction into armed forces not reviewable for defendant who did not exhaust all administrative remedies); Estep v. United States, 327 U.S. 114 (1946) (*Falbo* clarified and judicial review confirmed). On review in Selective Service cases, *see* Tigar & Zweben, *Selective Service: Some Certain Problems and Some Tentative Answers*, 37 GEO. WASH. L. REV. 433 (1969).

28. 367 U.S. 290 (1961), *discussed in* Spock, 416 F.2d at 171–73.

29. *See, e.g.*, Freedman v. Maryland, 380 U.S. 51 (1965).

30. 424 U.S. 669 (1976).

31. For information on a case involving Muslim charities, and in which several church groups are supporting the Muslim organizations, *see Criminalizing Compassion in the War on Terror: Muslim Charities and the Case of Dr. Rafil A. Dhafir*, mrzine.monthlyreview.org/hughes181106.html.

32. The article is available online at http://www.iht.com/articles/2006/12/04/opinion/edanna.php.

33. A good overview of any of these issues is HOWARD ZINN, A PEOPLE'S HISTORY OF THE UNITED STATES: 1492–PRESENT (2004). *See also* RICHARD DRINNON, REBEL IN PARADISE (1961).

34. See Professor David Cole's compelling historical narrative, *The New McCarthyism: Repeating History in the War on Terrorism*, 38 HARV. C.R.-C.L. L. REV. 1 (2003).

35. In addition to the Navasky book cited above, see two excellent books by the great civil liberties lawyer FRANK DONNER, THE AGE OF SURVEILLANCE: THE AIMS & METHODS OF AMERICA'S POLITICAL INTELLIGENCE SYSTEM (1980), and PROTECTORS OF PRIVILEGE: RED SQUADS AND POLITICAL REPRESSION IN URBAN AMERICA (1991). *See also* ALAN WESTIN, PRIVACY AND FREEDOM (1967).

36. Two thoughtful analyses of the first amendment issue are THOMAS EMERSON, TOWARD A GENERAL THEORY OF THE FIRST AMENDMENT (1966), and THOMAS EMERSON, THE SYSTEM OF FREEDOM OF EXPRESSION (1970).

37. This history is recounted in Boyd v. United States, 116 U.S. 616 (1886), a case that has since been overruled as to one of its legal doctrines but remains authoritative on the history and intent of the fourth amendment warrant clause.

38. John Wilkes had an exciting career: parliamentarian, dissident, pornographer. *See* ARTHUR CASH, JOHN WILKES: THE SCANDALOUS FATHER OF CIVIL LIBERTY (2006).

39. Silverman v. United States, 365 U.S. 505 (1961).

40. Katz v. United States, 389 U.S. 347 (1967). *See* WAYNE R. LaFAVE, JEROLD H. ISRAEL & NANCY J. KING, CRIMINAL PROCEDURE § 3.2 (4th ed. 2004).

41. The old requirement that a warrant cannot issue for "mere evidence," as distinct from contraband and fruits and instrumentalities of crime, has been abandoned. Warden v. Hayden, 387 U.S. 294 (1967).

42. FEDERALIST No. 45, *at* http://madison.thefreelibrary.com/Federalist-Papers-Authored-by-James-Madison/1-11.

43. 482 U.S. 691 (1987).

44. 18 U.S.C. §§ 2510–20 (2000). *See* WAYNE R. LaFAVE, JEROLD H. ISRAEL & NANCY J. KING, CRIMINAL PROCEDURE, ch. 4 (4th ed. 2004).

45. 394 U.S. 165 (1969). For some of the earlier history, in addition to the prior proceedings cited in *Alderman, see* Hoffa v. United States, 387 U.S. 231 (1967).
46. I presented an edited and annotated version of Edward Bennett Williams's oral argument in *Alderman/Ivanov in* PERSUASION: THE LITIGATOR'S ART, ch. 6, part 2 (1999).
47. 321 F. Supp. 424 (C.D. Calif. 1971).
48. United States v. United States District Court, 407 U.S. 297 (1972).
49. *See* James Risen & Eric Lichtblau, *Bush Lets U.S. Spy on Callers Without Courts,* N.Y. TIMES, Dec. 16, 2005, at A1 ("In 2004, according to the Justice Department, 1,754 warrants were approved under F.I.S.A."); Dan Eggen & Robert O'Harrow, Jr., *U.S. Steps up Secret Surveillance: FBI, Justice Dept. Increase Use of Wiretaps, Records Searches,* WASH. POST, Mar. 24, 2003, at A1 ("Attorney General John D. Ashcroft has also personally signed more than 170 'emergency foreign intelligence warrants,' three times the number authorized in the preceding 23 years, according to recent congressional testimony.").
50. The relevant procedural requirements are discussed in Matthew R. Hall, *Constitutional Regulation of National Security Investigation: Minimizing the Use of Unrelated Evidence,* 41 WAKE FOREST L. REV. 61 (2006). The inadequacy of minimization procedures in practice is borne out by my experience as counsel in national security cases.
51. Under the Speech or Debate Clause, members of both houses of Congress, "shall in all Cases, except Treason, Felony, and Breach of the Peace, be privileged from Arrest during their attendance at the Session of their Respective Houses, and in going to and from the same, and for any Speech or Debate in either House, they shall not be questioned in any other Place." U.S. CONST. art I, § 6, cl. 1. *See* United States v. Johnson, 383 U.S. 169 (1966) and United States v. Brewster, 408 U.S. 501 (1972).
52. The following discussion owes a great deal to the work of Natalie Hirt, my research assistant at Duke Law School.
53. RICHARD A. POSNER, NOT A SUICIDE PACT 7 (2006).
54. By analogy, consider the police and prosecutorial reaction to *Miranda v. Arizona,* which requires police warnings to an arrested person of rights to silence and to an attorney. Encouraged by judicial decisions taking a somewhat attenuated view of *Miranda,* police agencies devised stratagems to avoid its strictures. Consultants wrote manuals on techniques of evasion. This is a familiar pattern of behavior: bureaucratic resistance to norms that frustrate bureaucratic goals that are in tension with fundamental principle.
55. 372 U.S. 144, 160 (1963).
56. 378 U.S. 500 (1964).
57. Communist Party v. Subversive Activities Control Board, 367 U.S. 1 (1961).
58. 453 U.S. 280 (1981).
59. The analysis of what I have called the first myth owes a great deal to Louis Fisher, *President's Game: History Refutes Claims to Unlimited Power Over Foreign Affairs,* LEGAL TIMES, Dec. 4, 2006, as well as to the works that Fisher cites. In my article, *Judicial Power, the "Political Question Doctrine," and "Foreign Relations,"* 17 UCLA L. REV. 1135 (1970), *reprinted in* THE VIETNAM WAR AND INTERNATIONAL LAW, Vol. 3 (R. Falk ed., 1972), I discuss some of these issues.

60. 299 U.S. 304 (1936).
61. RICHARD POSNER, NOT A SUICIDE PACT 4 (2006).
62. *Id.* at 4.
63. Fisher notes that the Bush administration lawyers and a Boalt Hall law professor have made a similar error of analysis.
64. Louis Fisher, *President's Game: History Refutes Claims to Unlimited Power Over Foreign Affairs,* LEGAL TIMES, Dec. 4, 2006.
65. Zschernig v. Miller, 389 U.S. 429 (1968).
66. 299 U.S. at 318.
67. 175 U.S. 677 (1900).
68. Gilchrist v. Collector of Charleston, 10 Fed. Cas. 355 (No. 5,420) (C.C.D. S.C.).
69. Joseph Story, in his COMMENTARIES ON THE CONSTITUTION, noted both the embargo's constitutionality and its unwisdom. STORY, COMMENTARIES ON THE CONSTITUTION §§ 1284–86 (1833).
70. 10 Fed. Cas. at 359.
71. 10 Fed. Cas. at 361.
72. *Quoted in* David Wilson, Comment, 53 CAL. L. REV. 878 (1965), and *quoted in part in* Eric Schnapper, Book Review, 84 COLUM. L. REV. 1665, 1685 n.76 (1984), with a different source.
73. *See generally* Justice Ruth Bader Ginsburg & Susan Bloch, *Celebrating the 200th Anniversary of the Courts of the District of Columbia,* 90 GEO. L.J. 549 (2002).
74. You can hear a recording of that address on http://www.americanrhetoric .com/top100speechesall.html.
75. 299 U.S. at 319, *quoting* ANNALS OF CONG., p. 613 (6th Cong., 1st Sess., March 7, 1800).
76. John G. Kester, *Some Myths of United States Extradition Law,* 76 GEO. L.J. 1441 (1988).
77. 5 U.S. 137 (1803).
78. *See* United States v. Burr, 25 Fed.Cas. 30 (No. 14, 692d) (C.C.D. Va. 1807).
79. *See* United States v. Nixon, 418 U.S. 683 (1974).
80. Reynolds v. United States, 345 U.S. 1, 9-10 (1953).
81. 8 WIGMORE, EVIDENCE § 2379, at 809–10 (McNaughton rev. 1961).
82. GORE VIDAL, BURR (2000).
83. LRC2, at 309–11.
84. *See* David Cole, *The New McCarthyism: Repeating History in the War on Terrorism,* 38 HARV. C.R.-C.L. L. REV. 1 (2003).
85. JACOBUS TENBROEK, PREJUDICE, WAR AND THE CONSTITUTION: CAUSES AND CONSEQUENCES OF THE EVACUATION OF THE JAPANESE AMERICANS IN WORLD WAR II (2d ed. 1970). The journal LAW & CONTEMPORARY PROBLEMS devoted its Spring 2005 issue to the Japanese relocation cases, with a foreword by Professor Eric Muller. *See also* Muller, *The Japanese American Cases: A Bigger Disaster Than We Realized,* 49 How. L.J. 417 (2006).
86. *See* Duncan v. Kahanamoku, 327 U.S. 304 (1946); Harry N. Scheiber & Jane L. Scheiber, *Bayonets In Paradise: A Half-Century Retrospect on Martial Law in Hawai'i,* 1941–1946, 19 HAWAII L. REV. 477 (1997); Major Kirk L. Davies, *The Imposition of Martial Law in the United States,* 49 A.F. L. REV. 67 (2000).
87. *See* United States v. Dellinger, 472 F.2d 340, 348 (7th Cir. 1972).

88. 343 U.S. 579 (1952).
89. Jackson had been lead prosecutor at the Nuremburg trials.
90. 343 U.S. at 638 (concurring opinion).
91. *See* THOMAS EMERSON, TOWARDS A GENERAL THEORY OF THE FIRST AMENDMENT (1966).
92. Brandenburg v. Ohio, 395 U.S. 444 (1969).
93. Reynolds, 345 U.S. 1 (1953).
94. The Reynolds family filed a petition for writ of error *coram nobis*, containing the unsealed information. The URL is http://www.fas.org/sgp/othergov/reynoldspet.pdf. The petition was denied without opinion, 539 U.S. 940 (2003).
95. Information on the case of Wen Ho Lee, unjustly arrested and accused, is available at www.wenholee.org, and with a Google search. A Detroit case in which the Justice Department heralded convictions of two Islamic defendants as a victory in the war on terror was tossed out due to prosecutorial misconduct. *See* Hakim, *Judge Reverses Convictions in Detroit "Terrorism" Case*, N.Y. TIMES, Sept. 3, 2004 (online). Professor Geoffrey Stone of the University of Chicago attended a workshop with Judge Posner while the judge was working on NOT A SUICIDE PACT. During the workshop, Judge Posner agreed with the Supreme Court's decision in *Hamdi*, holding that a detainee being held in Guantanamo should be entitled to some judicial review. However, he continued to insist that the Japanese relocation, and the Supreme Court decision upholding it, was correct. Professor Stone cogently pointed out that the relocation was an even more egregious response to a perceived threat than the Hamdi detention, and that courts and the executive branch had expressly repudiated the rationale for relocation. http://uchicagolaw.typepad.com/faculty/2006/04/judge_posner_ha.html.
96. Richard A. Posner, *The Supreme Court, 2004 Term: Forward: A Political Court*, 119 HARV. L. REV. 31 (2005).
97. Professor David Luban has written a trenchant rebuttal to the notion that torture should and could be used to compel a terrorist to tell the location of a "ticking bomb." The hypothetical assumes that the authorities already know that the torture victim has that knowledge and that the bomb exists. *See* David J. Luban, *Liberalism, Torture, and the Ticking Bomb*, 91 VA. L. REV. 1425 (2005).
98. Rochin v. California, 342 U.S. 165 (1952), later rejected in favor of the incorporation doctrine. *See* WAYNE R. LAFAVE, JEROLD H. ISRAEL & NANCY J. KING, CRIMINAL PROCEDURE § 2.4 (4th ed. 2004).
99. Giaccio v. Pennsylvania, 382 U.S. 399 (1966), *discussed in* WAYNE R. LAFAVE, CRIMINAL LAW § 2.4 (4th ed. 2003).
100. Posner, at 56.
101. 232 F.3d 1166 (9th Cir. 2000), *cert. denied*, 534 U.S. 887 (2001).
102. 18 U.S.C. § 7 (2000).
103. Posner, at 99-100.
104. *See* FRANK DONNER, THE AGE OF SURVEILLANCE: THE AIMS & METHODS OF AMERICA'S POLITICAL INTELLIGENCE SYSTEM (1980), and PROTECTORS OF PRIVILEGE: RED SQUADS AND POLITICAL REPRESSION IN URBAN AMERICA (1991). *See also* ALAN WESTIN, PRIVACY AND FREEDOM (1967).

105. Posner, at 113.
106. Posner, at 115–19.
107. This detail is from the NYU ANNUAL SURVEY OF AMERICAN LAW, volume 61.
108. The text is available online at http://lexrex.com/informed/otherdocuments/warprayer.htm.
109. Professor Juan Cole's Web site, *Informed Comment*, contains daily discussion of Mideast issues. The particular references cited in the text are http://www.juancole.com/2006/03/bigotry-toward-muslims-and-anti-arab.html and http://www.juancole.com/2003/01/koran-and-fighting-unbelievers.html.
110. Posner, at 144-45.
111. *See* FRANK DONNER, THE AGE OF SURVEILLANCE: THE AIMS & METHODS OF AMERICA'S POLITICAL INTELLIGENCE SYSTEM (1980), and PROTECTORS OF PRIVILEGE: RED SQUADS AND POLITICAL REPRESSION IN URBAN AMERICA (1991). *See also* ALAN WESTIN, PRIVACY AND FREEDOM (1967).
112. Comment, *Who Let the Dogs Out?*, 37 RUTGERS L. REV. 377 (2006).
113. The Supreme Court's formulation and extension of a constitutional right of privacy was the subject of Symposium, 54 DePAUL L. REV. 657 (2005), and the many articles in that symposium discuss the relevant authority. See also the many discussions of first amendment-related privacy concerns in THOMAS I. EMERSON, THE SYSTEM OF FREEDOM OF EXPRESSION (1970), particularly chs. VIII, XIII, XIV.
114. 5 U.S. at 166.
115. In 2006, a California Congressman pleaded guilty to crimes arising from accepting bribes to influence legislation favorable to defense and intelligence contractors. He was able to conceal his crimes for a long time because of the Congressional practice of "black" or secret legislation. When Congress allocates money for some military and intelligence operations, or regulates how these are to be conducted, the legislation is secret and available only to certain "cleared" members and to their "cleared" staffers. Behind the veil of secrecy, this Congressman and others conducted their criminal activity.
116. Military Commissions Act of 2006, P.L. 109-366, Oct. 17, 2006 (codified to 10 U.S.C. § 948b(e)).
117. Gutknecht v. United States, 396 U.S. 295 (1970).
118. 317 U.S. 1 (1942).
119. 126 S. Ct. 2749 (2006).
120. The poll results are available at http://www.pipa.org/. This site also includes background information and related material.
121. *See generally* Richard J. Goldstone & Janine Simpson, *Evaluating the Role of the International Criminal Court as a Legal Response to Terrorism*, 16 HARV. HUM. RTS. J. 13 (2003); Richard J. Goldstone, *The Future of International Criminal Justice*, 57 ME. L. REV. 554 (2005).

INDEX

ABOUT THE AUTHOR

MICHAEL E. TIGAR has been a lawyer and law teacher for more than forty years. He has taught at UCLA, the University of Texas, Duke, and Washington College of Law, and has been visiting lecturer at dozens of law schools, judicial conferences and bar groups. He has also taught at law schools in Europe, Africa and Latin America. He was Chair of the ABA Litigation Section 1989–90. He is author of Fighting Injustice, Persuasion: The Litigator's Art, and Examining Witnesses, all published by the ABA, as well as several other books. His legal work has focused on seeking vindication for victims of terrorism, and on defending the rights of those targeted by the government in cases involving national security. Justice William J. Brennan, Jr. said of Mr. Tigar that his "tireless striving for justice stretches his arms towards perfection." In 1999, the California Attorneys for Criminal Justice held a ballot for "lawyer of the century." Mr. Tigar ranked third, behind Clarence Darrow and Thurgood Marshall.